Programming The Macintosh In C

PROGRAMMING THE MACINTOSH™ IN C

BRYAN J. CUMMINGS
LAWRENCE J. POLLACK

SYBEX®

Berkeley • Paris • Düsseldorf • London

Cover art by Jean-Francois Penichoux
Book design by Lisa Amon

We have taken great care in preparing this book. All information is deemed to be accurate at
time of publication. All programming examples have been thoroughly tested on a Macintosh
with two disk drives, the Consulair Mac C compiler (release 2.0), and the Macintosh Development System.

Aztec C68K compiler is copyrighted by Manx Software Systems.
The Consulair Mac C compiler is copyrighted by Consulair Corporation.
C/PM-80 and C/PM-86 are trademarks of Digital Research, Inc.
Macintosh is a trademark of Apple Computer Incorporated.
The Macintosh Development System is copyrighted by Apple Computer Incorporated.
MS-DOS is a trademark of Microsoft Corporation.
PC-DOS is a trademark of IBM Corporation.
UNIX is a trademark of Bell Laboratories.

SYBEX is not affiliated with any manufacturer.

Every effort has been made to supply complete and accurate information. However, SYBEX
assumes no responsibility for its use, nor for any infringements of patents or other rights of
third parties which would result.

Library of Congress Card Number: 85-63244
ISBN 0-89588-328-7
Printed by Haddon Craftsmen
Manufactured in the United States of America
10 9 8 7 6 5 4 3 2 1

For Judy, Lydia, Matt, and Steve

ACKNOWLEDGEMENTS

The production of a book requires many steps and many people. For ourselves, and on behalf of DATATECH Publications, the authors would like to thank those people who have helped to create this book. First of all, we want to thank Geta Carlson for her magnificent editorial support. At SYBEX, we would like to thank Dr. R. S. Langer and Karl Ray for managing this project so well. Also at SYBEX, thanks to Lisa Amon for her book design, Joel Kroman for technical support, Brenda Walker for typesetting, Dave Clark and Scott Campbell for word processing, Jon Strickland for proofreading, and Jannie Dresser for the tedious task of indexing.

B. C.
L. P.

TABLE OF CONTENTS

THREE

INTRODUCTION TO USING C

INTRODUCTION

This book was written for people who have an interest in designing and writing their own software for the Macintosh. We have developed this tutorial to the C programming language for you, the Macintosh user, and for programmers at all levels of expertise, whether you have done just a little programming in BASIC or Pascal or whether you are skilled in several languages. This book will guide you through all phases of computer programming and give you opportunities to learn, to be challenged, and to experience the success of writing and running your own programs.

The tutorial nature of this book makes it easy for a programmer at any experience level to learn a new language. When reading *Programming the Macintosh in C*, you will encounter many sample programs that should be treated as programming exercises. As you encounter the programming samples, enter them into your computer and run them. Make any indicated changes and note the results. As we all know, the best way to learn something is to do it!

HOW THIS BOOK IS ORGANIZED

Chapter 1 describes the structure of the computer from a programmer's viewpoint and defines basic elements such as the CPU, bytes, and words. It also discusses important topics like memory, memory management, storage representations, and the binary, octal, and hexadecimal numbering systems. Chapter 1 continues with a description of how to get data into and out of your C programs. The chapter concludes with a brief illustration of how to use the computer to write and operate C software. Those readers who feel comfortable with these concepts may quickly review the material and skip directly to Chapter 2.

Chapter 2 is devoted to the topic of the elements of a programming language and to the task of writing a program. The first part of the chapter describes what programming languages do, focusing on the task of machine-level language and on the need for higher-level languages. Next the chapter addresses the question of the differences between programming languages in regard to four key factors: the jobs the language is designed to accommodate; the levels of the language; the programming tools available in the language; and when language translation is performed. All of this leads up to an introduction to the special characteristics of the C programming language in which we explain why C is such a popular language among programmers today. Chapter 2 conludes with an overview of the programming process and a definition of some of the elements and conventions of C.

Chapter 3 lists the basic constructs used in all programming languages. For each construct, the appropriate C syntax, a description of its use, and an example are provided.

Chapter 4 details the organization of a C program. The basic component of a C program is the function. Chapter 4 describes the function and its various attributes with respect to the use of functions in a C program.

Chapter 5 continues the discussion of data storage by specifically detailing the method that C uses for data storage. The chapter begins with an introduction to the basic types of data that you may use in C. Topics such as constants, determining the data type to use, and converting from one data type to another complete the chapter.

Chapter 6 builds upon the information introduced in Chapter 5. Chapter 6 begins with the topic of addressing data and using pointers to access the data. The second and third sections of this chapter cover the more sophisticated data handling methods available in C, such as arrays and structures.

Chapter 7 presents the standard input and output routines. From a technical standpoint, these input and output routines are not part of the C programming language. Chapter 7 explains why these routines are provided and how to use them.

Chapter 8 completes our description of the process of writing a program in C. This chapter focuses on the utility programs you will be using to generate a working C program. The chapter begins with the compiler and its options. The linker is described next, followed by the librarian.

Chapter 9 is a reference guide for you to use while you are writing your C programs. The topics in the reference guide are presented in the same order as they are in Chapters 2 through 6. This portion of the book is intended to make the book a useful reference text as well as a learning tool.

This book is designed to teach you about the C programming language and how to use it with the Macintosh. It is beyond the scope of this book to teach you how to program the Macintosh (for example, topics such as creating windows and menus and using the graphics routines are not covered). In order to program the Macintosh, your programs must make use of the support routines built into the Macintosh ROM, called the User Interface Toolbox. Before you can write sophisticated programs of this sort, you need to know a language in which to program the Mac. By teaching you C, this book will give you the background you need before you move on to programming the Macintosh.

WHAT YOU NEED TO USE THIS BOOK

C is a compiled language and requires several auxiliary pieces of software in order to translate your program into a code that the computer can understand. Of course, before you can do any C programming, you need a computer that will run this software. The hardware required for this book is the basic Macintosh, an external floppy disk drive, and a printer. The basic Macintosh consists of 128 kilobytes of memory, a display screen, a keyboard, a mouse, an internal floppy disk drive, and the software required to make the computer function.

Although the basic Macintosh will suffice for some C development systems, the lack of the second disk drive means that you will be doing an extensive amount of disk swapping. The ideal Macintosh C development system hardware consists of a Macintosh with 512 kilobytes of memory, an external hard disk drive, and a printer. The larger memory allows the Macintosh to operate a little bit faster. The hard disk drive eliminates the need to swap disks while you are developing a program. In addition, the hard disk drive runs much faster than the floppy disk drive, which reduces the amount of time you spend waiting for your program to compile (see Chapter 2).

As for the software, the first program you need is a C *development package*. Several companies are now producing such packages for the Macintosh. The development package, also called a *development system*, will at least consist of a program called a compiler. Along with the compiler, you will need an editor, a linker, and possibly an assembler.

This set of software is used in various combinations in order to create a program file that can be executed by the computer. The *editor* is a program that allows you to type your C program into the computer and save it on disk. It is actually a specialized word processor that has features unique to the needs of a programmer. The *compiler* takes your C program and creates a file to be used by either the linker (a relocatable object file) or the assembler (an assembly file). If the compiler creates an assembly file, then the *assembler* must be used to create the relocatable file. The *linker* takes the relocatable file and generates an executable program file. (This is just a brief overview of what the development software does. For a more complete description, refer to Chapters 1, 2 and 8.) The editor, assembler, and linker programs—that is, the programs other than the compiler—may or may not be included in your development package, depending upon the manufacturer. Some systems will provide all of these programs plus some other utilities, while other systems will only provide a compiler.

To provide continuity through the many examples used in this text, we have selected the Consulair Mac C Compiler available from Consulair Corporation. The Consulair system is designed to be used with the Macintosh Development System (MDS). The Mac C compiler consists of the C compiler and several supplementary files (the use for these files will be explained in Chapter 8). The MDS includes the assembler, the linker, and the editor. For this book, it is irrelevant whose development system you choose as long as you have all of the necessary programs and as long as the compiler implements the standard Kernighan and Ritchie C programming language. Kernighan and Ritchie designed C and have provided a list of specifications about what programming constructs the compiler must support, and in some cases how the compiler must work. If your compiler's manual states that it supports the K® standard C, then it will work with this book and can be used for many of your programming tasks.

Take the security precautions necessary when dealing with any computer: make duplicate copies of all your important software. Never use your originals, and use only those disks that have information of relatively low value on them for experimentation. If you take these two simple precautions, it will be impossible to "break" your computer's software.

A Review
of Some
Programming
Basics

The purpose of Chapter 1 is to provide a refresher course on the basic concepts needed in order to program effectively. The chapter begins with a look inside the computer at the basic components called the CPU, RAM, and ROM. Next comes a discussion on numbering systems including decimal, binary, hexadecimal, octal systems, as well as converting values between the various systems. Following the discussion about numbers, the chapter covers data representation and memory usage. Chapter 1 concludes with a brief overview of the program development process. Those of you who already feel comfortable with this information may skip this chapter and move immediately on to Chapter 2.

A BRIEF LOOK INSIDE THE COMPUTER

All personal computers now available have essentially the same set of internal hardware: a central processing unit (called a CPU), a main memory storage unit, and various devices for communication with the operator (a keyboard, a mouse, and a video display terminal). From the point of view of programming in C, the hardware of primary concern is the CPU and the computer's memory.

THE CENTRAL PROCESSING UNIT

We will begin with the heart of the computer: the *central processing unit,* or *CPU* for short. This small silicon microchip controls the operation of your computer. Technically, it does not physically operate all the parts of the computer, since this would place a tremendous workload upon the CPU. Instead, certain instructions will cause the CPU to activate an auxiliary piece of hardware, which in turn has its own unique task that it can do much more efficiently than the CPU could. For example, to read data from a disk, the CPU will issue a read instruction to a microchip in charge of the disk drives.

The CPU contains an instruction set that programmers refer to as *machine language,* a language in which the instructions are immediately executable by the CPU. Machine language consists exclusively of ones and zeros representing "on" and "off" states within the circuitry of the machine. This makes machine language much too difficult for humans to remember and use. This language is sometimes confused with *assembly language*, which uses symbols (like ADD, MOV, and so on) to represent the machine instructions. We will discuss these languages later.

MEMORY

The CPU has significantly limited storage facilities, so programs and data are stored outside the CPU. This part of the hardware is called *memory*. Currently, most smaller computers contain two types of memory: read-only memory (ROM) and random-access memory (RAM).

ROM AND RAM

The term *read-only memory* is almost self-explanatory: ROM contains information that can be read by the CPU but not changed. Just as one might write in permanent ink, the contents of read-only memory are written once (usually by the manufacturer) and then are forever available for reading. This type of memory is also termed *nonvolatile memory*, indicating its persistence even after the power is turned off.

In contrast, RAM is *volatile memory* and will lose its contents when the power is terminated. Much like writing in pencil, the contents of RAM can be written and then changed. *Random-access memory* is the major memory portion of your personal computer. It is theoretically thought of as a separate unit that allows you to retrieve data independently of the order in which it was stored; hence the name "random" access. RAM also allows you both to read from and write to it, and is thus sometimes known as read/write memory. Throughout the remainder of this book, references to memory will imply the RAM portion of your computer unless otherwise specified.

You may have heard that a computer only uses two values: on or off. Electronically, this is a relatively easy task to implement. However, using only two values requires some creative thinking in order to represent data within a computer's memory. This problem has been solved through the use of various numbering systems.

Numbering Systems

The various numbering systems used when programming consist of the decimal, binary, hexadecimal, and octal numbering systems. The decimal numbering system is the one that we use daily. It is provided by the compiler as a convenience to the programmer. The binary numbering system is the numbering system used by the computer. In cases where you need to access the computer's hardware (for example, to control a modem or disk drive), you will use the binary numbering system. The last two systems, hexadecimal and octal, are just variations on the binary system.

The Binary Numbering System

In the section discussing the representation of data in the computer's memory (later in this chapter), a knowledge of the *binary numbering system*, also known as *base 2*, will be very helpful.

The decimal numbering system has ten digits labeled zero through nine with each digit representing a power of ten. As you can see in Figure 1.1, the decimal number 51,035 is equal to 50,000 plus 1,000 plus 30 plus 5.

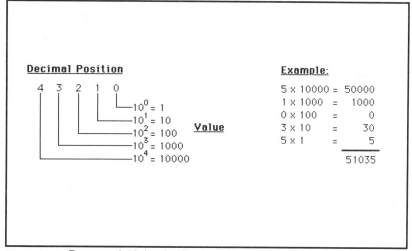

Figure 1.1: Powers of 10 for the Decimal Numbering System

CONVERTING FROM BINARY TO DECIMAL

The binary numbering system contains only two digits: zero and one. Each digit represents a power of 2 (see Figure 1.2). The binary number 10011 is equal to 19: that is, to 16 plus 2 plus 1.

This last example illustrates how to convert from the binary numbering system to the decimal numbering system. Converting from decimal to base two by hand takes a little more effort than converting from binary to decimal and consists of a series of repeated steps.

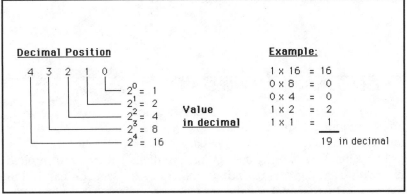

Figure 1.2: Powers of 2 for the Binary Numbering System

```
19 divided by 2 = 9,  with a remainder of 1;
                      so we write down the number 1:        1
 9 divided by 2 = 4,  with a remainder of 1;
                      so we write down the number 1:       11
 4 divided by 2 = 2,  with a remainder of 0;
                      so we write down the number 0:      011
 2 divided by 2 = 1,  with a remainder of 0;
                      so we write down the number 0:     0011

Add the number 1 to the left of the digits:            10011
```

Figure 1.3: Converting the Decimal Number 19 into Binary

CONVERTING FROM DECIMAL TO BINARY

Figure 1.3 shows a simple example of converting the decimal number 19 into binary. As you can see, 19 in decimal is 10011 in binary.

To convert a number from decimal to binary, follow these generic steps. As you perform the steps, write all the answers to the questions *backwards*: that is, right to left.

1. Divide the decimal number by 2.

2. If you have a remainder, write down the number 1. If you do not have a remainder, write down the number 0.

3. Discard the remainder you might have obtained earlier and use the quotient as the dividend in the next division.

4. Repeat steps 1 through 3 until you obtain 1 as the quotient. The number 1 will always be added to the left of the digits you have already obtained.

The easiest way to completely understand these procedures is to practice them. Table 1.1 contains a list of powers of two and Table 1.2 contains several conversion examples.

Common Powers of 2

n	2^n	n	2^n
0	1	11	2,048
1	2	12	4,096
2	4	13	8,192
3	8	14	16,384
4	16	15	32,768
5	32	16	65,536
6	64	17	131,072
7	128	18	262,144
8	256	19	524,288
9	512	20	1,048,576
10	1,024	21	2,097,152

Table 1.1: Common Powers of 2

Decimal	Binary
0	0
1	1
2	10
19	10011
101	1100101
255	11111111
10,354	10100001110010

Table 1.2: Decimal to Binary Conversion Examples

BINARY ARITHMETIC

Addition of binary numbers is analogous to addition in the decimal number system. If two digits, when added, generate a value that cannot be represented with a single digit, the rightmost digit is retained and the remaining digits are carried to the next column. Figure 1.4 shows some sample additions in binary.

Using the binary number system has important implications for in-depth computer use in, for example, engineering, programming, and design. But for the purposes of this book, you need only understand the principles discussed in this section.

OTHER NUMBERING SYSTEMS: OCTAL AND HEXADECIMAL

Along with the binary number system, you will encounter two other number systems: *octal* (*base 8*) and *hexadecimal* (*base 16*). These two

Conversion from Binary to Octal			
000 = 0		100 = 4	
001 = 1		101 = 5	
010 = 2		110 = 6	
011 = 3		111 = 7	

Table 1.4: Conversion from Binary to Octal

bases were chosen because their base values are powers of two, making conversion among all three numbering systems relatively easy.

For example, to convert from binary to hexadecimal, split the binary number into groups of four digits, starting from the right; the four binary digits will represent the values 0 through 15 of the hexadecimal system. Then convert each group to its appropriate hexadecimal value. By convention, the values 10 through 15 are represented by the letters A through F, respectively (see Table 1.3). Octal conversion is similarly easy. Split the binary number into sets of three digits, starting from the right, and then convert each set to its appropriate octal value (see Table 1.4).

These two numbering systems are used at various points in computer programming. For simplicity, decimal numbers will be used throughout the remaining chapters of this book, with any exceptions explicitly noted. In the next section of this chapter, we will see the binary system in use for data representation.

How DATA IS STORED

Information to be stored in a computer memory needs to be in a form the computer can use and manipulate with efficiency. After much experimentation, it became standard to use the two electrical conditions of on and off. (The words "on" and "off" do not necessarily correspond to an electric current; they merely represent the relative electric state of the unit.) Since a unit of memory can have only

Conversion from Binary to Hexadecimal	
0000 = 0	1000 = 8
0001 = 1	1001 = 9
0010 = 2	1010 = A
0011 = 3	1011 = B
0100 = 4	1100 = C
0101 = 5	1101 = D
0110 = 6	1110 = E
0111 = 7	1111 = F

Table 1.3: Conversion from Binary to Hexadecimal

```
Carry → 1      1111     11                    111111
        1101   1111     0110      1010        01110101
       +0001  +0001    +0110     +0101       +11011110
        ─────  ─────    ─────     ─────       ─────────
        1110   10000    1100      1111        101010011
```

Figure 1.4: Some Sample Additions in Binary

one of two values, it is called a *bit*, which is short for binary dig*it*. This representation works well for the computer and is also a relatively easy representation for humans to use if one of the states is defined to be the value 0 and the other state is defined as the value 1. Thus, the contents of any memory unit at a given time will have the value of either 1 or 0.

As we have seen in the previous section, placing several 0's and 1's (bits) together will form a positive integer number in binary. Unfortunately, other types of data also exist and need to be represented—for example, negative and real numbers or alphanumeric and other characters. By using standardized conventions, these other types of data can be represented with little difficulty. Before these conventions are discussed, however, you need to know some of the terms used for strings of bits—that is, you need to know about bytes and words.

The term *byte* refers to a string made up of a specified number of bits. The number of bits in a byte depends on the particular representation system chosen. Byte sizes can be six, seven, or eight bits in length, depending upon the computer. Most microcomputers and minicomputers use an 8-bit byte. We will deal with only 8-bit bytes in later sections of this book. The memory inside personal computers and the storage capacity of external storage devices are measured in bytes. Greek prefixes have been used to express large quantities of bytes: for example, a *kilobyte* (KB or simply K) equals one thousand bytes, and a *megabyte* (MB) equals one million bytes.

The term *word* indicates a division of memory. The size of the word equals the number of bits the CPU uses during the execution of an instruction. The Macintosh processes 32 bits per instruction and therefore has a word size of 32 bits; hence its designation as a 32-bit computer. Other common word sizes are 8 and 16 bits. The word is a machine-related concept that you will come across when you write complex systems software like an operating system, compiler, or a word processor.

There are some important points about the byte that you should know about. First, let's return to the point that initiated the explanation of bits and bytes: data representation.

How Numbers Are Represented

Positive integer numbers are easily represented through the binary numbering system: one byte can represent any number from 0 through 255 (00000000 to 11111111); two bytes together, or 16 bits, can represent any number from 0 through 65,535, and so on, using as many bytes as will provide enough bits to represent the number desired.

Negative integer numbers are a little trickier. The manufacturers of CPUs use the convention that the leftmost bit of a string of bits is used to indicate (flag) whether or not the number is negative (assuming the data represents a number). You will notice that the range of numbers that the binary string can represent doubles each time we add a digit to a binary string. For example, one digit can represent the two values 0 and 1. Two digits can represent four values, and three digits can represent eight values.

Now, if we dedicate the leftmost bit to be a *sign bit* that indicates the sign of the number, then the largest value that can be represented by the remaining bits will be half that of the original string of bits. For example, assuming you have an 8 bit string, you can represent the numbers 0 through 255, or 256 different values. Now take the leftmost bit and call it the sign bit. The remaining 7 bits can now only represent the numbers 0 through 127, or 128 different values.

Don't despair because what we lost in the positive range of values, we gained in the negative range of values. The sign bit plus the seven bit number can also represent the values −1 through −128, or 128 different values. Thus, an 8-bit string will always be able to represent 256 different values whether the values range from 0 through 256 or from −128 through +127.

Another consideration in representing negative numbers is the need to insure the proper numerical order, so that −2 comes before

−1, for example, and −1 comes before 0. The latter of these two conditions is more easily implemented. For negative versus positive numbers, the computer can simply compare the sign bit and conclude that a negative number will always be less than a positive number because a negative number has a 1 in the leftmost digit and a positive number has a 0 in the leftmost digit.

To allow the computer to compare two negative numbers, a more involved scheme of representation is required. The number −2 cannot be represented as 10000010 in binary since this would not be less than 10000001 in binary, or −1. Rather, a method called *two's complement* is used to generate negative binary numbers. This is a three-step process, carried out as follows:

1. Take the binary representation of the positive of the number to be converted.

2. Convert all 1's into 0's and all 0's into 1's.

3. Add 1 to the resulting number.

One property of the two's complements (and complements in general) is that the conversion of a two's-complement negative number into a positive number can be done using exactly the same procedure!

Two's-complement numbers satisfy the requirement of having the number −2 (11111110 binary) be less than the number −1 (11111111 binary). For these reasons, the two's-complement representation of negative numbers has been adopted for almost all programming uses.

Figure 1.5 shows two examples of creating negative binary numbers in two's-complement form. Figure 1.6 shows two examples of converting negative binary numbers in two's-complement form into positive binary numbers.

Another property of the two's complement makes it easy to add binary numbers (where negative numbers are represented in two's complement). The numbers are added as if they were both unsigned binary numbers. No special alterations are needed. Figure 1.7 shows some binary arithmetic using two's-complement numbers. Any carry beyond the seventh digit is ignored.

Real numbers—also called rational or floating point numbers—have an even more involved method for representation, which we will not discuss here. If you are interested, the Consulair Mac C has an internal floating point format and also supports the IEEE 80-bit standard format.

Example 1:

8 decimal	=	00001000 binary
Convert	=	11110111
Add 1	=	+ 1
−8 decimal	=	11111000 binary

Example 2:

47 decimal	=	00101111 binary
Convert	=	11010000
Add 1	=	+ 1
−47 decimal	=	11010001 binary

Figure 1.5: Examples of Creating a Two's-Complement Number

Example 1:

−8 decimal	=	11111000 binary
Convert	=	00000111
Add 1	=	+ 1
8 decimal	=	00001000 binary

Example 2:

−47 decimal	=	11010001 binary
Convert	=	00101110
Add 1	=	+ 1
47 decimal	=	00101111 binary

Figure 1.6:Converting Negative Number to Positive Using Two's Complement

```
  8 decimal  =    00001000          47 decimal  =    00101111
 -8 decimal  =  + 11111000          -8 decimal  =  + 11111000

  0 decimal  =    00000000          39 decimal  =    00100111


  8 decimal  =    00001000         -47 decimal  =    11010001
-47 decimal  =  + 11010001          -8 decimal  =  + 11111000

-39 decimal  =    11011001         -55 decimal  =    11001001
```

Figure 1.7: Binary Arithmetic Using Two's-Complement Numbers

CHARACTER REPRESENTATION

Binary numbers are also used to represent text characters. Computers, as we have seen, work exclusively with numbers. Therefore, the easiest way to present text so that the computer can understand it is to transform the text into numbers. Several character set representations exist today, the most popular of which are ASCII (American Standard Code for Interface Interchange) and EBCDIC (Extended Binary Coded Decimal Interchange Code). The EBCDIC representation system was developed by IBM and is used primarily on their larger computer systems. The ASCII system is widely used among most other computer systems, and we will only discuss this system here.

Since character representation requires only that a character be converted to some unique numeric value, the ordering of characters within the set tends to be arbitrary. Appendix A contains an ASCII chart showing each character and its associated numeric value in decimal, binary, octal, and hexadecimal. The arrangement of the chart breaks the character set into eight 32-character segments. The first segment (0 through 31 decimal) contains nongraphic (unprintable) characters used for device and information control. The next three segments (32 through 127 decimal) contain graphic (printable) characters, including the alphabet, punctuation characters, and other symbols. The remaining four segments are not defined by ASCII convention. Some devices will use these segments to duplicate the first four segments into the second four segments. However, most programs and other devices will distinguish between characters with values less than 128 and those greater than or equal to 128.

AN OVERVIEW OF MEMORY ORGANIZATION

At this point we are ready to return to the subject of memory. Understanding the mechanisms at work while your program executes, or carries out its tasks, will help you to understand the tools available in the programming language, to design more efficient programs, and to determine why, where, and how programming errors occur.

Memory itself consists of a large block of stored bits divided into bytes or words. Each byte in memory has an address, used by the CPU to request data from the location or store information at that location. Since the memory contains only the binary representation of the data, the data stored in memory may be used to supply a program with information, or it may be a program instruction for the CPU to execute. Thus, the term "data" refers only to the contents of a memory location and not necessarily to what the contents represent.

At one point in computer history, data and program instructions resided in physically separate units of the machine; this was inefficient and wasteful. Today, the data and program instructions reside in the same physical piece of hardware and are differentiated merely by their location within the memory. The program instructions reside in a contiguous block of memory that the CPU processes in sequence (according to address), with the remaining available memory containing the data for the program. In this case, the program will tell the CPU where to find the data it requires by supplying the address of the data to the CPU.

Fortunately for the programmer, a language like C frees you from all this addressing and internal data structure. The placement of your program and its data are taken care of by subordinate programs (the compiler, for example).

In languages like C, the programmer deals with variables rather than with addresses in memory to be used by the computer. A *variable* is an identifier that allows the programmer to name a place in memory. The name, for convenience purposes, associates the contents of the location with the meaning of the contents. You can call the location "partnumber" or "total" instead of just using the address which might be 08A0 or F08D (both in hexadecimal). The numbers don't tell you what is at that location, whereas a variable can give you an exact meaning of that location's contents.

The variable can be used like a variable in an algebraic or mathematical expression. For example:

(1) x = 6
(2) y = 2
(3) z = x + y

Here x, y, and z are variables. In line 1, x is assigned a value of 6. In line 2, y is assigned a value of 2; and line 3 contains an expression that assigns z the value of the contents of x added to the contents of y. Thus, z will have a final value of 8.

A variable can be used on both sides of the assignment symbol (=) within the same expression:

(4) z = z + x;

This takes the value of the contents of z and adds it to the value of the contents of x—in this case, 8 + 6. The resulting value of 14 is now put back into location z. Note that when a variable is used in an expression, its value will not change unless it is being assigned a value. For example, the values of variables x and y in lines 3 and 4 of the preceding example remain the same.

Variables are just simply a method of naming a location in memory. The data at that location is literally a string of bits, or perhaps a string of bytes if a larger data space is required. The data may be interpreted in any way that is appropriate for the context. It may be a number, a character, or some other object you want to call it. In Chapters 3 and 5 you will see how the compiler knows how to interpret the data associated with a particular variable.

FILES, OPERATING SYSTEMS, AND OTHER ESSENTIALS

The tutorial nature of this book virtually requires you to use your computer to create, compile, and execute programs. Therefore, you should have some familiarity with operating your computer. Specifically, you will need to be familiar with the use of the desktop, the file editing program, and your peripheral and other hardware in general (the Macintosh itself, disks, printers, and so on). If you do not have this familiarity, learn it now! Read the manuals and practice using your machine. From this point on, we will assume that you have a basic knowledge of computer operation.

In the following sections, we will explain what you will need to know about files and the Macintosh operating system—that is, the desktop environment—in order to begin programming in C on the Macintosh. As a programmer, you will eventually need to use either files, or the operating system, or both, within a program. Both of these terms—files and operating system—are discussed here as concepts rather than tangibles.

FILES

Files provide a place within the computer system's architecture to store vast amounts of data permanently. Files usually exist on a secondary storage unit such as disks, tapes, or punch cards (the main memory is considered the primary storage unit of the computer). The most popular of these devices in use today is the disk, which is available in two varieties: floppy and hard. We will be concerned only with files residing on disks in drives. From a programmer's perspective, there is no difference between a file on a floppy disk and a file on a hard disk, except for the size limitation of the file itself.

HOW FILES EXIST IN MEMORY

Conceptually, a file consists of a block of contiguous data. Storing data in a file is not very different from storing data in computer memory, although data storage within a file is not done as automatically as storing data in memory because of the way files are designed and used.

Two types of files exist: *sequential files*, which require data to be read or written in a sequential manner, and which do not allow specific placement of data within the file; and *random-access files*, which allow data to be read or written at any specified point within the file. Random-access files require some overhead in programming (like determining how much space the data will require) so that the point where data will be read or written can be specified. In either case, file accessing has some strict rules associated with it which will be discussed later.

From the program's point of view, the file is an extended area of memory with the added benefit of being nonvolatile. Like random-access memory, a random-access file permits the programmer to place data at any desired location. For now, all you need to know about files is the overall data organization within the file.

How Files Are Organized

A file may contain any set of data—a program, for example, or data for a program. Whatever the file contains, the program using the file must be able to understand the nature of the data the file contains. In other words, the data within a file will have a specific format that satisfies the particular program's expectations. For example, a file that contains data for a program (called a *data file*) will usually consist of data records.

Let's take a closer look at how data records organize the information in a data file. A *data record* is a logical grouping of pieces of data, all of which describe or pertain to a particular item. The pieces of data that make up a record are collectively referred to as *fields* of the record. An employee record is an example of a data record (the employee being the item described). This record contains fields for the employee's name, his or her address, telephone number, social security number, and any other information used by the program for processing. The record will be constructed with the fields in a fixed order for ease of use. In other words, the employee's name will always be found in the same place within the record. Finally, the file will contain a set of data records (for several employees, for example), and the records in the file will all be of the same format, thereby eliminating the programming overhead that would be needed to determine the format of the record (each time a record is read). This also makes the file much easier to use.

We have described the most general case for a data file. In practice, other types of files can take on any format the programmer chooses. As a rule, the format of a file will imitate the format of the application. For example, a program file ready for execution will look like that portion of memory in which the program will reside; or the files containing the C programs you will write will consist of a continuous sequence of characters. In essence, the *format* of the file is the organization of the data within the file.

The Operating System

Operating systems control hardware. Actually a program in itself, the operating system resides within the computer while other programs execute. The operating system provides preprogrammed sets of instructions to perform specific hardware functions such as writing to the disk or displaying data on the video screen.

For the programmer, the operating system provides a standardized environment in which to create programs. Each system of computer hardware has intrinsic operating characteristics. The author of the operating system takes as many of these differences into account and supplies the user of the operating system with a consistent set of functions that will perform defined operations in conjunction with the various pieces of hardware. Thereafter, when the operating system is used on different machines, the programmer need only know the operating system's commands and need not know about the operation of the hardware.

This, in turn, reduces programming time and provides a consistency among programs written by different programmers. On the Macintosh, for example, the windows are handled through special routines that are part of the Interface Toolbox. If each programmer had to write his or her own window routines, each program produced might have windows that look different from one another. Some programmers might not even supply windows. However, with the Toolbox, each programmer can use the same window routines so that all of the programs written for the Macintosh have a consistent look.

Most computer users do not even realize that the *disk operating system*, or *DOS*, is a program and that it is separate from the hardware and controls the operation of the computer. The term disk operating system is used to differentiate the operating systems used on the smaller personal computers from those used on larger computers. The larger computers' operating systems contain many more facilities for the programmer and the user, and control many more functions than just operating the disk drives. When you program with a language like C, you will not need to use the operating system directly, because much of the operating system interfacing is provided for you by the compiler. When you have learned C, you may want to access these fundamental controls of the computer directly. Then you will be able to create menus and windows, control the mouse, and so on.

Programmers also need to know something about the external view of the operating system—that is, how the operating system is perceived by the general user. For aesthetic and functional reasons, this is an important consideration in designing a computer program. The program cannot violate the rules set by the operating system; for example, all file names must be of valid construction. Also, a program that looks similar to other application programs will seem "friendly" to the user. Since the programmer uses the operating system (as a user, that is) while writing a program in order to edit and compile the program, he or she will become familiar with using the operating system quite rapidly.

WRITING A PROGRAM

This section defines the overall process of creating and executing a program in C, and then discusses the way in which programming errors are handled.

THE PROGRAMMING PROCESS

Creating a program requires a goal. Once you decide what aspect of life you want to automate, the program can be designed. After the design stage, the program can be written. To write or *code* the program, you use a text editing program to create a file containing the necessary programming language instructions. This file is called the *source file;* it contains the *source code,* or programming statements.

After completion of the program coding, you will need to execute at least two programs in sequence to create a program file the computer can understand. In most cases, the first program, the *compiler,* takes your source code and creates a *relocatable file.* The second program, usually called the *linker,* links the relocatable file to create the *executable file.* You can now execute this file just as you would any other command (commands are really programs) available on the system.

Other compilers, like the Consulair Mac C, generate an *assembly file* that contains the source code translated into assembly code. Therefore, you must run an intermediate program, called the *assembler,* to convert the assembly file into a relocatable file. This multistep process provides the very valuable facility of being able to write and test the program in small sections.

The relocatable file contains the machine-language instructions corresponding to your source code. However, no addresses have been specified for the location of the program or the variables. The linker takes the relocatable file, locates the actual address in memory where the program will execute, and appends these actual addresses to the machine code and variables.

The term "link" rather accurately describes the process taking place, especially with multiple relocatable files. When large programming systems are developed, they are usually coded in small, individualized sections, with each source file defining a unique function within the system. Each section can be tested separately to make sure it works. When all sections have been tested, they are linked into one program so that all functions can work together as a system. (We will not go into any further detail about programming large systems. This explanation simply provides the reason for the linking step when an executable file is created.)

DEALING WITH ERRORS

Either the compiler, the assembler, the linker, or the executable file may produce an error, which for our purposes is a message that indicates a problem. An error that occurs during compilation is called a *compile-time* error. Such errors indicate that the compiler did not understand a source code instruction in the source file, an error usually due to a typographical mistake on the part of the programmer, such as omitting a closing parenthesis or mistyping a variable name. Other errors include the misuse of variables, inconsistent use of terms, and incorrect use of program instructions. The compiler will tell you, via an error message, what the problem is, and where it occurred.

The linker may also produce errors, but these errors will be rare in your situation since (for the duration of this book, in any case) you are neither linking nor referencing multiple files to produce one program. The most common error message that results during a link process indicates a reference from one file to another for a function or variable that does not exist.

Errors that occur while your program is running are known as *run-time errors*. Some compilers place diagnostic code within the executable file to handle any errors that occur during execution. Your compiler may or may not have this added feature. If it does, your compiler's manual should contain a section, table, or appendix describing run-time error messages. At the time the error occurs, your program will display an error message, usually describing the reason for termination, and then abort the program. If your compiler does not have this facility, your program will probably terminate abruptly when the error occurs, or stop execution of the program and the whole computer system as well. When the latter happens, you must restart (reboot) your computer.

Some languages provide methods of *trapping* errors. With this technique, you can place instructions within the source code to indicate a specific action to be taken when an error occurs. This is known as *error handling* or *exception handling*. C does not provide an error trapping facility.

If you have had any difficulty understanding any section in this chapter, reread that section and then continue with Chapter 2. If you still have difficulty understanding the bit, the byte, the character sets, or memory organization, you should find and read some reference materials in these areas before proceeding.

TWO

PROGRAMMING
LANGUAGES

In this chapter, we will take an overall look at programming languages: what they are designed to do, how different levels of languages evolved, and what factors are taken into account in categorizing a language. We will also explain how C fits into this overall context. In the second part of the chapter, we will focus in on some of the specific characteristics of C. We will expand our discussion of the features that make C such a popular language to work with. We will also describe C's syntax and briefly discuss the basic logical flow of programs and the purpose of program statements.

WHAT PROGRAMMING LANGUAGES DO

Your Macintosh is a data processor. Processing data, however, covers a broad range of tasks. In practice, a programmer evaluates a particular task and determines whether or not it is suitable for a computer program. The assignment could be as simple as balancing a checkbook or as complex as "reading" and summarizing a full-length novel. Most tasks are easily definable and repetitive, making them ideal for computerization, because a computer can perform calculations much faster and more accurately than a human can. By computerizing such repetitive assignments, we can apply more manpower to other areas, which can result in significantly higher productivity.

Although computers are versatile, there are many jobs they cannot yet perform: for example, driving an automobile in heavy traffic. Computers are bound by the limitations of current technology.

How does a job become computerized? Not all tasks can be. Tasks that can be well-defined as a sequential progression of activities, match the computer's ability to perform a series of instructions in a specified order. The set of instructions that anyone would have to follow to complete the task is the essence of a computer program. Since the computer cannot select the instructions it will perform, however, someone must select the appropriate instructions and express them in computer language. This is the function of a computer programmer. The programmer examines the job and determines what actions the computer will have to take in order to complete the job.

Suppose that you wanted the computer to balance your checkbook. For a computer to balance a checkbook, you must instruct it to find the total of all uncashed checks and other debits listed in the checkbook and not listed on the bank's printed statement. Then the computer must find the total of all deposits and other credits listed in the checkbook and not listed on the bank statement. Next it must add the statement balance to the credit total, and subtract the debit total. If this new total equals the balance in the checkbook, all is well. Otherwise, a mistake has occurred somewhere in the checkbook, and another process begins to find the mistake.

Most of us would find this description clear and straightforward. Computers, on the other hand, have a language far removed from the abstract concepts humans use to communicate. Their language consists exclusively of 1's and 0's. For example, the instruction set of a computer does not include the concept of "find" (as in "find the total") in its limited vocabulary. The computer's commands allow adding, subtracting, even multiplying and dividing, moving, and comparing pieces of data. The computer programmer must now define for the computer what our English word "find" means, and he must tell it what series of instructions will perform this operation.

The programmer could, in effect, "teach" a computer how to perform a new task by communicating to it in its own machine language—the language of the CPU. This language consists of a set of instructions provided by the designer of the CPU. These instructions will be one data word in length; any required data (depending upon the syntax of the specific instruction) will follow the instruction. Most machine language instructions have a very simple action, such as adding or moving. Each bit in the word has a specific meaning, and the machine language programmer must construct each instruction manually; this can be a very laborious and error-ridden task.

Since this method of communication is so repetitive and time-consuming, however, programmers decided to computerize the very art of communicating with the CPU. Today's programming languages are the result of such computerization. In the early stages of programming language development, the programmer only required a format easier for humans to read. This gave rise to a program called an *assembler*. The programmer creates a source file containing the CPU instructions in a format humans can read, like ADD, SUB, and MOV. The programmer executes the assembler program, which converts these commands into their respective machine codes (1's and 0's). Thus, assembly language provides ease of use, but only with respect to the commands provided by the CPU; it does not make representing the concepts of the programming task at hand any easier. For this reason, assembly language is considered a low-level language.

It's important to note at this point that the level of a language does not necessarily reflect its quality; that is, a high-level language is not necessarily better than a low-level language. The term "level" refers to the ability of a language to represent abstract concepts used in explaining and defining the programming task. Thus in our previous example, for instance, the computer does not know that a check contains information regarding the payee of the check, the amount of the check, the check's number, and the date of the check. But if a programming language has the ability to define the word "check" to collectively refer to the associated data, the programmer may use the word in his or her description of the task to the computer.

Being able to use the word "check" yields two benefits. First, programming will proceed more rapidly, because the programmer is no longer required to monitor every bit of data that comprises a machine-language program. The programmer can now collectively refer to groups of data with a single, natural word. Second, the program becomes maintainable or easily readable. This second point is important because often relatively small programs are written with little regard for readability. At some later time, when the program requires alteration (that is, maintenance), the original programmer may either be unavailable or have forgotten the details of the logic used when writing the program. In both cases, a programmer will have to waste valuable time learning the program from scratch. If you have had experience with programming, you have probably encountered this situation already. If not, you will become aware of the possible difficulties with such situations as we begin programming later in the book.

To provide for the kinds of expanded capabilities we have been discussing, programming languages more complex than machine language or assembly language were developed. The vocabulary of a programming language is often closely related to the kinds of tasks the language was designed to perform. Since it would be rather cumbersome to design a programming language that included enough commands to perform all specific tasks, most programming languages provide programmers with the tools to construct their own commands. These new commands may be called *functions, procedures, subroutines,* or *subprograms.* A created command of this sort is really a structure made up out of simpler, single-word commands that have either been provided by the language or previously created by the programmer. With this ability to create commands, one can define, for example, what the English word "find" means. Moreover, because the programmer can define new commands, the initial vocabulary of the programming language can be relatively small, making it easy to learn for first-time users of the language.

THE DIFFERENCES BETWEEN PROGRAMMING LANGUAGES

Why do so many different languages exist? There are four major differences between programming languages: 1) the jobs the languages were designed to accommodate; 2) the levels of the languages; 3) the tools available within the languages; and 4) when language translation is performed. Let's take a brief look at each one of these differences and how the C language fits into this picture.

THE JOBS A LANGUAGE IS DESIGNED FOR

First of all, let's consider the matter of the tasks that programming languages are designed to accomplish. Programming languages have been designed to facilitate the translation of ideas into instructions the computer will use to perform the task. The languages FORTRAN (for FORmula TRANslator) and APL (for A Programming Language) have extensive mathematical functions that make them ideal for scientific programs. A language called LISP (for LISt Processing), on the other hand, has the ability to define more abstract concepts, and is used in many applications based on artificial intelligence. Because of certain characteristics that will be explained later on, the C language is ideal for writing system programs. Many operating system programs and real-time applications (for example, a program that controls a robotic welding machine) are written in C.

THE LEVEL OF A LANGUAGE

The level of a language, the second factor in determining the differences between languages, is often more difficult to identify. Level has in fact become a vague term. In general, there are high-level languages and low-level languages. The lower the level of the language, the closer it is to the actual workings of the machine. The higher the level of the language, the further removed the instructions get from the underlying design of the computer. C is considered a mid-level language. While C originally began as an elevated assembly language, today's version of C can match the capabilities of high-level languages.

A LANGUAGE'S SPECIAL TOOLS

The third factor involved in classifying a language is the tools or special programming features that the language offers. The tools available within the language affect the ease with which the language can be used to write programs. As we mentioned earlier, a programming language may be quite general and provide the ability to define new commands and data groups. C is such a language. It provides a relatively small set of tools that can be combined (and even altered) by the programmer. These new tools may be designed either for general use or to meet the specific requirements of the job at hand. Other languages try to include all the specific tools required for the task for which the programming language was designed. These languages are less flexible than C and are often difficult to extend to other tasks.

INTERPRETED VS COMPILED LANGUAGES

Translation, the final category that differentiates languages, can be done by an *interpreter* or a *compiler*. When a language is interpreted, the source code files (see Chapter 1) that are written by the programmer are loaded into the computer's memory in a form readable by humans. The computer then begins execution by taking the first instruction of the source file, translating it into the appropriate machine code, and executing the machine code instructions. Actually, two programs are being executed: the applications program itself and the program to interpret the source code. In general, an interpreted program executes much more slowly than a compiled program, and usually lacks the complex abilities and constructs of a compiled program, such as being able to define the data object "check" or the command "find." However, interpreted languages do not need to be pretranslated so you don't need to wait before running your program. This makes finding and correcting errors faster and easier than with compiled languages.

In a compiled language, like C, the programmer writes instructions in a source file, and then runs a program called a compiler to translate the source code into machine code. When the program is to be executed, the machine code file can be loaded into the computer and used without delay. One advantage of a compiled language is that because compiled programs are, in effect, pretranslated, they will run faster than interpreted programs. A second advantage of compiled languages is the access to the more abstract and complex concepts that make general and large-scale programming easier to do. The drawback is the time spent waiting before a program can be tested and run.

THE SPECIAL CHARACTERISTICS OF C

At this point, it might be helpful for us to explain some of the special characteristics of C in a little more detail. These special characteristics include C's data storage and definition capabilities, its portability, its flexible and consistent set of tools for building new commands, its modular structure, and the ease with which programs can be documented internally.

Don't be concerned if you don't completely understand the concepts we will be presenting in the next few pages. Our intention here is simply to give you an overview of C's advantages as a programming language. As you learn more about C in upcoming chapters, the significance of the characteristics we are about to describe will become clearer.

DATA STORAGE AND DEFINITION

In regard to data storage and definition, C combines the advantages of assembly language with those of a higher level language. Let's take a brief look at why this is so.

As we mentioned previously, programs and data reside in the same memory. The computer does not know the difference between bytes of a program and bytes of data. Some languages, like assembly language, require the programmer to explicitly define the location of the instructions and the location of the data. This requirement increases the complexity of programming as different types of data become necessary, because different types of data have different storage requirements. For instance, a number between 0 and 255 needs only eight bits of storage space, whereas the word "HELLO" requires at least five bytes. Higher-level languages relieve the programmer of the tedious practice of allocating space for the data, and so does C.

On the other hand, a programmer may want to know where and how the data resides in memory. The semantics of a programming language define how each data type is stored, and this usually cannot be changed. The semantics also determine the storage location of a piece of data. Many languages will provide some method of determining the addresses of the data. These methods vary as much in ease of use as the programming languages themselves. C provides a very capable and flexible set of operators used to manipulate pieces of data and to determine the location of data storage. We will discuss this topic in depth in Chapter 6.

PORTABILITY

Processing power would be useless without the ability to receive the original sets of data (input) and the ability to return the new sets of data (output) to the outside world. The input/output facilities of a language determine the ease with which the programmer can access or communicate with the standard peripheral devices connected to the computer, such as the video display terminal (VDT) and the keyboard. But what happens when the computer has to communicate with a nonstandard device—for example, when another machine such as a CAT-scan (computer-assisted tomography) device wants to supply data to the computer, or when a device such as a robotic welding machine is dependent upon instructions from the computer, or when both situations exist, for example, in a Cruise missile?

Not all languages allow communication with nonstandard input/output (I/O) devices. In fact, this facility is quite difficult to implement, because different devices have different requirements for communication and operation. Some programming languages have no facilities for adaptation to new devices; other languages, like C, can adapt easily. While in general, the ability to adapt lies predominantly within the operating system, the programming language must also be able to communicate with the operating system so that meaningful data can be exchanged.

The C language specification contains no input/output facilities. This means the language does not have any "wired-in" data accessing mechanisms, with the result that the language is not hardware dependent—that is, tied to particular machinery. Most C compilers include a set of commands for accessing some peripherals like the keyboard, VDT, disk drives, and printer. This means that a programmer's source code can be moved directly from one machine (with its hardware-dependent compiler) to another (with its own compiler) and be recompiled with few, if any, changes. This is a big plus for a programmer's productivity.

Tools for Building Commands

Earlier we mentioned that C is quite general and provides the ability to build new commands and data groups. Why is this the case?

C deals with the same data objects used by most computers—for example, numbers, characters, and addresses. While the C language provides a wide variety of mathematical operators to manipulate these objects, however, C does not supply complex data objects. Instead, the programmer has the ability to define additional data objects as needed. Neither complex data objects nor operations on these data objects are provided for in C; so the programmer must create new commands to define operations for the data objects in use. In summary, C has a relatively small vocabulary with a well-defined and consistent set of operators.

Writeability: Structured Programming

When writing a program, a programmer must plan carefully and keep a multitude of thought tracks organized. Unplanned programs tend to reflect the complexity of the workings of the programmer's mind, with the result that the program itself tends to become confused. Unplanned programming leads to error-prone, unmanageable source code.

Structured programming was developed to help programmers avoid the pitfalls of unplanned programming. In structured programming the programmer breaks up the entire task into logical segments or modules. Each segment consists of a single-step function used in processing the task. For example, a single step during checkbook reconciliation involves totaling all uncashed checks. Structured programming breaks down and describes the task to the computer in a defined and logical manner, and simultaneously clarifies and organizes the source code for the programmer. The result: decreased program development time, improved performance, and fewer errors in the program logic.

Because of the advantages of structured programming, many of the newer programming languages, including C, have been designed to use this modular programming style. By providing a framework for grouping programming instructions into processing segments, these languages create an environment for structured programming. We will discuss the organization of source code in greater depth when we begin examining the use of these constructs.

READABILITY: INTERNAL PROGRAM DOCUMENTATION

As we just saw, structured programming yields a two-fold benefit. It aids the programmer both in segmenting the task and in describing the task to the computer. This, in turn, provides for more readable programs that are also easier to maintain. However, the mere fact that a program is structured may not always mean that there is enough information for you or a subsequent programmer to make changes to the system. A good structured programming language like C will in addition provide a method for you to place comments— explanations that you can read but that the compiler ignores—within your code.

As a rule, comments are most helpful in the following areas of your program:

- *At the beginning of the source code file.* These comments will contain the title and function of the program, the name of the programmer(s), and the date on which the program was written (or started). These comments may be followed by information regarding any major changes made to the program after it was written. This subsequent information contains the name of the programmer who made the change, the date of the change, and why and where the change was made.

- *At the beginning of program segments.* This highlights the beginning of a segment. It could include a description of the function the segment will perform, as well as any useful information about the logic of the segment itself.

- *At all points of the source code where the purpose may be anything less than perfectly clear.* In some cases, for example, you may need to use a "programming trick." Programming tricks are small portions of code that have an effect that is not obvious to a person reading the code. Comments should be used extensively with these programming segments to make their purpose clear.

We will provide examples of how to use comments throughout the programming exercises in this book.

DEVELOPING PROGRAMS: SYNTAX, LOGIC, AND THE ROLE OF STATEMENTS

We will wrap up this chapter with a brief examination of some of the syntax of the C language. We will also discuss programming logic and the role of statements in programs. Before we get down to specifics, however, some general remarks about writing programs may be helpful.

THE PROGRAMMER'S AXIOMS

The syntax of a language, operating system, or program describes the format in which the computer expects to receive data. Being very "dumb" machines, computers do not understand typographical errors or commands that the programmer has inadvertently rephrased. For example, if you want to open a file called FILE and you type FIEL instead, the operating system will give you an error message. If in your source code you type x = y instead of x - y, the compiler accepts the command as valid, but your program may not perform as you had intended. This tendency of the computer to take instructions literally leads to two important axioms for computer programmers.

Axiom 1: Garbage in, garbage out. This is a point for a programmer to consider when designing a program. If an operator supplies meaningless data, the results of the program will also be meaningless. However, this should not be justification for the programmer to avoid building data error checking in the program. The programmer has the responsibility to protect the operator from entering values that will cause abnormal termination of the program or unpredictable results due to invalid data. For example, you don't want the operator to enter in any alphabetic characters when an amount is expected. For the sake of clarity, the programming examples given here provide very little data validation because data validation requires extra code that would clutter our examples.

Axiom 2: Computers do what you tell them to do, not what you want them to do. The language computers use must be very precise in order to be specific. When checking your programs for errors, you may often find that you have not completely articulated what you wanted the computer to do in language the computer could understand. Structured programming aids significantly in finding these sorts of errors.

THE SYNTAX OF C

As a matter of convention, various special characters and types of terms are part of the syntax of a language. Here is an overview of some of the syntactical elements of the C language.

WHITESPACE CHARACTERS

Blanks, tabs, newlines, and comments are collectively termed *whitespace* and are ignored by the compiler, except when they are used to provide separation of elements. *Blanks* and *tabs* are self-explanatory; they are analogous to the same functions on a typewriter. A *newline* is a character or set of characters that separates lines of print on the display or listing. This character is analogous in effect to the carriage return on a typewriter.

There are also special characters or sets of characters used to introduce the *comments* that provide description of the source code for purposes of readability and understanding. In C, comments begin with the first occurrence of the characters /* and end with first occurrence of the characters */. In general, a comment will look like this:

```
/* This is a comment and will be ignored by the compiler */
```

This format is generally used to clarify your program statements within the program. At the beginning of the source file or before a major program segment, you will want a more noticeable comment format like:

```
/ * * * * * * * * * * * * * * * * * * * * * * * * * * * * * * * * * * *
*                                                                     *
*       This text will name the program segment and                  *
*       provide the reader with information about what                *
*       the segment does, what data it needs for input,              *
*       and what data it provides as output.                         *
*                                                                     *
* * * * * * * * * * * * * * * * * * * * * * * * * * * * * * * * * * * */
```

You may place any valid characters and as many lines as you want between the /* and */ *delimiters*. Remember that the first /* encountered will start the comment, and the first */ found will end the comment.

The comment format you choose is not important as long as it is easy to see and read. You should also choose a format that is relatively quick to type. You don't want to spend all of your time writing comments.

Also, specific to the Consulair Mac C compiler is the character set //. If this character is found on a line, any characters following the // on that line are ignored. The /* and */ comment delimiters may include several lines of comment, but the // comment indicator is active only until the end of the line.

IDENTIFIERS

An *identifier* is simply a name. One kind of identifier is a group of letters and digits created by the program to identify a specific object. An example of such an identifier, as we learned in Chapter 1, is a variable name. An identifier may contain any combination of letters and digits as long as the first character is a letter. Note that the _ (underscore character) is also considered a letter and the uppercase letters differ from lowercase letters. You can use as many characters as you want for the identifier.

Most compilers, including the Consulair, will use up to 31 characters to determine the uniqueness of an identifier. The authors of the C programming language require that the compiler use at least the first 8 characters to differentiate between identifiers. Thus the identifier **abcdefghooo** would be the same to the **abcdefghzzz**. Therefore, the more characters your compiler uses, the more combinations you can have for identifier names.

The term *keywords* refers to the set of identifiers that are used for specific C functions and commands, and may not be used otherwise. Chapters 3 through 7 cover all of the keywords used in the C programming language.

A *constant* is an explicit defined value that never changes during the program's execution. For example, in the statement

    x = 36

the number 36 is a constant and the character x is an identifier for a variable. Throughout the rest of the program, the variable x may be assigned new values, but each time this statement is executed, x will be assigned the constant value 36.

Each type of data (numbers and characters) has a special format for creating a constant of that type. Chapter 5 discusses how to make constants for the different data types.

PUNCTUATION CHARACTERS

Programming languages give special definitions to many punctuation characters in order to create code that describes its own function visually. In C, the most commonly used punctuation character is the semicolon (;). The semicolon is used to signify the end of an instruction. This allows an instruction to be formatted in the way that best suits the meaning of the instruction. For instance, you could have an instruction formatted in either of the following two ways. First,

```
x = 6;
```

And second,

```
x
=
6
;
```

Obviously, the first format is much easier to read, although both formats are completely valid. This example just demonstrates that every instruction must end with a semicolon.

PROGRAM FORMAT

As we know, structured programming is emphasized under C. In structured programming, the programmer writes code in a logical fashion by dividing the code into blocks. Each block contains a set of instructions pertaining to a single idea or purpose. C uses the open brace character—{—to indicate the beginning of a block and the close brace character—}—to signal the end of a block. Blocks may be contained within blocks; this is known as *nesting*. Structured programming will be discussed in detail in Chapter 4.

Finally, all C programs must contain the following segment somewhere within the source code:

```
main()
{
    program code
}
```

The heading main() names the block of code. This is known as a function definition. All C programs must have a function block entitled main() to indicate the program starting point. We will address the subject of blocks and functions in Chapter 4.

BASIC PROGRAMMING LOGIC

Once you have conceptualized a program, you can provide a natural structuring of your program by simply describing each step required to accomplish the goal. Beginning with the first step in the task and coding each subsequent step in order yields a program that is written from the top down. Each large step can then be broken into substeps for further structuring. You should stop this fine tuning when you reach a point when the substep definition describes a single process.

In our example for a check reconciliation program, we have already split the problem into its major steps as follows:

1. List all checks, debits, and credits written in your checkbook, as well as those checks outstanding since the last bank statement.

2. List all checks, debits, and credits on your bank statement.

3. Remove each item that appears on both lists from both lists.

4. Total the remaining debits in the first list. Total the credits in the first list.

5. Add the credit total from the first list to the statement balance. Then subtract the debit total.

6. If this new balance equals your checkbook balance, then all is well. If not a mistake has been made.

This outline by no means defines all the individual processes needed to reconcile a bank statement. It does, however, list the major divisions of the task at hand. With experience, you will be able to describe the steps and substeps within a task with greater accuracy.

DEVELOPING A PROGRAM STATEMENT

After the program has been outlined and subdivided into single process steps, we can begin writing the code for each process. Each process consists of a sequence of programming statements or instructions, each of which in turn consists of some combination of operators and expressions. An *expression* may include any combination of constants and identifiers. An *operator* performs a function on an expression or set of expressions. For example, the plus sign and minus sign for addition and subtraction are operators. They perform an operation on two expressions such as *expr1* + *expr2* and *expr1* − *expr2*. The terms *expr1* and *expr2* can represent a variable, a constant, or even another expression.

A program statement performs one of three actions: data processing, data input or output, or program flow control.

- *Data processing* uses data known to the program and alters it to produce the desired result. A data processing routine we might use in our example would take the checks written during the month and total their amounts.

- *Input* and *output* greatly enhance a program's usefulness.

- *Flow control* heavily influences the capabilities of a programming language. Normally, the flow, or order, of execution begins with the first statement, continues to the second statement, and so on. Flow control statements alter this natural sequence by allowing for repetition and conditional execution of selected statements. They also make it easier to write structured programs.

The remainder of this book details the tools available in the C programming language for creating program instructions. We will begin with simple arithmetic operators and introduce some of the programming overhead (like defining the main() segment) needed to get a program to run, and follow with program control statements. We will first treat the process of defining custom-tailored functions; then we will discuss why and how to use a structured algorithm in a program. Next we will discuss how to structure the data used by your program to complete the requirements of a structured program. Finally, we will examine the input and output functions and other miscellaneous functions supplied with the compiler for use in your C programs.

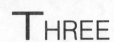

THREE

INTRODUCTION
TO USING C

Now it's time to get to work. This chapter begins with a more explicit example of how to use comments in your programs. The next section of the chapter deals with the actual process of writing, compiling, and executing your program. Read the corresponding section in your user's manual for the compiler you are using before continuing in this book. That way you will have an idea about the variations that might exist between our explanation and your actual system. For example, your compiler might come with its own editor and linker, or the entire process may be invoked by a single command instead of a series of commands. It's important to be sure you understand the steps you need to take to get a program running. If you do not understand your manual, find some assistance (perhaps a local user's group or a computer store); otherwise, you will not be able to try the examples given throughout this book.

The remainder of this chapter introduces you to the basic tools of the C programming language. These tools include arithmetic operators, program flow control, and statement blocks.

USING COMMENTS TO OUTLINE YOUR PROGRAM

We have already discussed the need for defining the goals of a program; this should be done before the program is written. For smaller programs (like those exemplified and mentioned here), one method of planning your program involves using comments to outline the program in the source file. For instance, a preliminary source file for a program that prints a list of all even numbers starting with zero might look like this:

```
/* EVEN—A program to print even numbers starting with zero */
/* Initialize starting point                              */
/* Display even number                                    */
/* Add 2                                                  */
/* Continue displaying                                    */
```

Using comments to outline your program has several additional benefits, one of which is that you avoid the hassle of trying to put comments into your completed program. Commenting before coding also helps to insure that your algorithm will be correct and encourages you to find errors in logic early in the programming process. If you do not comment before or while you write your code, the chances of becoming confused increase. Moreover, if you don't look for errors until the program executes, you waste time and effort.

Creating a specified comment format will help you get the most use from your comments. For example, start your comments at a specified column (somewhere in the middle of the screen). This makes them readily recognizable as comments rather than program statements. You may also want to use a decorative format to highlight the comment; for example:

>>>Wow! What a comment! <<<

Any such highlighting should be quick and easy to type; otherwise, you might stop using comments in your programs. Overall, your comments should be short and informative.

Using comments in your programs is important. Do not fool yourself into thinking you will remember everything about a program you write without including comments.

CREATING, COMPILING, AND EXECUTING SOURCE CODE

Before we explain the different operators available in C, we will present a sample program to familiarize you with the program generation, compilation, and execution processes. Use your text-editing program to create a file called list301.c and enter Listing 3.1 into this file.

```
/********************************************************
      list301     First programming example
********************************************************/

#include "stdio.h"

main()
{
      printf("Welcome to the world of programming");
}
```

Listing 3.1

The basic procedure you will follow after typing in the code as it appears in the listings is as follows. First you should confirm that you have typed everything exactly as shown in the listing. Next, exit your editor and execute the compiler. The compiler requires the name of the source code file that it is to translate. (Check your manual for the proper procedure to execute your compiler.) When the compiler has completed its processing, you will use the program called the *linker* to generate the actual program file. (Again, check your manual for the proper procedure.)

If you are using the Consulair Mac C compiler, you will be using the Macintosh Development System to compile, assemble, and link your programs. To facilitate automatic processing of the compilation procedure, you should create the following two files. First, using the editor, create a file called **output.link**. This file will tell the linker how to create your program. It contains the following statements:

```
;Linker control file
!start

;Include the following libraries
fstdlib
stdfileio
stdioprim
floatlib
floatconv
MathLib
sanelib

;Place program name to link on the next line
list301
$
```

The next file you need to create controls the process of compiling, linking, and running your program. It assumes that you have the Mac C compiler disk in the internal drive, and a disk called "Source" in the external drive. You may change the name of the external drive if you desire. The file is called **output.job** and it contains the following:

```
c           list301.c        exec       edit
link        output.link      exec       edit
Source:output
```

To initiate compilation from the EDIT editor, make output.job the active window and from the Transfer menu, select Exec Source:output.job. This will compile, assemble (an action automatically initiated by the compiler), link, and run the program in file list301.c. Now, each time you want to recompile this program, simply open the output.job file and initiate the Exec command.

For the remaining programs in this book, follow this procedure:

1. Enter the program using the EDIT editor.

2. Open the output.link file and change the program file name list301.c to the current program name.

3. Open the output.job file and change the program file name to the current program name.

4. Choose the Exec command from the Transfer menu.

If you perform these steps in the order listed, you should have an automated compiling sequence. If the compiler or linker should encounter any errors, you will be returned to the editor to make the necessary changes. Hereafter, for the sake of brevity, we will use the term "compile" to refer to the process of both compiling (and optionally assembling if necessary) and linking your source code file into an executable file.

When the compilation is complete, execute your program by selecting it from the desktop. You should see

This is a C program.

You will quickly return to the desktop right after the line is printed. You have just compiled and linked your program. Of course, the compiler and linker provide many options other than those we have demonstrated, which we will see in Chapter 8, but let us take one step at a time.

Now edit your list301.c file again and change it to read like Listing 3.2. In this listing we introduce the characters \n used by C to indicate the end of a display line. Now recompile and link your program. After the new program is compiled and run, you should see the following on the screen:

This is a C program.
Welcome to the world of programming.

```
/********************************************************
     list302     Second programming example
 ********************************************************/
#include "stdio.h"

main()
{
    printf("This is a C program.\n");
    printf("Welcome to the world of programming.\n");
}
```

Listing 3.2

Next, remove the \n from the first line, and compile and execute your program once more. You will see this:

This is a C program.Welcome to the world of programming.

A *metacharacter* is a special symbol that changes the meaning of the character following it. In C, the backslash (\) is a metacharacter when used in a text or character constant (see Chapter 5) or in a string used for input and output (for example, in a printf statement). In the preceding example, the backslash followed by a lowercase "n" is the symbol for the newline character, which causes any subsequent output to be placed at the beginning of the following line.

Because of technical difficulties in writing the compiler, there are certain characters that cannot appear in a string or character constant. Therefore, the metacharacter is used to tell the compiler to "escape" from its normal interpretation of the next character and replace it with a specified alternate charater. Thus, the metacharacter followed by another character is called an *escape sequence*. Appendix C lists the escape sequences available in C and their actions.

The instruction printf used in the program provides for output of data. All of the following examples will utilize some form of the printf print function and you will have to use it without specific description until Chapter 7, which presents and explains the formats for input and output instructions. A brief explanation will accompany most of the new forms of the printf instruction as they are encountered.

To experiment with the newline character, try Listing 3.3. After compilation, run the program. You should see the following display:

This is a C program.
Welcome to the world of programming.

```
/**********************************************************
      list303      Third programming example
**********************************************************/

#include "stdio.h"

main()
{
    printf("This is a C ");
    printf("program.\n");
    printf("Welcome to ");
    printf("the world of programming.");
    printf("\n");
}
```

Listing 3.3

Notice that the printf instruction does not output a newline character until explicitly told to do so. This allows an output line to be constructed dynamically while the program executes. We will discuss the use of dynamic construction later.

BASIC OPERATORS

Every programming language has a basic set of words and symbols that are used in writing programs. The C programming language has a relatively small set of words with a great amount of flexibility. This section introduces most of the operational words and symbols used by C. The words are divided into distinct groups. The first group mentioned here is the arithmetic operators. These symbols are used to change the data used by the program. The purpose of the second group we will introduce is to control which program statements are executed. Once you have mastered these two groups of basic elements in C, you can easily write many simple programs.

ARITHMETIC OPERATORS

The simplest operators to understand are the arithmetic operators +, −, *, and /. The + and − are the symbols for addition and subtraction, respectively. However, the standard cross symbol used for multiplication would too closely resemble the letter "x", and the division symbol does not exist on most keyboards. Therefore, the asterisk (*) is used to signify multiplication and the slash (/) is used for division.

All of these operators are binary operators, meaning that they require two expressions to perform their operation and that they yield only one result. For example, x + y gives the single result of adding y to x. A binary operator will always be used in the form

   expression1 operator expression2

More complex formulas are formed similarly. The expressions used with an operator can even be other formulas, as in the following example:

   a * b + c * d

In this case, the expression a * b can be thought of as replacing the variable x in the first example; the expression c * d would be the variable y. This more complex example should raise some question regarding its evaluation. Would a * b, b + c, or c * d be evaluated first?

This question introduces the concept of *precedence,* or the order in which expressions are evaluated. Under mathematical convention, multiplication and division have a higher precedence than addition and subtraction and are always evaluated first. Multiplication and division have equal precedence with respect to each other and will be evaluated left to right in the order of their occurrence in the equation. Addition and subtraction also have equal precedence with respect to themselves. In this example, a * b is first to be evaluated, and then c * d. The results of these expressions are then added together to yield the final result. If we were to replace the variables with actual values, for example, the expression would be evaluated like this:

   6 * 5 + 4 * 3   30 + 12   42

Parentheses have the highest precedence and can be used to alter the precedence of any other operators. This is the explicitly parenthetical version of our example:

   (a * b) + (c * d)

In this example, the parentheses provide for readability. As far as the compiler is concerned, however, they are redundant. As a matter of style and habit, when expressions begin to get complicated, parentheses should always be used to provide clarity.

If the use of parentheses alters the precedence of other operators, expressions within parentheses will be evaluated from the innermost set to the outermost. Sets of equal precedence are evaluated left to right, in the natural order of the equation.

```
(a * (b + c)) * d
(6 * (5 + 4)) * 3      (6 * 9) * 3      54 * 3      162
```

Each operator in C has a precedence. Appendix D gives a list of the operators, their precedence, and their associativity (order of evaluation) in a nonparenthetical expression.

One other arithmetic operator is the *modulo* operator (%). This operator yields the remainder of an integer division. Thus, for example, 5 % 3 equals 2. Modulo can be defined as follows:

```
x modulo y = x - (y * floor( x/y ))
```

where floor(x/y) is the highest integer less than (x/y). The modulo operator comes in handy when you need to determine if x is evenly divisible by y (that is, when x % y equals 0) and in various advanced programming applications.

The final arithmetic operator is the assignment operator, the equal sign (=). The assignment operator assigns the value of the expression, which is to the right of the = symbol, to the identifier (usually a variable) on the left side of the operator. For example:

```
z = x + y
t = 3.1416 * (d / 2)
a = a + b
c = c + 1
d = d / 2
i = i - 1
```

COMBINED FORMS OF ARITHMETIC AND ASSIGNMENT OPERATORS

Arithmetic and assignment operators account for a substantial percentage of all operations within a program. Some combinations of arithmetic and assignment operations occur quite frequently in program code. To make the code less wordy (and to reduce the amount of typing), C has special combined forms of the assignment and arithmetic operators.

One common assignment operation is

variable = variable operator expression

which changes the value of a specific variable. The shorthand version combines the arithmetic and assignment operators into a single form, as follows:

variable combined-form operator expression

Here are some examples of these combined forms:

a + = b	*equivalent to*	a = a + b
c + = 1	*equivalent to*	c = c + 1
d / = 2	*equivalent to*	d = d / 2
i − = 1	*equivalent to*	i = i − 1

The most common of these combined operations is the *increment* operation (for example, c + = 1), which increases the value of a variable by one. This operation is often used for counting repetitions of a program step. The opposite combined operation is the *decrement* operation (for example, i − = 1); this decreases the value of a variable by one.

A further simplification of the increment/decrement operators is provided by two more combined operators. If you want to increment or decrement by one, you can use these forms: + + to increment by one, and − − to decrement by one.

c + +	*has the same function as*	c = c + 1 *and* c + = 1
i − −	*has the same function as*	i = i − 1 *and* i − = 1

C allows you to place the increment or decrement operator before the variable (+ +c or − −i) to perform the incrementing or decrementing before the variable is used, or to place the operator after the variable (c + + or i− −) to use the value of the variable first, and then increment or decrement the variable. We will be using these two forms extensively in the programming examples, so you should become quite familiar with their different uses.

INTRODUCTION TO DATA TYPES

In Chapter 1 we discussed how data is represented in the computer's memory. C and other structured programming languages require declaration statements that define for the compiler the data type each variable will represent. With this information, the compiler allocates the amount of memory required to store the variable and generates the most efficient machine code for performing operations on this particular data type.

In this chapter, we will be using the integer, floating point, and character data types. An *integer* variable can be any number with no fractional part from − 32,768 through 32,767 (for most compilers), inclusive. A *floating point* number is a rational number. (A rational number is a number that is an integer, or that can be expressed as the quotient of two integers.) The range for floating point numbers is machine-and-implementation-dependent. *Character data* is a set of characters from the ASCII character set.

Floating point notation is the computerized version of exponential notation. For example, 23,445,389,001 is represented by **2.3445389001E+10**, where the value preceding the E signifies the value of the mantissa, and the value following the E indicates the exponent as expressed as a power of ten. This notation evaluates to $2.3445389001 \times 10^{10}$ This format is commonly used throughout the computer industry because most computer displays cannot form a superscript character for the exponent.

The other data types that exist within C are extensions of the three basic types. We will introduce these other types in Chapter 5.

A *declaration instruction* consists of a data type declaration followed by the list of variables that have this particular data type. The items in the list are separated by commas. Integer data is represented by int, floating point data is represented by **double**, and character data is represented by char. For example:

```
int      i, j, k;
double   x, y, z;
char     a, b, c;
```

In this example, i, j, and k have been declared as integers; x, y, and z represent floating point values; and a, b, and c have character values. Notice the use of blank space in the example. The blank space means nothing to the compiler, but it makes the program easier to read.

A SAMPLE PROGRAM

With the small amount of information we already have about C programming, we can write a program to demonstrate the effects of assignment operators and the differences in data types. Our sample program will use the declaration statements. We will initialize the variables by assigning them appropriate constant values, perform a series of operations on them, and display the results after each operation.

The format of the printf statement we will use contains some new information. Using %d causes a decimal value to be printed. The %c symbol signifies that a character will be printed, and the %f indicates a floating point value printed in decimal notation.

The term *constant* holds the same meaning in computer programming jargon as in the general vocabulary: a constant does not change its value during the course of a program's execution. It is usually used to initialize variables, and we will use it that way in our program. The data type of the variable being assigned will determine the format of the constant. Appendix E has a listing of the different formats for constants for each data type. For the purposes of this program, notice that character constants are enclosed in single quotation marks, or apostrophes. Floating point constants have a trailing fractional part (although the fraction may be zero) to highlight the use of a floating point value.

The printf statement used in this program demonstrates the necessity of matching data types within an expression. In many expressions, especially assignment expressions, the type of the identifier being assigned must match the type of the result from the expression. If it does not, the memory space allocated for the assigned identifier may not provide enough room for the value. Some languages perform dynamic memory allocation automatically. This means that memory is allocated as it becomes needed, so that the "size" of the information to be stored determines how much space is alloted. Arguments can be made for and against this practice. C does not automatically allocate memory. However, it can dynamically allocate memory if explicitly told to do so, as we will see in Chapter 6.

When an expression contains two or more different types of data, it is called a *mixed-mode expression*. C will convert the operands of the expression based upon the conversion procedures outlined in Appendix E. Allowing C to perform automatic conversion is considered poor programming practice. C does let you explicitly convert from one data type to another (if the conversion is logical). We will show you how to do all of this in Chapter 5.

Listing 3.4 shows how operations vary for different data types. Enter and compile this program now.

Notice what happened when we performed arithmetic operations on character variables. The character variables were first converted to integer types and then operated on (see Appendix A for the mapping of characters to integers). Our sample program has also demonstrated the division of the source code into segments.

```
/*******************************************************
     list304     Program to practice usage of data types
*******************************************************/

#include "stdio.h"

main()
{
int     i, j, k;           /* integer variables        */
double  x, y, z;           /* floating point variables */
char    a, b, c;           /* character variables      */

                           /* variable initialization  */
        i = 10;            /* integer assignments       */
        j = 5;
        k = 3;

        x = 10.7;          /* floating point assignments */
        y = 5.0;
        z = 3.0;

        a = '0';           /* character assignments     */
        b = 'A';
        c = 'a';

                           /* print initial values      */
        printf("Integers: i = %d, j = %d, k = %d\n", i, j, k);
        printf("Floating Point: x = %f, y = %f, z = %f\n", x, y, z);
        printf("Characters: a = %c, b = %c, c = %c\n\n", a, b, c);
                           /* last printf provides      */
                           /* for double spacing        */

                           /* integer manipulation      */
        i++;
        printf("i has been incremented to %d\n", i);
        printf("Combine increment of i in printf statement %d\n", i++);
        printf("i incremented after value was used. New i is %d\n", i);
        printf("Increment i first. i = %d\n", ++i);
        printf("i after above statement = %d\n", i);
        printf("Integer division j / k = %d\n", j/k);
        printf("Modulo operator j %% k = %d\n", j%k);
                           /* Note %% is correct */
        j += k;
        printf("After j += k, j is %d\n", j);
        i = j + k;
        printf("After i = j + k, i = %d, j = %d, k = %d\n\n", i, j, k);

        printf("Press Return to continue program\n");
        scanf("%*s");

                           /* floating point */
```

Listing 3.4

```
      x++;
      printf("Increment of x is %f\n", x);
      printf("Floating point division y / z = %f\n", y/z);
      x *= y;
      printf("After x *= y, x is %f\n", x);
      x = y * z;
      printf("After x = y * z, x = %f, y = %f, z = %f\n\n", x, y, z);

                        /* character manipulation */
      a++;
      printf("Increment of a is %c\n", a);
      a += b;
      printf("After a += b, a is %c\n", a);
      a = b + c;
      printf("After a = b + c, a = %c, b = %c, c = %c\n\n", a, b, c);

      printf("Press Return to exit program\n");
      scanf("%*s");   /* hit the Return key to end the program */
      printf("End of program.\n");
}                           /* End main()                  */
```

Listing 3.4 (continued)

Notice that the program includes a function called **scanf()**. This is like the **printf** statement mentioned earlier except that it accepts input instead of producing output. The statement is used to suspend the program execution so that you have time to look over what is shown on the screen before it scrolls off the top. Many of the programs in the rest of this book will use this pause feature. The **scanf()** function will be covered in depth with the **printf** function later on.

At this point, let's experiment with the program in order to see the effects of some other operators and operations. This is an important step toward understanding the uses of what you have just learned. As you make changes to the program, try to predict the results before running the program in order to test your understanding of these operators.

First let's alter the program by deleting the sections that manipulate floating point numbers and characters. Recompile the program and run it to check your work. Now change the program to test other operators, such as the decrement operator. Using only the integer section of the program reduces the possibility of errors. Using the **printf** statements in the sample program as models, create your own **printf** statements to reflect the changes you make. After you have tested the integer manipulation, experiment with floating point and then character variables. Using many **printf** statements will make it easier to understand the order of execution and the functions of the operators.

You should also try some mixed-mode operations. If the compiler gives you error messages regarding illegal operations, determine which operation caused the error and either fix it, if possible, or remove it. Before you run any of these programs, write down what you think the computer will display at each printf statement. Use Appendix E to help in the conversion of mixed-mode operands. Do these experiments now.

Relational and Logical Operators

One of the most powerful capabilities a programming language has to offer is the ability to perform a specified set of tasks based upon a certain condition. For example, if you were to write a program for an automatic bottle-filling machine, you might say, "Fill the bottle *until* it contains 12 ounces." Thus, your program continues to pour the product into a bottle under the condition that less than 12 ounces have been output. When 12 ounces of product are in the bottle, the program will move to its next task.

There is some good news and bad news in all this. The bad news is that it is very difficult for a computer to understand a complex condition like "If it looks like rain or snow." The computer can only understand a comparison between two numeric values. The good news is that we can break apart the statment and represent each segment as a value either numerically or as a true or false statement. For example, we could rewrite "If it looks like rain or snow" as "If the chance or rain is more than 80 percent or the chance of snow is more than 80 percent". The branch of mathematics that deals with these types of statements is called logic.

Definition and Background of Logic Statements

Logic is very important in computer programming. The logic used in today's computers is based on Boolean algebra, developed by the English mathematician George Boole. In Boolean algebra, an operand or expression may be equal to one of two values, either true or false. The four common logical, or Boolean, operators are NOT, AND, inclusive-OR (called simply OR), and exclusive-OR (called XOR).

The NOT or negation operator performs the same function as it does when used in spoken language. If an element P has the value of true, then NOT P will yield false, and vice versa. Figure 3.1 shows the results of the logical operators in the commonly used truth table format.

The AND operator corresponds to the conjunction of two operands. Note that for the expression to yield a "true" value, both operands must have the value of true; otherwise, the entire expression evaluates to false.

The inclusive-OR operator corresponds to the common use of the word "or" in spoken language (a disjunction). When either operand has a value of true, the expression will evaluate to true. The exclusive-OR, commonly referred to as XOR, is true when either operand, but not both, is true.

All programming languages provide for implementation of these operations, and some even provide a special data type called *Boolean* to handle variables that will be used in these operations. To understand how these operations function in a programming language, notice that an operand can represent one of two binary values and that we can equate the operand to be a binary digit. By convention, the value of true is equal to 1, and the value of false is equal to 0.

Furthermore, by definition in Boolean algebra, a series of elements—in our case bits—can be operated on element by element, or bit by bit. For these operations the C programming language uses

P	NOT P
T	F
F	T

P	Q	P AND Q
T	T	T
T	F	F
F	T	F
F	F	F

P	Q	P OR Q
T	T	T
T	F	T
F	T	T
F	F	F

P	Q	P XOR Q
T	T	F
T	F	T
F	T	T
F	F	F

Figure 3.1: Truth Tables

bitwise operators: the bitwise AND (called &), the bitwise inclusive OR (called ¦), and the bitwise exclusive OR (called ^). These operators use integer values as operands and perform their respective operations in a bitwise manner (see Figure 3.2). See Appendix F for the numerical representation of the truth tables.

Two more bitwise operators perform a shifting of bits within an integer operand. These bitwise operators have a relatively small set of uses in general programming. They are restricted to hardware manipulation, and their use requires advanced data structuring techniques. Bitwise operators will be discussed in greater detail in Chapter 6.

Logical operators follow the same truth tables as their bitwise counterparts, but operate on the entire value of the operand. Valid operands for a logical operator evaluate to either true or false. In C, any nonzero value operand is considered true, and a zero value operand is considered false. Logical expressions equal 1 if the expression evaluates as true or 0 if it is false. The logical operators include logical AND (&&), logical inclusive OR (¦), equal to (==), NOT (!), and not equal to (!=).

Relational operator expressions also result in a 1 or 0, depending on whether the specified relation is true or false, respectively. The four relational operators are less than (<), greater than (>), less than or equal to (<=), and greater than or equal to (>=).

FORMING LOGICAL EXPRESSIONS

The objective of a programming language is to relate a task to the computer. The more similar the tools of the programming language and the language spoken by the programmer, the faster and easier it is to program the task. The relational and logical operators provide a great deal of flexibility in expressing the conditional requirements of a procedure. For example, to determine if your checkbook balances

```
      Bitwise AND          Bitwise OR          Bitwise XOR

          01101001             01101001             01101001
   &      11100011      ¦      11100011      ^      11100011
          --------             --------             --------
          01100001             11101011             10001010
```

Figure 3.2: Examples of Bitwise Operators

after reconciliation, you would ask, "Is my reconciled checkbook balance equal to (= =) the balance on the bank statement?" Expressions containing relational and logical operators form the basis for conditional processing and controlling the flow of program execution.

CONTROLLING PROGRAM FLOW

Program flow control in C consists of a statement to evaluate some condition and set of statements to be executed when the condition evaluates to true. The evaluation statements for C come in three varieties: conditional execution, loops, and forced flow interruption. Let's first begin by looking at the general structure of a flow control code segment, and then move on to the specific types of statements.

CONTROL STATEMENTS

As we mentioned earlier, a program is simply a sequential execution of instructions. Besides carrying out these instructions, the computer may have to evaluate certain conditions, data, and relationships between conditions and data. Statements in C that cause such evaluation and conditional execution are known as *control statements.*

Control statements provide increased programming structure. Each control statement has associated with it a conditional expression and a statement or block of statements. In C, a block of statements appears as a single statement in relation to the rest of the program. This compound statement structure removes code from the main flow of the program, making the program easier for the compiler and programmer to read.

STATEMENT BLOCKS

If a statement block appears in a program, it will be executed as if it were a statement itself. We will discuss the advantages of this in Chapter 4.

If a statement block follows a control statement, then the block will be executed only if the conditional expression in the control statement evaluates to true. If the conditional expression evaluates to false, then the entire block will be skipped and the statement following the block will be executed.

Statement blocks can also be defined within other blocks. This use of a block within a block illustrates the principle of nesting, something we will use in several programs.

CONDITIONAL EXECUTION STATEMENTS

Conditional execution statements are used for one-time execution; either the statement block associated with the statement is to be executed (the condition is true) or it is to be skipped (the condition is false). Once the condition has been evaluated and the statement block is executed or skipped, the next statement in the program is processed. Thus the conditional flow returns to the statement). The basic construct for conditional execution is the if statement.

THE IF STATEMENT

Control statements, the most fundamental of which is the if statement, are based on conditional expressions and determine program flow. The construction of an if statement is quite simple.

    if (expression)
        statement;

The if statement will execute the statement (which may also be a statement block) when the expression evaluates to a nonzero value, which, of course, we call true. The expression must be enclosed within parentheses. Because an if statement implies a then portion of the statement, C assumes the existence of the word "then," and you do not need to write it in your programs. Figure 3.3 shows some examples of if statements.

```
        Example 1:           Example 2:            Example 3:
        if (x == y)          if (x != 0)           if (--i > 0){
              z /= 2;               z = y / x;           z = i * 2;
                                                         a = b + c; }
```

Figure 3.3: Examples of the **if** Statement

The third example in this figure shows the use of the decrement operator within an expression. The variable i will be decremented first and then compared to 0. If the new value of i is greater than (and not equal to) 0, then the statement block will be executed. Note the placement of the braces to structure the format of the source code. As the examples become more complex, you will see how this indentation and formatting aids in the readability of your program.

The conditional expression following the if statement can be as complex as you need it to be. You may use virtually any combination of relational and logical operators.

Suppose, for example, that you needed to know if x is greater than y, and i is less than or equal to 7; or if x is less than 3 and y is less than 3. In either case you would perform some set of instructions. Here is a conditional expression you could use:

```
if ((x>y && i< =7) || (x<3 && y<3)){
    statement block;
}
```

Here the outermost parenthetical set is required by the syntax of the if statement. The two inner sets of parentheses are used to divide the two possible conditions, just as the semicolon was used in the text sentence above. The first set corresponds to the case in which x is greater than y, and i is less than or equal to 7. The second set requires x to be less than 3 and y to be less than 3. If either of these conditions evaluates to true, then the whole statement is considered true (as prescribed by the OR condition).

Relational operators have a higher precedence than logical operators, making parentheses around the relational expressions unnecessary. Of course, the statement we just considered could also be explicitly written as

```
if (((x>y) && (i< =7)) || ((x<3) && (y<3))){
    statement block;
}
```

However, when parentheses become too deeply nested, the expressions become difficult to read. Because the logical OR operator has a lower precedence than the logical AND operator, this expression does not need any parentheses except those required by the syntax of the if statement.

```
if (x>y && i< = 7 | x<3 && y<3){
    statement block;
}
```

But this again makes a difficult-to-read expression. Find a happy medium. You should use parentheses for syntax, precedence, and to enhance readability.

By definition of the C programming language, when a program evaluates an expression containing a logical operator, evaluation stops when the truth of the expression has been determined. In a logical AND expression, if the first operand is false, then the entire expression must be false. Comparison halts and this saves execution time. In a logical OR expression, if the first operand is true, then the entire expression must be true, and again additional testing is not performed on the rest of the if expression.

THE IF-ELSE STATEMENT

On many occasions, you will want to execute one set of statements if the condition is true and another set of statements if the condition is false, but not both. In English, we would use the phrase "if . . . then . . . otherwise . . . ." In C, we use the following syntax:

```
if (conditional expression)
    statement-1
else
    statement-2
```

This is the full-length version of the if statement we were using before; the else is optional, and statement-1 and statement-2 may be statement blocks. The if-else statement operates in the same manner as in English: if the conditional expression is true, statement-1 is executed; otherwise, statement-2 is executed. Both statements will never be executed under the same condition.

This if-else statement will set z equal to whichever value is greater—a or b:

```
if (a > b)
    z = a;
else
    z = b;
```

The fact that if statements can be nested means that an if statement can appear in the statement portion of another if statement. For example:

```
1   if (n > 0)
2       if (a > b)
3           z = a;
4       else
5           z = b;
6   else
7       if (x < y)
8           x = y;
```

Here the indentation is used to indicate that the else in line 4 belongs to the if in line 2; the else in line 6 matches the if in line 1. Another else statement in our example would then pair with the if in line 7. By definition, an else always pairs with the closest previous nonpaired if. This is a very important point, as multiple (nested) if statements can become quite confusing.

Consider the following example:

```
1   if (n > 0)
2       if (x < y)
3           x = y;
4   else                        /* INCORRECT MATCHING */
5       if (a > b)
6           z = a;
7       else
8           z = b;
```

Although the indentation in this example shows what the programmer intended, the compiler will generate code based upon the definition of the C language. The else in line 4 will be matched with the if in line 2 since it is the closest previous if without an else. The proper formatting of this code is as follows:

```
1    if (n > 0)
2         if (x < y)
3              x = y;
4         else
5              if (a > b)
6                   z = a;
7              else
8                   z = b;
```

The if in line 1 has no corresponding **else** statement.

The use of braces to identify statement blocks tells the compiler to produce code of the correct intent. Braces are to program flow as parentheses are to expression evaluation: they tell the compiler to segment the code and treat everything between the braces as if it were a single statement. Another version of our last code example is

```
1    if (n > 0) {        /* Start of block */
2         if (x < y)
3              x = y; } /* End of block */
4    else
5         if (a > b)
6              z = a;
7         else
8              z = b;
```

The **else** in line 4 is paired with the if in line 1. In effect, the **else** does not know about the if in line 2 because of the braces. Remember: the braces hide what is inside from the rest of the program.

THE **ELSE-IF** STATEMENT

The **else-if** statement is not a special statement by definition. Instead it arises from the ability to nest **if-else** statements. The **else-if** construct, written as

```
if (expression-1)
     statement-1
else if (expression-2)
     statement-2
```

```
        else if (expression-3)
            statement-3

                .

                .

                .

        else if (expression-n)
            statement-n
        else
            no-match statement
```

is simply a more clearly formatted version of

```
    if (expression-1)
        statement-1
    else
        if(expression-2)
            statement-2
        else
            if (expression-3)
                statement-3
            else if

                .

                .

                .
```

```
            else if (expression-n)
                statement-n
            else
                no-match statement
```

This indented format tends to push the code off the edge of the screen during coding and does not communicate the one-to-one correspondence of conditional expression to statements. The first expression evaluating to true will have its associated statement executed, and it will be the only statement executed; this is called a *multiway decision*. The final **else** statement with its associated no-match statement will be executed if and only if one of the previous statements has not been executed.

No-match statements are useful as default procedures that execute if no special conditions have arisen. They can also be used to catch any "impossible" situations; for example, you may expect one of the listed expressions to be true, and for some reason none of them is. This can be an important tool in debugging (that is, removing the errors from) your program. This type of no-match statement can be as simple as printing a message indicating that no matches occurred, or as elaborate as printing a diagnostic message and then executing a special error-handling routine. Of course, the form of the statement will depend upon the programming assignment.

THE ?: OPERATOR

A special three-operand assignment operator is available in C. It functions exactly like the if-else statement used earlier to find the greater value of two numbers. The ?: operator has the form

(*conditional expression*) ? *expression-1* : *expression-2*

Should the conditional expression be true, the ?: operator evaluates expression-1; otherwise it evaluates expression-2. The value of the expression evaluated can be assigned to a variable. Thus, the if-else statement from before

```
if (a > b)
    z = a;
else
    z = b;
```

can be rewritten as

```
z = (a > b) ? a : b;
```

Because the ?: operator is an expression itself, it can be used anywhere an expression is required. Notice that it differs from the if-else in that it cannot have statements within its construction: the ?: is an operator that returns a value and that must contain valid expressions.

Listing 3.5 is somewhat skeletal, allowing you to experiment with the statements introduced in this section without too much overhead. Enter and compile this program. When you are satisfied you understand the operation of the statements contained in this segment of code, make changes, and observe the results. What happens if you remove the braces in the else-if section? Or if you move the ?: operator into the printf statement following it and use the ?: operator instead of the variable i?

REPETITION STATEMENTS

Most programming tasks will require a number of repetitions of some kind within your program. A structure that performs repetition is called a *loop*. C has three types of loop statements: **while**, **for**, and **do-while**.

THE **WHILE** STATEMENT

A **while** statement has the following format:

while (*expression*)
    loop body
rest of program

```
/*******************************************************
     list305     Experimenting with If
*******************************************************/

#include "stdio.h"

main()
{
int    i, j, k;

    j = 2;                          /* initialization    */
    k = 10;

    i = (j > k) ? j : k;          /* find max(j, k)      */
    printf("Maximum of %d and %d is %d\n", j, k, i);

    i = 5;
    if (i == 1)
        printf("*> This should not be printed. <*\n");
    else
        printf("This should be printed.\n");

    k = 3;
    if (j > k)
        printf("j is greater than k.\n");
    else if (j < k) {
        printf("j is less than k.\n");
        j++;                        /* notice this does not */
                                    /* cause the next       */
                                    /* else-if to be        */
                                    /* to be executed       */
    }
    else if (j == k)
        printf("j equals k.\n");

    scanf("%*s");
}                                   /* end main */
```

Listing 3.5

When the while statement is encountered, the expression is evaluated. If the expression is true (nonzero), the loop body is executed and control returns to the while statement for reevaluation of the expression. This process will be repeated until the expression becomes false, at which point program execution continues with the rest of program segment. If the expression was false on the first encounter, the loop body is skipped and the rest of program is executed. The loop body may be a single statement or a statement block.

Listing 3.6 demonstrates the while loop with a program that is similar to Listing 3.5. Notice that the while statement executes the statement block as long as the variable j is less than 10. How many iterations will this loop perform? If you removed the instruction that increments j, the loop would never terminate.

The while statement is used in situations where the program is waiting for a particular condition either to arise or to cease. For example, if the program is to do analysis on a set of data and the quantity of data is unknown, the while statement could be used as follows:

end of data is false
while *(not end of data)*
get more data

```
/************************************************************
     list306     Experimenting with the While Loop
 ************************************************************/

#include "stdio.h"

main()
{
int     j, k;

    k = 5;                      /* initialization       */
    j = 1;

    while (j < 10) {            /* begin loop body      */
        printf("j = %d, k = %d: ", j, k);

        if (j > k)
            printf("j is greater than k.\n");
        else if (j < k)
            printf("j is less than k.\n");
        else if (j == k)
            printf("j equals k.\n");

        j++;
    }                           /* end while (j < 10)   */
    scanf("%*s");
}                               /* end main             */
```

Listing 3.6

In this symbolic example, the loop body (get more data) would be required to retrieve the data and to set the end of data flag when it encounters that situation.

The **while** statement can also be used in converting a decimal number to a binary number. Try writing an algorithm to do this using the **while** statement. Use the **printf** statement to output a 1 or 0 when appropriate.

THE **FOR** STATEMENT

The **for** statement simply reorders the while statement. Compare the two constructs. On the one hand, the **for** statement:

> **for** (*expression-1; conditional expression; expression-2*)
>   *loop body*

And on the other hand, the **while** statement:

>   *expression-1;*
> **while** (*conditional expression*) {
>   *loop body*
>   *expression-2;*
> }

As you can see, the **for** statement will execute expression-1 before entering the actual loop. The expression is usually an initializing assignment statement, although it can be any valid expression. The loop continues to execute as long as the conditional expression evaluates to true. Expression-2 is also any valid expression, usually an expression to change the values used in the conditional expression.

Thus we can use the **for** statement to rewrite the **while** loop from program list306. The **for** statement centralizes the loop-controlling statements, making the program clearer and more concise. The **for** statement and the **while** statement can be nested and can also appear within the loop body of any other loop statement. Under these conditions, centralizing controlling statements becomes essential for making a program understandable.

Any of the expressions in the **for** statement can be omitted, but the semicolons must remain. If either expression-1 or expression-2 is left out, no special action is taken. If the conditional expression is omitted, it is assumed to be permanently true. The statement

```
for (;;) {
     loop body
}
```

has no intialization, no loop end expressions, and no exit condition. This is known as an *infinite loop* because it will execute *ad infinitum*, or until the loop is terminated by outside intervention.

Expression-1 and expression-2 can consist of multiple statements separated by the comma (,) operator. The for statement in Listing 3.7 can be written as

```
for (j = 1, k = 5; j < 10; j+ +) {
```

which incorporates the initialization of k into expression-1. The comma operator may appear in any expression. It has the lowest precedence of all operators.

Listing 3.8 uses the for statement in this way to print a table of the powers of 2. The table will include all powers of 2 between 0 and 10. The inner for loop initializes j and p to 1. What happens when i equals 0 on the first iteration? If we look back at the while equivalent

```
/*********************************************************
     list307       Experimenting with the For Loop
*********************************************************/

#include "stdio.h"

main()
{
int     j, k;

    k = 5;                          /* initialization    */

    for (j = 1; j < 10; j++) {   /* begin loop body     */
         printf("j = %d, k = %d: ", j, k);

         if (j > k)
              printf("j is greater than k.\n");
         else if (j < k)
              printf("j is less than k.\n");
         else if (j == k)
              printf("j equals k.\n");
    }                               /* end for (j)        */
    scanf("%*s");
}                                   /* end main           */
```

Listing 3.7

of the **for** statement, we see that first the two statements of expression-1 are executed, and then the conditional expression is executed. In this case, the condition evaluates to false, and the inner loop is not executed at all. This sets 2 to the 0 power equal to 1, which, by mathematical definition, is correct.

The inner **for** statement also has only one statement within its loop body. In this specific example, this statement could be placed in expression-2 of the **for** statement by using the comma in this manner:

```
for (j = 1, p = 1; j <= i; p *= 2, j++)
    ;
```

Although this format performs the same function as the original version, it clouds the intent of the **for** statement, its control statements, and the purpose of using the loop. The semicolon is required because a **for** statement must be followed by a loop body, either a statement or statement block. Since we do not have anything in the loop body, we need a placeholder for the statement. A pair of empty braces can also be used to indicate the nonexistent statement.

THE DO-WHILE STATEMENT

The **for** and **while** statements test their conditional expressions at the top of the loop. The expression is tested before the loop ever

```
/*****************************************************************
   list308      Print a table of powers of 2
*****************************************************************/
#include "stdio.h"

main()
{
int i, j, p;

    printf("Powers Of 2\n\n");  /* print a title            */

    for (i = 0; i <= 10; i++) {  /* range of powers to calc  */
        for (j = 1, p = 1; j <= i; j++)
            p *= 2;              /* calculate power          */

        printf("2 to the power of %d = %d\n", i, p);
    }                            /* end for (i)              */
    scanf("%*s");
}                                /* end main                 */
```

Listing 3.8

begins; this means that the loop body might never execute, as in our program Listing 3.8. On occasion, however, you may wish to execute the loop at least once regardless of the evaluation of the conditional expression. The **do-while** statement provides this ability.

The **do-while** statement is used as follows:

```
do
    loop body
while (conditional expression);
```

Upon reaching the **do** portion of the **do-while** statement, the program will immediately execute the loop body and then test the conditional expression. As in the **for** and **while** statements, the program will continue to process the loop body as long as the conditional expression remains true.

THE CONTINUE STATEMENT

A **continue** statement causes the next iteration of the enclosing loop. In the case of **while** or **do-while**, a **continue** will cause immediate execution of the conditional expression controlling the loop, and program execution will continue from this point. In a **for** statement, a **continue** statement causes expression-2 to be executed, and program execution continues from there.

A **continue** statement is generally used to avoid nesting large portions of the program within an **if** statement. For example, if you want to process only one certain item from a large list of possibilities, you could write

```
for (appropriate values) {
if ( !condition ) /* skip items not matching condition */
    continue;
    /* process items otherwise */
}
```

Use of the **continue** statement is entirely the programmer's prerogative. If using the **continue** statement clarifies the intentions of the code, then it should be used; otherwise, use a different construct.

THE **BREAK** STATEMENT

The **break** and the **continue** statements are related by the nature of their usage. While the **continue** statement will start the next iteration of its enclosing loop, the **break** statement actually "breaks out of," or exits, the enclosing loop.

The **break** statement may be used in a loop that continues processing until a certain condition is met, after which control passes to the statement following the loop.

For example, Figure 3.4 shows a program fragment that demonstrates a crude method of checking incoming data. An external device may have difficulty communicating with a computer due to poor conditions such as long cable distances; or the device may be in a hostile environment. In these instances, the data received by a computer will need to be checked for quality by some prearranged method. In this example, the program receives a list of characters. Under the error-checking routine installed, if it is determined that any charater is invalid, the entire list is considered invalid; otherwise, each character needs to be processed.

The algorithm gets a list of characters. Each character can be referenced by an index, and in this example we use i (ignore how this is done for now). The variable n is the number of characters in the list. We process each character in the list using the **for** loop. The **for** statement sets a flag, **listok**, to true, to signify that the list is OK to begin with. If we find a bad character, **listok** is set to false, and the loop is broken since there is no need to process further characters. The remainder of the **while** loop checks the status of the **listok** flag. If the list was completely processed, a new list is requested; otherwise, a retransmission of the list is requested.

```
while (more character lists) {
    get list of characters;
    for (i = 1, listok = true; i < n; i++) {
        if (current character is invalid) {
            listok = false;
            break;
        process this character;
    }
    if (listok)
        signal for new list;
    else
        signal to repeat list;
}
```

Figure 3.4: Use of the **break** Statement

THE SWITCH-CASE-DEFAULT STATEMENT

A specialized form of the **else-if** construct can be found in the switch-case-default statement, which we will simply call **switch**. The **switch** statement is written as follows:

```
switch (integer expression) {
case constant-1:
    statement-1
case constant-2:
    statement-2

    .
    .
    .

case constant-n:
    statement-n
default:
    default statement
}
```

The integer expression in the **switch** statement can be any expression that evaluates to an integer value. Each **case** statement must have a unique integer or character associated with it. This statement will match the integer expression in the **switch** statement to the constant of the **case** statement.

One of the two major differences between this construct and the **else-if** construct is that this construct is limited to the use of integer constants. The second major difference is the execution of subsequent statements. With the **else-if** statement, only one statement (or statement block) will be executed from the entire construct. In a **switch** statement, execution begins with the first matching **case** statement and will continue until the end of the block (notice the braces). To stop execution of the rest of the block, use the **break** statement to force the program flow out of the block. Finally, execution will begin at the default programming segment if no other **case** statements match the integer expression. The **default** case may appear anywhere within the block. If no matches occur and no **default** statement exists, then no action is taken.

Figure 3.5 shows a sample program fragment that validates a date. This program fragment receives a date with the components **year**, **month**, and **day**, which are treated as separate variables. The **year** is assumed to be a complete 4-digit year.

```
/* Date verification routine */

int      month, day, year;

     if (day > 0) {
          switch (month) {
          case 1:               /* January */
          case 3:               /* March */
          case 5:               /* May */
          case 7:               /* July */
          case 8:               /* August */
          case 10:              /* October */
          case 12:              /* December */
               if (day > 31)
                    printf("Invalid Day\n");
               break;

          case 4:               /* April */
          case 6:               /* June */
          case 9:               /* September */
          case 11:              /* November */
               if (day > 30)
                    printf("Invalid Day\n");
               break;

          case 2:                /* February */
               if (year % 4 == 0)
                    if ( (year % 100 != 0) || (year % 400 == 0) )
                         if (day <= 29)
                              break;

               if (day > 28)
                         printf("Invalid Day\n");
               break;

          default:
               printf("Invalid Month\n");
          }                        /* end switch */
     }                             /* end if */

     else
          printf("Invalid Day\n");
```

Figure 3.5: Date Verification Routine

Examine this segment of code now. Notice that the first test checks to see if **day** is greater than zero. The **switch** statement then passes control to the **case** statement containing the **month**. The first set of **case** statements processes the months that have 31 days. The second set processes those months with 30 days. The final case statement processes February, which can have 29 days in all leap years (those years divisible by 4 and not divisible by 100, unless they are divisible by 400), and 28 days in all other years. The **default** statement catches an invalid month reference. The **printf** statements could be altered to change the truth value of a date validity flag instead of just printing the diagnostic message in the sample.

THE GOTO STATEMENT

The **goto** statement consists of two parts. The first part consists of the keyword **goto** and the name of the line where the program should go to. The second part of the **goto** statement is the line that is named by the label.

A *label* is an identifier terminated by a colon (label:). The label gives a name to a particular line within your source code file. The only use for a label is to target a line for a **goto** statement.

The **goto** statement immediately transfers execution to the location of the label following the **goto**. For example:

```
goto wayout;
        .

        .

        .
wayout:
```

The **goto** statement disrupts the continuity of a program's structure. When a **goto** is encountered, it causes an explicit jump to some other location. The **goto** itself does not provide any information about why the jump is to be made, nor about why the particular location named was chosen as the target of the **goto**. Abuse of the **goto** statement can easily lead to "spaghetti-code"—that is, code in which if you trace the path of the program's flow with a pencil, your page quickly begins to resemble a plate of spaghetti.

The **goto** statement should be used in specialized situations: for example, if you want to exit from more than one loop with one statement. The **break** statement will not work as it only exits the enclosing loop. The **goto** statement has little allegiance to the program's structure and will allow you to jump to a point outside the loops you wish to exit. Unless you have a compelling or unique reason for using the **goto** statement, you should try to avoid it. In most circumstances, code that uses a **goto** statement can be rewritten without it.

F_{OUR}

P_{ROGRAMMING}

T_{ECHNIQUE}

Chapter 4 presents you with the actual nitty-gritty of writing a complete program in C. We will begin by examining the organization of a program. The organization technique presented here, called structured programming, is the most widely accepted practice for designing and writing programs.

The principle structuring device in a C program is called the *function*. The function provides the programmer with the tool to develop a larger vocabulary for his programming use. For example, the function can be used to define the procedure of getting a date from the program operator and checking to see if it is a legitimate date (for example, that February does not have 31 days).

Associated with the function are several concepts that need to be studied in order to be able to understand how a program works. These concepts include scoping of variables, defining storage classes, parameters, and recursion. All of these concepts will be covered in this chapter.

STRUCTURED PROGRAMMING

When writing a program, even the most experienced programmer rarely writes an algorithm from top to bottom without making some alterations or backtracking to include some detail he or she forgot. The algorithms shown in this book were not written with a single pass of our cursor!

Programming usually follows a path from the general to the specific. Beginning with an idea, the program designer starts with an outline of the algorithm. (The program designer is sometimes the same person who will later write the code for the program and sometimes a different person.) Relatively short programs, such as most of the examples presented here, require only an outline of comments in your source code file as a first step. Larger programs written for larger systems require more extensive and rigorous planning.

The outline covers the general program flow. Each section of the outline represents a separate task within the program for which a section of code will be expressly written. For example, the date routine used in Chapter 3 would be considered a separate task within a larger program.

The process of writing code is divided into stages corresponding to the sections of the outline. For larger programs, each major stage may have an outline, and each part of each stage may also have an outline. The depth of the outline depends upon the size of the program (the number of functions it must perform) as well as its intricacy. The outline will illustrate the different procedures within the program and clearly define the requirements of each procedure. At this point, coding can begin.

As the programmer begins coding, he or she is actually finalizing the outline. In essence, the coding begins from the innermost level of the outline. The completion of each sublevel provides a base upon which the next level can be built.

Explaining the process in English will clarify the outline. In telling someone else how to proceed with check reconciliation, you may begin with something like "Get a check," and we would use this as a section heading for our outline. However, the computer is relatively dumb and does not know how to get a check; it requires more detail. A check is simply a piece of paper with bits of information on it and getting a check implies obtaining this information. Now our outline looks like this:

    Get a check
        Get the check number
        Get the date
        Get the payee
        Get the amount

This would provide sufficient information to a programmer, who in turn would continue to refine the outline to include data validation:

    Get a check
        Get the check number
            Get a number
            Is this a valid number (nonnegative; within range)?
            Is this an unused number?
        Get the date
            Get a date input
            Is this a valid date?
        Get the payee
        Get the amount

Our outline for getting a check is now ready to be used to write the section of the program it describes. If the questions (which become conditional statements in the program) evaluate to true, the procedure continues. If any of these statements evaluates to false, then the program would take special action.

For example, if the response to "Is this an unused number?" is false, your program can perform any of a variety of procedures. The program can give an error message indicating the number has already been used and then request another number. Or it can display the check corresponding to the number entered and then request another number (this would allow the user to verify whether the check has already been entered or whether the check number was entered incorrectly). Or finally the program can display the corresponding check and allow the user to change the information on this check (that is, essentially allow the operator to use an editing facility). The method chosen would appear in the outline under the heading of the conditional statement.

As you can see, the outline can become extremely complex. As a rule of thumb, the final level of any section will refer to a single step in that section of the program. The section "Get the amount" refers to one self-explanatory segment of the program. This level of detail is by no means developed on one pass. The general outline and a few sublevels are produced, and as each sublevel is coded the details are supplied. The structure of the code follows from the structure of the outline.

The final step in developing the outline is to specify the data requirements of each section. This means that you must specify what data the section needs from other parts of the program once the task is completed. For example, in the "Get a check" section of our hypothetical check-balancing program, the routine does not require any data from other parts of the program. When the routine finishes, it provides the check information entered by the operator, which can be used by another part of the program (perhaps a routine to permanently store the data on disk).

Now that a program outline has been written and data requirements for each section have been specified, the program design is complete. Notice that the design does not explain or list how to write the program; the outline only explains what the program will do. Essentially, the outline defines the flow and processing of data, and not the manner in which it is processed. This is called the *black box principle*.

A black box is an object (or in this case a portion of programming code) into which a known set of data enters, is altered through some mechanism, and exits. The alteration mechanism is purposely hidden from the outside world. By defining the input data and output data, and leaving the processing unexplained, each subsection in our outline corresponds to a black box in the program, whose only requirement is to follow the data structures assigned to it.

The division of the program in the outline stage into single-concept portions forces program structuring once actual coding is underway. The designer should give a well-defined description of the program subsection, leaving the programmer to write the actual code. The definition of input and output data requirements is the first step in the process of data structuring (which we will cover in the next section). Program sections can then be given to several programmers on a programming team, or if a single programmer is coding the project, the work can be scheduled. The flexibility of this method of program production makes it applicable to any size or level of programming task.

The C programming language provides constructs called functions that make this type of design easy. We have already seen the use of the braces to block program statements together. The braces group the enclosed statements into a form resembling a single program statement. From the point of view of the rest of the program, this single statement has known inputs and outputs with a hidden mechanism for processing the data. We will use these statement blocks more and more frequently. The function is, however, C's major structural division.

FUNCTIONS

Functions are named blocks of code within a program. All C programs consist of sets of functions. At the top of all the programs we have written, we have used the statement main(), which is the name of the function first executed upon initialization of a program. The function statements are then enclosed with a pair of braces.

Thus, a trivial program could be written as:

```
main()
{
}
```

This code is just a shell, of course, serving no purpose except to exercise your disk drives in order to load the "program" and return to the desktop.

The intent of using a function is to move repeated code outside of the program's main flow. Thus, in practice, programs are usually organized so that main() contains the program's general outline, and each major program section is written as a function. Suppose, for example, that you were writing program requiring our date validation routine in several places. Rewriting the date-checking code each time would greatly increase both the size of the code and the chances for typographical or logical errors. But if the date-checking code were contained in a function, you would only need to use the name of the function when you want to check a date, as in this program fragment:

```
main()
{
. . . some program statements . . .
datecheck();
. . . more program statements . . .
datecheck();
. . . more program statements . . .
}

datecheck()
{
code for date validation
}
```

When a function name is used to transfer program flow to the start of the function, it is said that the function is *called*. Any valid identifier may be used as a function name, but a good function name will indicate the purpose or nature of the function. This is because the function definition code may not be located near the calling statement. The function definition code may occur following main(), preceding main(), or in another source file altogether (see Chapter 8).

Functions separate the code that defines them from the code that calls them. In a program, for example, we may have the function main() call the function datecheck() to validate the correctness of the date entered. Immediately after main() calls datecheck(), program execution jumps to the start of datecheck(). Likewise, if our program has other functions, these other functions could also call datecheck() at any time and vice versa.

You will notice that the function main() is always followed by at least one pair of braces. These braces act, in effect, to hide what is contained inside them from the rest of the program. Therefore, when datecheck() is called, it does not know what main() contains. What the function main() would contain is, of course, some data declaration statements, as you will recall from our work with main() in Chapter 3.

And just as the program statements within a pair of braces are invisible to any other function, so are these data declarations.

Scoping

This leads us in fact to an important principle in C programming called *scoping*. The scope of a variable is restricted to the enclosing braces in which it is defined. Variables declared within braces are called *local variables*. A data declaration can also appear outside any particular set of braces, however. This kind of declaration produces *global variables*.

Local Variables

Any variables declared within a set of braces are considered *local* to the block defined by the braces. Figure 4.1 demonstrates the scoping of local variables.

The scope, or range, of statements over which a variable is accessible greatly facilitates the ease of programming in a structured

```
main()
{                             /* begin main */
int i, j, k;
    ...AAA...                 /* statements in main */

    {                         /* begin block 1 */
    double x, y, z;
    char i;
        ...BBB...             /* statements in block 1 */
    }                         /* end block 1 */

    {                         /* begin block 2 */
    double a, b, c;
        ...CCC...             /* statements in block 2 */
    }                         /* end block 2 */

    ...DDD...                 /* more statements in main */
}                             /* end main */
```

Figure 4.1: Scoping of Local Variables

format by allowing you to hide the data you are using under the black box principle. In the function shown in Figure 4.1, we have declared the variables i, j, and k as integers. These integers are then accessible only within function main(). Processing continues through statements *AAA*, and we reach block 1, where x, y, and z are floating point variables and i is a character variable. The variables x, y, z, and i from block 1 and the variables j and k from main() are accessible for processing within the statements for *BBB*, and so on. In short, the scope of a variable is the block in which the variable is defined and any other blocks nested within the defining block.

Note that in our example there is a duplication of variable identifiers—namely, of the variable i. The rule in such cases states that the last declared variable is the one that the program uses for reference. In essence, the i declared in main() has been "layered over," or hidden, by the i declared in block 1, but the original i still exists in memory.

Upon exiting a block, all variables declared within the block are removed from access (literally erased from memory in most cases), and the active variable list prior to entering the block is reinstated. As our program exits block 1, the floating point variables (x, y, and z) and the character variable i are removed, leaving the original three integer variables (i, j, and k) active. The same process applies to block 2, which has access to three floating point variables (a, b, and c) declared within the block and three integer variables (i, j, and k) declared in main(). Upon exit from block 2, variables a, b, and c are removed and i, j, and k remain during the processing of statements *DDD*.

To sum up, then, the rules for local variable scoping are as follows:

- Variables are only accessible within the block in which they are defined and all blocks nested therein.

- If more than one variable has the same identifier, the variable declared last has precedence in any reference made to that identifier.

- Upon exiting from a block, all variables declared within the block and their associated data are removed from the system.

A function will always have an associated statement block; therefore these scoping rules apply not only to blocks but to functions as well. Two major differences exist between functions and blocks.

First, a block can only be entered through the natural flow of the program (one can use a goto to jump into a block, but this would most likely confuse the programmer, the compiler, and the program execution). A function, on the other hand, can be entered from anywhere by referencing its name. Second, blocks can be nested and functions cannot. C will not allow a function to be defined within another function.

You may be wondering why someone would use the same variable name in a subordinate block? Actually, this is not such a good idea, as it tends to confuse anyone reading the program, including the programmer! Although you may want to use this facility for loop-control variables (so you don't have to keep inventing new names), it is not recommended. And if you are using the Consulair Mac C Compiler, it is illegal to redefine local variables in a subordinate block. The manual tells us, in effect, that the designers of the Mac C Compiler decided not to allow this practice by defining the following example as illegal:

```
p()
{ int i;
    { int i;
    }
}
```

This should not cause you much difficulty, however, unless you are transferring a C program from another compiler.

GLOBAL VARIABLES

Global variables, as the name implies, are accessible to all parts of the program. A C program can be separated into several source files. The files themselves act like function blocks and provide a degree of privacy among variables. If a variable from one source file needs to be transported into another source file, or if a variable is required among several functions within the same source file, then a global variable should be used.

A variable is made global by placing its declaration outside any function block. Such a variable can be used in any program statement following the declaration until the end of the source file. C calls variables of this type *external* variables, because of the placement of their declaration. In the source file shown in Figure 4.2, functions fun2() and fun3() have access to the variables i, j, and c. If fun2() makes a change to any of these variables, then fun3() will be affected by the change when it uses the variables, and vice versa. The fun1() function has no access to these variables because it occurs before the variable declaration. Functions fun2() and fun3() can use these variables with no further declarations required.

Now assume that fun3() resides in a second source file, as shown in Figure 4.3. The function has been written to use variables i, j, and c as external variables; therefore, some kind of declaration needs to be made in the second source file.

The variables are defined in file **SOURCE1** and declared in **SOURCE2**. This brings up the fine point of distinction between defining and declaring an external variable. The variable's *definition* includes a data type and the optional storage class (storage classes will be discussed in a moment). This definition actually reserves space within memory for the variable. If this definition occurs outside of a function block, then the variable can be used as an external

```
fun1()
{ statements }

int i, j;
char c;

fun2()
{ statements }

fun3()
{ statements }
```

Figure 4.2: Examples of External Variables in the Same Source File

```
file SOURCE1:                         file SOURCE2:

    fun1()                                extern int i, j;
    { statements }                        extern char c;

    int i, j;                             fun3()
    char c;                               { statements }

    fun2()
    { statements }
```

Figure 4.3: External Variables Used Across Two Source Files

variable. The variable's *declaration* indicates to the compiler the existence of the variable's name somewhere among the program's source files. For practical purposes, this difference in terminology applies only to external variables.

Declarations for external variables can appear in any source file. The declaration indicates to the compiler the type of the variable and the fact that it has been defined (that is, storage has been allocated) somewhere else among the program files. If one or more external declarations appear within a set of program files, then that variable must have one and only one definition.

When writing large systems using many source files or creating a library of files containing useful functions, you may have a file with several related functions requiring external variables between them (a series of functions to process a graphics screen for example). Assume that these functions follow the black box principle so that you don't need to look at them for several months—you just use them. By this time, you probably don't remember what variable names you used. Now, when you are writing a new program that uses these functions, it is quite possible for you to redeclare a global variable name in your program that was made global in your function file. You now have two declarations for the same variable name and this is not allowed. You therefore need a variable type that will make the variable global throughout the function source file and invisible to other source files. In such a case, you can use a *static external* variable in order to limit the external variable's scope solely to the file containing your functions. (We will explain what "static external" means in more detail in a moment.)

Figure 4.4 illustrates the use of such a static external variable. In file **SOURCE2**, variables i, j, and c have been defined. They are external because they are defined outside any function. And, because they are static, no other files have access to the same data referred to as i, j, and c in file **SOURCE2**. Another programmer's file, **SOURCE1**, is part of the same program as **SOURCE2** and has defined the same variable names to refer to completely different data. There will be problems, however, as the variables in **SOURCE2** have been defined as static. As you can see, this particular conjunction of scoping rules represents a very powerful tool for reducing variable name duplication errors in programs spanning multiple files.

STORAGE CLASSES

Each variable has a *storage class* associated with it. The storage class tells the compiler how and when the storage space for the

```
        file SOURCE1:                      file SOURCE2:

            int i, j;                          static int i, j;
            double c;                          static char c;

            funa()                             fun2()
            { statements }                     { statements }

            funb()                             fun3()
            { statements }                     { statements }
```

Figure 4.4: Using Static External Variables

variable is to be allocated. C has four storage classes: automatic, external, static and register.

The *automatic* storage class is the default storage class for local variables. If a function or statement block declares automatic variables, the storage space for the variables will be allocated when the function of statement block is entered during program execution. When the function or statement block is exited, the storage space is released from use by these variables (hence the ability to have local variables). You may use the keyword **auto** before the variable declaration. Since automatic is the default storage class, however, the keyword is redundant.

The second storage class, *external,* tells the compiler that the storage space for the variable is allocated somewhere else. A variable is declared to be external by placing the keyword **extern** before the variable declaration. We have seen the external storage class in action to declare global variables.

The third storage class, *static,* is kind of an oddball. It actually has two functions. The first application is to set the storage class of a local variable. Instead of creating and removing the data space from memory each time the function or block is entered, a static variable is given storage space at the start of the program and remains active as long as the program is running. The advantage to this is if you want to retain a specific value (perhaps a running total of an account), you don't need to use a global variable. With a static variable, you can maintain the black box principle of programming.

The second application for a static variable is to limit the scope of a global variable to the source file in which it is defined. We saw an example of this in the previous section on external variables. To define a variable as being of the static storage class, use the keyword **static** in front of the definition.

The final storage class is known as the *register* class. A register variable is stored in one of the data registers within the CPU. The advantage of using a CPU register is that it operates much faster than normal memory. If you have a very time-sensitive situation, therefore, you would probably want to use a register storage class for a variable. To define a variable as a register variable, use the keyword **register** before the variable definition.

There are some limitations to using a register variable. First, the number of register variables you may use is limited (usually four or six different variables). Second, only certain types of data may be stored in a register variable (that is, integers, characters, and pointers). Finally, not all compilers support the use of register variables. You should check your compiler manual for the restrictions on using register variables.

PARAMETERS

Although it is possible to use external variables to make data from one function accessible to another function, this defeats the entire structuring design of the program. If all of the variables were declared outside of any function, then their reason for existing would be vague, if not lost entirely, since there would no longer be any association between the variable and its use. When declaring variables, you should always declare the variable within the block (and subblocks) in which the variable will be used. This announces to anyone reading the program that the particular variable contains data necessary for the task currently being performed.

On the other hand, if the data is kept hidden within its declaration block, how can this data be used by another function without making the variables global? Notice that following the function name is a pair of parentheses. Within these parentheses, the programmer can place data from the calling function which causes the values of data to be "passed" to the called function. The pieces of data listed within the parentheses are called *parameters*. The full function definition looks like this:

> *function name(formal parameter list if required)*
> *formal parameter declarations if required*
> {

```
    declarations if required
        statements
        return();
}
```

(In case you were wondering how to get back to the main flow of the program, the return() statement is what causes program flow to resume at the point from which the function was called. The return() statement is discussed in greater detail in the next section.)

Figure 4.5 shows an example function declaration using parameters. This test function has three parameters or *arguments*, as they are called in C. Parameter declarations follow the function declaration and perform two roles. The parameter declaration 1) tells the compiler what type of data to expect and 2) declares the arguments to be used within the function. Thus the parameter declaration permits these parameters to be used exactly like local variables. In fact, you may not declare a local variable to have the same name as an argument. And just like locally declared variables, the parameters are removed from use when the function returns. There are some restrictions on the types of data that can be passed using parameters. These restrictions will be discussed when we introduce pointers and addresses.

The parameters listed in the function declaration are called *formal parameters*. They formally define what data the function requires when it is called and serve mainly to provide a variable name for the data supplied. When a function is called, the function name is listed, followed by an *actual parameter* list. The actual parameter list contains expressions for all the formal parameters named, separated by commas (,). An actual parameter must evaluate to the same data type as its formal parameter. They are matched in order, from left to right,

```
test(i, z, c)
int      i;
double   z;
char     c;
{
     function body
}
```

Figure 4.5: Example of a Function Declaration Using Parameters

with the formal parameters. The expressions used as actual parameters are usually simply variables that are currently being used by the calling function.

A SAMPLE PROGRAM

Listing 4.1 is a new version of the LIST308 program that appeared in Chapter 3. Moving the power calculation into a function designed expressly for this task has provided increased flexibility. For example, the program now prints five tables for the powers of the numbers 1 through 5. This is done through a nested for loop. The outer loop, using the variable i, controls which table is being printed, and the inner loop controls which power is calculated. The second printf statement uses the function power_() as an integer expression.

You may be wondering why there is an underscore character following the name of the power function. You will recall from Chapter 3 that in order to translate your source code into an executable program, you need to use a compiler and linker. The output.link file specified in the last chapter referred to other files such as fstdlib, stdfileio, and MathLib. These files are called *libraries*, and they contain routines used by the compiler. The routines cover such varied tasks as handling input and output, initializing memory, calculating mathematical routines, and so on. Since there already exists a function called power in one of these libraries, the linker would give you an error message stating that the name is "multiply defined" if you were to use the name without the underscore for the function in Listing 4.1. The message means, of course, that the same name has been used to reference two different items in the program. To avoid this problem, we simply add the underscore to our function name. (See Chapter 8 for more information about libraries and linking.)

Notice that the method for calculating a power has also been changed slightly from that used in Chapter 3. The for loop in the function power counts backwards by decrementing the parameter i. The loop could have been written as follows:

```
for (j = 1, p = 1; j < = y; j + +) /* calculate power */
    p * = x;
```

This, however, requires an extra local variable, j. While the variable-saving process we have used in Listing 4.1 is not a requirement for

```
/********************************************************
    list401      Print tables of powers
********************************************************/

/*
    This version prints tables for base values 1 through 5
    and powers of each of these number from 0 through 5.
*/

#include "stdio.h"

main()
{
int     i,                      /* base value counter   */
        j;                      /* power value counter  */

    for (i = 1; i <= 5; i++) { /* base value loop     */
        printf("Powers Of %d\n", i);

        for (j = 0; j <=5; j++)     /* power value loop     */
            printf("%d to the power of %d = %d\n", i, j, power_(i,j));

        printf("Press Return");     /* pause between tables */
        scanf("%*s");
        printf("\n\n");             /* space between tables */
    }                               /* end for(i)           */
}                                   /* end main             */


/********************************************************
    power_          compute x to the power of y
********************************************************/
power_(x, y)
int     x, y;                   /* formal parameters    */
{
int     p;                      /* local variable       */

    for (p = 1; y > 0; y--)     /* calculate power      */
        p *= x;

    return(p);                  /* return calculated power */
}                               /* end power            */
```

Listing 4.1

good programming, it does save space for the disk and computer. You should select whichever method produces the most understandable program. Our primary reason for using this decrementing method is to show how parameters are passed to and used within the function.

One of the primary things you should notice in this example is that the variables i and j in main() correspond to the formal parameters x and y of power_(). When power_() is called, the value of j is copied to the variable y, allowing y to be altered without affecting j. The same is true for i and x. This is consistent with our black box methodology, because it maintains the locality of variables declared to a function.

Returned Values

The return() statement causes program flow to resume at the point from which the function was called. Execution continues with the next statement to be executed in the calling program. The return() statement may contain an expression within the parentheses whose value will be returned to the calling function. The function need not receive nor return data, of course, but it is a good idea to return at least one value to indicate whether the function performed its operation correctly or not. If the return() statement does not exist, then when the function reaches the right brace, the function will return to the calling program with some undefined value. If the calling function expects a proper value, this undefined value may cause problems or erroneous data.

In our example, the function power_() returns the value of p. By default, all functions are assumed to return an integer data type. To make a function return a different data type requires two steps. First, the type of the function must be declared as part of the function declaration itself. Do this by simply preceding the function declaration with a type declaration. Since integers limit our ability to calculate powers of a number, we will change our function data type to double, so that the function can return a floating point value.

```
double power(x, y)
```

When the function reaches a return() statement, the expression inside the parentheses will be converted to the data type of the function (in this case, a double type) before returning to the calling function. Within the functions, we also need to convert the local variable p to a double, so that it too can calculate the larger powers.

The second step for changing the data type returned by a function is to tell the calling function what data type will be returned. To do this, simply declare the function with the appropriate data type, this time listing only the parentheses, not the formal parameters. The new program now looks like Listing 4.2 (Notice the change in the printf statement to handle the printing of the double data types. The substitution of %f for %d allows for the output of double and floating-point numbers as fixed-decimal numbers.)

Test the new ranges that you can calculate by changing the limits of the for loop. For example, change the maximum power value to 10. Now recompile and test your new version of the table power program.

```
/******************************************************
    list402     Print tables of powers (using 'double')
******************************************************/

/*
    This version prints tables for base values 1 through 5
    and powers of each of these number from 0 through 5.
*/

#include "stdio.h"

main()
{
int     i,                          /* base value counter   */
        j;                          /* power value counter  */
double  power_();                   /* power returns a double  */

    for (i = 1; i <= 5; i++) {  /* base value loop    */
        printf("Powers Of %d\n", i);

        for (j = 0; j <=5; j++)     /* power value loop     */
            printf("%d to the power of %d = %f\n", i, j, power_(i,j));
                                    /* change last %d to %f */

        printf("Press Return");     /* pause between tables */
        scanf("%*s");
        printf("\n\n");             /* space between tables */
    }                               /* end for(i)           */
}                                   /* end main             */


/******************************************************
    power        compute x to the power of y
******************************************************/
double power_(x, y)
int     x, y;                       /* formal parameters    */
{
double  p;                          /* local variable       */

    for (p = 1.0; y > 0; y--)          /* calculate power      */
        p *= x;

    return(p);                      /* return calculated power  */
}                                   /* end power            */
```

Listing 4.2

USING FUNCTIONS

When we talk about using functions in C, we are really talking about two things: first, using functions of the standard input/output library supplied with your compiler, and second, creating your own functions specifically tailored to meet the needs of your program. We have already gotten a basic sense of how to create customized functions, and we will study customized functions in greater depth throughout the rest of this book. With some sense of how functions work, we are ready to learn about the library functions, which will, by the way, expand our programming capabilities.

LIBRARY FUNCTIONS

The design philosophy of C emphasizes *portability*, which means that programs written on one machine will operate in the same manner on another machine. In other words, the programmer can write a program, compile and test it on a development machine, and then transfer the source code file to the target machine and compile the source code there by making only a few changes, if any. This greatly increases a programmer's efficiency, as well as the program's usefulness and life span. For example, when a company switches to a larger computer system, the software can be moved with relative ease.

In moving a program from computer to computer, we encounter certain logistical and physical problems, such as differences in operating systems and differences in the capabilities of the hardware. Because of these differences, the designers of C chose not to include any input/output facilities in the language itself. However, most applications require input and output.

To accommodate this need for input and output, C compilers are accompanied by a standard I/O library. For some C compilers, including the Consulair, this library may be a file called **stdio** which contains a variety of functions used for input and output. Using the functions supplied by the library is as simple as using a function you create yourself. Your compiler manual will list all the functions available in your library file and how to access them.

The library functions are referred to as "standard" because most C compilers have them, and the method of calling them and their parameters will be the same for all compilers and all machines. The inner workings of the functions may differ from machine to machine, but as programmers in C, we need not concern ourselves with what is actually happening inside the computer. Because these functions are in fact fairly similar from the programmer's point of view, we can give an idea of how to use the range of library functions you are likely to encounter by zeroing in on some of the basic ones.

Because the standard library resides in a separate file, you must tell the compiler to load this file at the same time it compiles your source code program. To do this, use the following *compiler directive:*

   #include <stdio.h>

or

   #include "stdio.h"

The number symbol (#), which must appear in the first column of
your source file, instructs the compiler to perform a specific action
before or during compilation. The #include directive tells the compiler to include the file named in the broken brackets (< >). Note that
broken brackets or quotation marks (" ") are *required*. The file named
in the #include statement contains source code that will be included
in the compilation of the source file in which it is named. (We will
encounter a few other compiler directives throughout the rest of this
book. A complete list of the directives available under C is given in
Chapter 8.)

THE GETCHAR() AND PUTCHAR() FUNCTIONS

The first two library functions we will explore are console I/O
functions: getchar() and putchar(). As you might assume, these functions are opposites, performing complementary tasks. getchar()
returns a character from the standard input and has no parameters,
whereas putchar() sends its one-character argument to the standard
output and returns no useful information. (Note that the terms *standard input* and *standard output* for the Macintosh refer to the
keyboard and the screen, respectively.

Listing 4.3 exercises the functions getchar() and putchar() by getting a character from the console (that is, from the keyboard) and
displaying it back to the user. In the program, the function getchar()
returns a defined character called *EOF* (for "end-of-file") to indicate
that no more characters are available for input and that the end of
the file has been reached. We must check for this flag to know when
to stop reading characters from the keyboard. The algorithm under-
lining this procedure looks like this:

   while *(another character is available)*
      output the character

Although short, this algorithm does everything we need it to do.

```
/******************************************************
    list403      Using getchar() and putchar()
*************************************************/

#include "stdio.h"

/**** Use only if your system cannot generate a standard EOF signal ***/
#undef      EOF
#define     EOF 4
/*********************************************************************/

main()
{
int c;

    while ((c = getchar()) != EOF)
        putchar(c)                    /* remove this line if echoing      */
        ;                             /* this completes the line above    */
                                      /* so it can be removed if necessary*/
}   /* end main */
```

Listing 4.3

The program as written follows our algorithm perfectly. The expression within the **while** statement first assigns the character returned by **getchar()** to variable **c** in case it is needed. Then the character returned is evaluated. If it is valid, (that is, not an EOF character) the character is displayed and another is fetched from the console; otherwise, the program ends.

You may experience an echo effect on your display depending upon the implementation of the **getchar()** function in your compiler. Because **getchar()** is not a specified part of the C programming language, the developer of the compiler has several options for the design of this function. If you are experiencing duplicate characters on your screen, then your **getchar()** version *echoes* the characters it receives. In this case, you do not need the subsequent **putchar()** function. Take it out now and in following programs where it causes echoing.

Notice that we use the **#include** statement to obtain the I/O functions. When you test this program, press the Command key (the one with the cloverleaf on it) and the D key simultaneously to produce the required EOF character. (The Command key on the Macintosh emulates the function of the Control key on other terminal keyboards.) This key sequence creates the character code for *Control-D* which is the end-of-file character used by UNIX. (Control-D is a carry-over from UNIX because C was developed for UNIX.)

At this point, we need to take note of a special problem associated with the EOF value for users of the Consulair Mac C compiler. C handles all characters through the numeric representation of the character set that is in use by the machine. In the case of the Macintosh, this is an extended ASCII set. The values of the characters range from 0 to 255. Therefore, the EOF character is usually assigned the value of − 1 to avoid confusion with an actual character. Most compilers will arbitrarily use the Control-D character sequence to indicate the end-of-file character. This sequence causes the **getchar()** function to return the EOF value instead of the value of the character entered.

Because of this, the Consulair compiler does not assign any character to signify the end-of-file character. To get around the problem of the lack of an EOF character, add the following two lines to your program immediately following the **#include** line like this:

```
#include "stdio.h"

#undef EOF
#define EOF 4
```

This sets the EOF character to have the value of 4 (the ASCII value of a Control-D) so you can use the Command-D key sequence to emulate an EOF character. Include these two lines in your program until Chapter 7, where we will use a different technique.

In demonstrating the use of the **getchar()** and **putchar()** functions, we introduce a concept used in many C programs to develop compact and fast running code. When an assignment statement is used as an expression, it evaluates to the data being assigned. In other words, the expression

```
a = b = c;
```

explicitly written as

```
a = (b = c);
```

causes the assignment of **c** to **b**, which evaluates to the value of **c** and is assigned to **a**. At first, using an assignment statement as an expression may seem a bit confusing. Give the program some thought and write an alternate algorithm without using this concept. The alternate program will undoubtedly be longer than this program and may be more difficult to read. Make sure your alternate algorithm does not output the EOF character.

OUR GETNUM() FUNCTION

In an example of using standard library functions, we will create a function to accept and validate a positive integer entry. Our new function is called **getnum()** and it has no arguments. **getnum()** returns either the integer depressed or an EOF character if an EOF was entered.

Listing 4.4 shows **getnum()** in action. The **do-while** construct is appropriate for this situation since we require the loop to be done at least once. A new standard library function, **isdigit()**, is used to check if its argument has an ASCII value ranging from the digit 0 through the digit 9. A \n, generated by the carriage return key or an EOF character signals the termination of our function. If the \n was entered, then the number is returned. If an EOF character is entered,

```
/*******************************************************
    list404      Input test program
*******************************************************/

#include "stdio.h"

/**** Use only if your system cannot generate a standard EOF signal ***/
#undef    EOF
#define   EOF 4
/********************************************************************/

main()
{
int     i;

    while ( (i = getnum()) != EOF)
        printf("\nThe number entered = %d\n", i);
}   /* end main */

/*******************************************************
    getnum       Get an integer from the console
*******************************************************/
getnum()
{
int     c, num = 0;

    do {                            /* begin character fetch    */
        c = getchar();
        if (isdigit(c)) {
            num = (num * 10) + (c - '0');
            putchar(c);             /* remove if getchar() echoes */
        }
    } while (c != EOF && c != '\n');

    return(c == EOF ? EOF : num);
}
```

Listing 4.4

it is returned. Although this function is not very useful, since it allows us to input only positive integers, we will soon design a function for general numeric input.

Finally, our declaration statement for the variable num also contains an assignment expression. Any statement which sets the initial value of a variable is called an *initialization statement*. This format—that is, combining the declaration and the initialization—provides a shorthand method for setting a declared variable to a specific value.

It's important to note that in C and most other programming languages, a variable that has not yet been assigned a value contains an undefined value. Thus, you should not assume that a variable starts with a value of zero. To test this feature, first remove the assignment expression from the declaration statement in Listing 4.4. Then run this program and enter just a carriage return to see what value is returned by the function. Remember that it can be quite dangerous to use uninitialized variables in a program since you cannot be sure what values (if any) the computer may have assigned them.

RECURSION

Recursion, derived from the Latin word *recurrere*, meaning to run back or return, is an extremely powerful tool in both mathematics and computer science. It is even found in everyday life. For example, on television when a studio camera takes a picture of the monitor showing the camera's point of view, you will see the monitor with a picture of a monitor, with a picture of a monitor, and so on. Essentially, something which is recursive will contain part of itself in its definition. In some programming languages, functions can be written so that within the function there is a call to the function itself. This is known as a *recursive call*.

When a function calls itself, all of the scoping rules apply. Program execution begins at the start of the function and assigns a completely new set of local variables. This is like calling another function that does exactly the same task as the function the program is currently in.

To illustrate how recursion works, we will write a program to print a recursively-defined mathematical sequence of numbers. One such sequence, the Fibonacci number set, is defined as

$$\text{fib}(n) = \text{fib}(n-1) + \text{fib}(n-2) \text{ for } n > 0,$$

where fib(1)=1 and fib(0)=0. This algorithmic definition means that the next number in the mathematical sequence is the sum of the previous two numbers of the sequence. The sequence begins as follows:

```
Counter:    0 1 2 3 4 5 6  7  8  9 10 . . .
Fibonacci:  0 1 1 2 3 5 8 13 21 34 55 . . .
```

The *counter* refers to the position of the Fibonacci number within the sequence; thus, the number 13 is the seventh Fibonacci number. In Listing 4.5 our function fib() will be supplied with the counter (also called an *index*) and will calculate the Fibonacci number corresponding to that index.

```c
/**********************************************************
    list405     Calculate Fibonacci numbers using recursion
**********************************************************/
#include "stdio.h"

/**** Use only if your system cannot generate a standard EOF signal ***/
#undef      EOF
#define     EOF 4
/**************************************************************************/
main()
{
int    n;                       /* Fibonacci index        */

    printf("Enter Fibonacci Index: ");
    while ((n = getnum()) != EOF) { /* Cannot use index four if EOF=4 */
        printf("\n");
        printf("fib(%d) = %d\n", n, fib(n, 0));
        printf("\nIndex: ");
    }
}  /* end main */

/*******************************************************
    getnum       Get an integer from the console
*******************************************************/
getnum()
{
int    c, num = 0;

    do {                        /* begin character fetch    */
        c = getchar();
        if (isdigit(c)) {
            num = (num * 10) + (c - '0');
            putchar(c);
        }
    } while (c != EOF && c != '\n');

    return(c == EOF ? EOF : num);
}

/*****************************************************
    fib      Calculate Fibonacci sequence recursively
*****************************************************/
fib(n, level)
```

Listing 4.5

```
int     n,                           /* Fib number index   */
        level;                       /* level counter      */
{
int fnum, indent;                    /* local variables    */

                                     /* print indentation  */
    for (indent = 1; indent < level; indent++)
        printf(".");
    printf("Calculating %d\n", n);

    if (n > 1)                       /* recursive call      */
        fnum = fib(n-1, level+1) + fib(n-2, level+1);
    else if (n == 1)
        fnum = 1;
    else if (n == 0)
        fnum = 0;

    return(fnum);
}                                    /* end fib             */
```

Listing 4.5 [continued]

Let's scrutinize what happens when Listing 4.5 executes. First, the function **getnum()** is called to retrieve a positive integer number, which is the total number of Fibonacci numbers to be displayed. If **getnum()** returns EOF, then the program ends. (If your compiler must use the EOF modification mentioned above, then you cannot use the Fibonacci index with a value of 4.) After the program retrieves this number, it calls **fib()** to calculate the associated Fibonacci number.

The function **fib()** demonstrates several important concepts. First, the function is recursive just like the definition of the sequence. It calls itself to determine the two preceding numbers in the sequence by using two arguments. The first holds the index of the Fibonacci number to be calculated. The second is used to trace the number of recursions the function makes to calculate the value.

This tracing technique is used frequently in program error detection and error correction. It uses what we might tell the "locality principle" of variables. It is important to understand that when a function calls itself, it is as if it calls another function that performs the same operations. In both cases, the called function is oblivious to where the call came from—whether from **main()**, another function, or itself—and the arguments and locally-declared variables are *local* to the called function. Our Fibonacci number program demonstrates this very well, because each recursive call is considered a level of recursion in which a new set of variables is allocated.

Figure 4.6 shows the levels of our function for an index of 4. The addition symbols (+) indicate the two calls resulting from the statement

fnum = fib(n − 1, level + 1) + fib(n − 2, level + 1)

Recursive calls will continue until the first argument reaches the value of 1 or 0. Because the sequence is defined for these two values, they will be returned without further calculations. If these definitions did not exist, the function would call itself continuously.

To indicate the level being calculated, the for loop at the beginning of the function indents a "level status" message. The number of dots printed equals the level number. Enter and run this program if you have not already. From the display output, manually trace the execution of the program. Although we will not be using recursion in any other examples in this book, you should understand its use because it is a powerful tool.

In this chapter, we have seen how to construct progrms written in C. We began with the concept of structured programming and creating an outline of the program. This led to the use of statement blocks and the black box principle, which eventually provided us with C's most powerful structuring tool—the function.

Using the function required an understanding of local and global variable scoping, as well as of the use of various storage classes. With

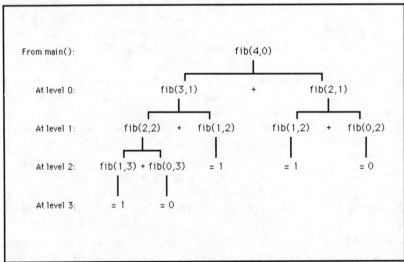

Figure 4.6: Four Levels of Recursive Calls to fib()

this information we created our own function and used some of the functions provided in the standard I/O library. Finally, we examined the powerful technique of recursion.

The purpose of this chapter has been to introduce you to the tools for writing a program in C. As you progress through the rest of the book, you will see how these tools are used to create complete and structured programs.

F IVE

D ATA
T YPES

In Chapter 1 we briefly looked at how data is represented in a computer's memory. At this point, you should note that different types of data require different amounts on memory. For example, a character represented by a number in the ASCII character set uses only eight bits, which equals one byte, while an integer will use two bytes to represent values from 0 to 65,535. In order for the compiler to know how much memory space to allocate for a particular variable, each variable's data type is specified in a declaration statement.

So far we have explored only three basic data types available in C; the other predefined data types are merely extensions of these three. In this chapter, we will discuss all of the data types in more detail, how to determine when to use these types, and how constant values are created for different types.

THE DATA TYPES

There are several variations on the int (for integer) data type that act more like adjectives than data type declarations: the short int, long int, and unsigned int. These alternative integer data types are used to indicate the amount of storage (in bits) you wish to provide for a particular integer variable. The actual number of bits used for any data type is both machine- and implementation-specific; however, a long integer will usually be twice as large as a plain integer. Check with your compiler manual for the exact size and numeric range of data types used in your compiler.

These alternative integer data types are used in the same way as an int. Whenever no specific data type is stated, the type is assumed to be int, as is shown in this example.

```
short        i;
long         j;
unsigned     k;
```

Also, if an identifier has not been declared, then by definition it is assumed to be of type int. If you forget to declare a variable in your program, the compiler will give you a warning message that identifies the undeclared variable and that tells you that this variable is assumed to be of type int. Depending upon what you are using the variable for, this assumption can cause many more errors throughout your program. It is considered poor programming style to leave any variables undeclared.

This assumption that an undeclared type is an integer also applies to the values returned by functions. In the last chapter, the original power() function had no declaration type and it could only return an integer value. As a matter of style, it is acceptable to leave out the declaration type in a function declaration if the function returns an integer or no values at all.

A char type variable will hold the numeric representation of the character assigned to the variable. This generally equates a char to an int (a short int most likely) and allows char type variables to be used in arithmetic expressions.

Floating point values can be represented by the float or double data types. The term double implies *double precision* which allows for a large range and precision of values to be represented. Floating point values can represent any number up to a certain amount of precision (the number 6.12345 is considered more precise than 6.123).

The final data type, called a pointer, will be discussed in the next chapter because it is most often used with data structuring techniques. The sizes for data types under the Consulair compiler are listed in Table 5.1.

Data Type	Size in Bits
char	8
unsigned char	8
short int	16
unsigned short int	16
int	32
unsigned int	32
long int	32
unsigned long int	32
float	32
double float	64
pointer	32

Table 5.1: Sizes for data types used by the Consulair Mac C Compiler

CONSTANT VALUES

A constant is a value that never changes and is explicitly defined prior to compilation. In our previous program examples, all the explicit values used have been constants. As there are different data types for variables, so too are there different types of constants.

Integer constants can be represented by a sequence of digits. The digit sequence may define a decimal number, an octal number, or a hexadecimal number, depending upon the leading characters. If the sequence is preceded by the digit zero (0), it is considered to be an octal number. If the sequence is preceded by "0x" or "0X," the number is considered to be a hexadecimal constant and may contain the digits "a" through "f" or "A" through "F," as well as 0 through 9 numbering systems.

Integer constants evaluate to **int** data types. If an integer constant exceeds the range of values associated with the data type, the constant will be considered a **long int** type. If an octal or hexadecimal constant exceeds the largest unsigned integer value, it, too, will be considered a **long int** type. You may explicitly define a constant to be a **long int** type by appending the letter "L" to the constant. Figure 5.1 shows some examples of integer constants.

Character constants consist of a single character enclosed in apostrophes ('). As we explained in Chapter 1, this expression translates into the ASCII integer value corresponding to the character. The special character sequences listed in Appendix C can also be used as character constants.

Floating point constants consist of a sequence of at least one digit, with an optional decimal point appearing anywhere within the digit sequence. The sequence may be followed by an exponent of the form, "E *integer-number.*" If an exponent is used, the letter "E" must be present in the exponent and may be in either upper or lowercase.

Octal	Hexadecimal	Decimal	Long decimal	Long octal
0123	0x3E4C	−2548	125496L	055432L

Figure 5.1: Examples of Integer Constants

The integer number must fall within the range of precision available with your compiler.

All this yields a number of the form: n.nnnnnnExxx. This format is the computerized version of the familiar scientific notation n.nnnn-nnn × 10^{xxx} which says "take the number n.nnnnnn and multiply it by 10 raised to the xxx power." This format is used instead of superscripts because most computer displays have a difficult time generating superscripts. Figure 5.2 shows some examples of floating point constants. All floating point constants are assumed to be double.

DATA TYPE DETERMINATION

A general set of rules determines which data type to use. Integers, named for the integer number set from mathematics, handle values without fractional parts. Because integers can be represented internally to the computer with a straightforward bit pattern, the int data type can be manipulated with great speed and can be stored efficiently. The application determines which kind of integer type to use. Basically, you should use the integer type which best fits the range of values you expect your program to require. Integers should be used for control variables in loops, Boolean values (true or false), and counters that do not reach large values (for example, our variable level in Listing 4.5 from the last chapter.)

Floating point values represent numbers with fractional quantities. The float data type can also represent a much larger range of values than integer data types, at the price of reduced speed and increased storage requirements.

Character data types are represented as integers within memory and can be used as integers in expressions. However, the use of a char type makes the program easier to read and understand since

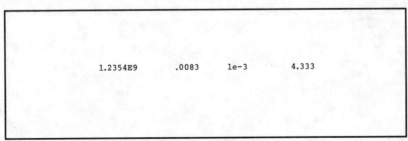

```
        1.2354E9      .0083    1e-3      4.333
```

Figure 5.2: Examples of Floating Point Constants

anyone reading the program would know that the variable declared as char could only represent a character value. This data type uses the most efficient storage size for a character on the machine being programmed. The usual size of a char is one byte, but it may be longer if a larger size is more efficient for speed and storage space. Obviously, the character data type is used in situations requiring manipulation of text.

Listing 5.1 illustrates the differences in efficiency of manipulation obtained with various data types. The program's objective is to provide a common algorithm that tests the speed (and therefore the efficiency) at which the different data types are manipulated. The program shown uses an integer variable. In running this program, you probably will not detect the elapsed time between the printing of "Begin" and the printing of "End" as the integer data types work extremely fast. After testing the execution time of this program, change the data declaration type to a float, and time the interval again. This time you will notice a much longer pause. As a third test, use a double declaration; you will need to give the program some time to run with this data type. The actual execution speed will depend upon the compiler you use.

DATA TYPE CONVERSION

Earlier in this book we saw the automatic data type conversion done by C in expressions involving operands of differing data types.

```
/****************************************************
    list501     Test data type manipulation efficiency
*****************************************************/

#include "stdio.h"

main()
{
double     i;                        /* change this declaration */

    printf("Press Return to begin. . .");
    scanf("%*s");
    for (i = 1; i <= 10000; i++)
        ;
    printf("End.\n");
}                                    /* end main          */
```

Listing 5.1

Although the practice of using mixed-mode expressions is not recommended (some languages or compilers may even give you error messages), C will handle such an expression by converting the values of the operands into a common data type. The conversion is well-behaved and follows the set of rules outlined in Appendix E. In general, the common data type selected will be the largest data type (with respect to the number of bits) found within the expression.

The conversion process works only on the values of the operands and not on the operands themselves. In the following expression, assume that the variable x is of type **float**, and that the variable i is of type **int**.

$$x = x + i;$$

This statement will convert the value of both x and i to a **double** based on the conversion rules. The result of x + i is now a **double**, so what happens when the result has to be placed into x, which is a **float**? The result is "squeezed" into the data type of the variable. In this case, the **double** result is rounded to fit into a **float** variable. The rules for other result conversions are also listed in Appendix E.

Function parameters are also regarded as expressions requiring data types; the data types of the parameters are converted into alternative data types based upon the conversion rules during a function call. Even though you may call a function with a parameter of the **char** type, its value will be converted to an **int**, and **float** parameters will be converted to **double**. The two sample functions listed in Figure 5.3 indicate the data type conversions performed during a function call. The formal parameter declarations use the converted data type.

```
test1(c)        /* called with a char */
int  c;         /* declared as an int */
{ function body }

test2(x)        /* called with a float */
double   x;     /* declared as a double */
{ function body }
```

Figure 5.3: Type Conversion During Function Calls

Under certain circumstances, you will be required to supply a specific data type. For instance, mathematical library function calls will usually require a **double** type parameter. Supplying an integer may cause some very strange results.

Experiment with Listing 5.2. You may need to include a file like the **stdio.h** file in order for your compiler to recognize the **sqrt()** function. Use the **#include** statement for the **stdio.h** file as a guide and add the line required by your compiler. (The Consulair compiler uses the file **sane.h** to define the functions and data types used.) The program itself finds the square roots of the numbers 1 through 10. The important point is that the function **sqrt()** requires a **double** type parameter.

Now run the program and see how your compiler handles the **sqrt()** function. Several possibilities exist: your compiler may give you an error message (this is unlikely); your program may give you an error message; your program may print very strange results; or your program may not run at all (if this happens, we suggest that you restart your computer). Of the tools listed so far in this book, the only one which will make this program operate properly is changing the declaration of **n** to a **double**. This would make for an extremely inefficient program, as we have seen from our comparison of execution speeds using the different data types.

```
/********************************************************
    list502      Using math library functions #1
********************************************************/

#include "stdio.h"

/********************************************************
WARNING! This program may cause strange results depending upon
your compiler. Be prepared to reboot your computer.
********************************************************/

main()
{
int     n;

    for (n = 1; n <=10; n++)
        printf("The square root of %d = %f\n", n, sqrt(n));
    scanf("%*s");
}                                       /* end main             */
```

Listing 5.2

To avoid this inefficiency, C provides a *cast* operator for such an occasion. Its form is:

(type name) *expression*

The parentheses indicate the *cast* operator and convert the expression into the data type named within. Unfortunately, C has a tendency to use characters like the parentheses in several different contexts. You will have to read the programs with care and define the characters based upon the context in which you find them. For the most part, their definition will be obvious; they should also be well-documented by the programmer.

Now let's rewrite Listing 5.2 using the cast operator. The revised program, shown in Listing 5.3, should operate properly. Note that the cast operator converts only the value of the expression and not the expression itself, allowing n to remain an integer and to continue to be used by the for statement.

Cast operators provide a mechanism for explicitly telling the reader what data type is expected in an expression. Of course, the compiler could provide the necessary conversion (at the expense of a longer compilation time and probably less efficient code), but this would

```
/********************************************************
    list503     Using math library functions #2
********************************************************/

#include "stdio.h"
#include "sane.h"

main()
{
int     n;

    for (n = 1; n <=10; n++)
        printf("The square root of %d = %f\n",
            n, sqrt( (extended) n ));

/*
    Most systems use sqrt( (double) n). The Consulair uses a special data
    type called extended which is an 80-bit, floating point value.
*/

    scanf("%*s");
}                               /* end main              */
```

Listing 5.3

obscure the intent of the statement. Casts are used mostly in dynamic storage allocation. Dynamic storage allocation is used quite often with complex data structures, which we will examine in the next chapter.

SIX

DATA STRUCTURES

When we discussed structured programming, we mentioned two parallel structuring concepts: structured code and structured data. So far we have covered the basic principles involved in structuring the source code of a program, including the use of functions and statement blocks. In this chapter we will discuss the fundamentals of *structured data*. As a subject, structured data in fact comprises a broad range of topics. After defining the term structured data itself and explaining why it is an essential aspect of programming in C, the chapter will discuss the two fundamental tools used for handling your data: pointers and addresses.

Our examination of actual data structure techniques will begin with the simple structure called an *array*. With the array, we will see how large sets of similar types of data can be manipulated in a consistent and rapid manner. Our focus on the array will then lead us toward an explanation of the numerous applications for pointers, including pointer arithmetic, using pointers as function parameters, and using pointers to call a function.

Having dealt with arrays and pointers, we will go over the method used for handling several objects of different data types as a single group called a *structure*. A structure is what will allow us to define the more abstract concepts of human thought (like the term "date") in basic terms that the computer will understand (like a value for the month, day, and year).

All of this information will be summed up in a program that demonstrates how to implement a data structure called a *linked list*. The program demonstrates such techniques as dynamic memory allocation and the use of C structures, pointers, and addresses.

The chapter concludes by presenting some tools related to data structuring that are available in C. These tools include bit-oriented operators and a statement that allows you to give C structures a name for easy reference.

Before we begin this chapter, we will look at how data is stored in the computer's memory and why data structuring is important. Those readers who have had experience with data structures may skip this section and proceed to the section entitled "Working with Pointers and Addresses."

STRUCTURING YOUR DATA

This book has stressed the importance of writing structured programs as a means of controlling the quite complex process of programming a computer. The task that you want to computerize can have several steps where each step can have substeps, and each substep can have sub-substeps, and so on. By programming the lowest substeps first and combining these to form the next level of substeps, you begin to build a structured program.

What benefits does this programming method have? First of all, you can easily visualize how to represent the major task to the computer. You tell the computer that the major task requires some subtasks to be performed. The subtasks, in turn, are defined in sub-subtasks. Once the program is written, you can review it and follow the steps that the computer is taking. This allows you to quickly verify that the program is operating properly. If you haven't written your program in a structured fashion, however, you may find yourself jumping from statement to statement trying to follow what the program is doing.

Other benefits of structured programming include more efficient programs and faster program generation. Because each subdivided task consists of a single process performed by a C function, it can be reused by the program whenever needed. In addition, because you don't need to rewrite the same code over and over, new programs can be generated more quickly. Once you have developed a set of common functions (for example, for input, display, and data verification), then you can simply include these functions in the new programs you write.

Using structured data is just as important as writing structured programs. Structured data works on two levels. First, it allows you to define a term that refers to a collection of data that can be logically grouped together. For example, a date would contain three numbers representing the month, day, and year. C allows you to group data items together into a structure under one name.

The second level of data structuring operates in a more theoretical manner than the first level. At this level, structuring your data allows you to define how you want to represent that data to your program, much in the same way as your program structure represents the task to the computer. There are many different types of data structures, each having a set of tasks that it is best suited for. For example, if you just wanted to manipulate a list of data objects (another term for the first level of data structuring), you could use a structure called an *array*, which is the first data structure we will look at.

When you design a data structure, it should be a natural representation of the data that you are working with. After all, the reason why a language like C provides a data structuring ability is to make the task of programming the computer easier. Before we investigate data structures any further, let's look at the concepts of addresses and pointers, which play an important role in data structures.

Working with Pointers and Addresses

In Chapter 1, we saw that memory actually consists of many individual bits. These bits are grouped together, eight at a time, into a unit called a byte. When the CPU needs data from memory, it fetches the data one byte at a time. (Actually, the hardware itself might fetch several bytes at a time, but we will only consider the processing of individual bytes.)

In order for the CPU to know which byte to fetch out of the thousands of bytes in memory, each byte is given a unique number called an *address*. You might think of a byte as a post office box where each box has a number associated with it. And just like in the post office, the addresses are listed sequentially, so that the byte with address 100 is followed by the byte with address 101.

Of course, not all of the data types provided by C will fit into one byte. An integer (data type int), for example, uses 16 bits to represent the number, which requires two bytes of storage. A long int uses 32 bits, or four bytes. When the program uses a data type that requires more than one byte, it will use consecutive bytes. Thus, if a long integer starts at address 150, it will utilize the four bytes at addresses 150, 151, 152, and 153.

Because the compiler takes care of allocating space and addressing the data associated with variables, we do not need to concern ourselves with these matters unless we want to manipulate memory directly. For example, if a program has the following two statements,

```
int x, y, z;
z = x + y;
```

the compiler will generate the instructions necessary to create space to hold the data for x, y, and z. At the same time, because the space for the data is located in memory, it has an address. Let's assume, for example, that the data space for x is at address 204, the space for y is at 202, and the space for z at 200. When the compiler translates the addition statement, it will generate instructions that tell the computer to take the data from locations 204 and 202, add them together, and then put this result into location 200.

Through this example, you can see that the variable is just another name for the memory location used to store the data. Conversely, we say that a variable has an address associated with it. Therefore, the address of the variable x is 204, while the address for variable y is 202 and for variable z 200.

THE ADDRESS OPERATOR: &

C allows us to determine the address of a variable by using the *address operator*, the ampersand (&). Thus the expression &x, for example, returns the address of variable x. Remember: an address is just a number used to locate a position in memory. The data type used to declare the variable does not affect the address because the data type only determines the number of bytes required to store the data, not where the data will be stored.

POINTERS

A *pointer* is a data type used to store an address. Thus, if px is declared to be a pointer, you can assign it the address of a variable using the address operator, like this:

    px = &x;

The variable px now contains the address of the variable x.

THE POINTER OPERATOR: *

Because a pointer is a specific data type, a pointer variable needs to be declared as such. The pointer operator, the asterisk (*), tells the compiler to use next variable as a pointer. Thus the pointer declaration

    datatype *identifier*

uses the pointer operator to declare the *identifier* as a pointer.

Notice that the identifier specifies a specific type of variable. If we have the declarations

```
int x, *px;
double y;
```

then the statement

```
px = &y;
```

would be illegal since the declaration for px is associated with an integer data type and the statement px = &y is associated with a double. The statement we presented at the outset of our discussion of pointers

```
px = &x
```

is the one that would be associated with this declaration. The main point then is that although an address for one data type is effectively the same as an address for another data type, the compiler must know what data type is at the location pointed to when we want to use the data stored there.

Now that we know what a pointer contains (an address) and how to give it a value, what do we do with it? Obviously, as the name implies, a pointer is used to point to something. In order to get at the purpose of pointers, let's look more closely at the use of the pointer operator. In order to do this, we will use the following declarations:

```
int x, y, *px, *py;
```

In the declaration statement, the pointer operator indicates which variables are to be used as pointers and to what data types they point. With these declarations, we can make the following assignments:

```
px = &x;
py = &y;
```

The address of x is placed into the variable px and the address for y in py. Using the pointer operator, we can assign a value to variables x and y, like this:

```
*px = 5;
*py = 3;
```

In this example, the pointer operator says to place the value 5 into the location pointed at by px, and the value 3 into the location pointed at by py. Since px contains the address of x and py contains the address of y, the statements place the value 5 at the location of x and the value 3 at the location of y. This procedure is therefore the same as writing x = 5 and y = 3. Because in using the pointer operator we have indirectly referred to variables x and y, the technical term for using the pointer operator and a pointer variable is *indirection*.

Indirection can be used almost anywhere you want to use a normal variable. You can use it in an expression such as x = *px + *py or as a parameter for a function like test(*px).

When using pointer variables, you must be careful to include the pointer operator when you are referring to the data at the address contained in the pointer variable and not to the address itself. The statement y = px/10 is not the same as y = *px/10. In the first statement, you would be dividing the address of variable x by 10. Performing division or multiplication on an address does not make any sense because of the way memory is organized (and in fact, these two operations are not allowed on pointer variables). Changing the value of an address indiscriminately can cause problems. The resulting address may be referring to a location used for program code. If you start changing this memory location, you will be changing the instructions that the program uses, and this will probably cause your program to stop running.

Do not confuse the pointer operator with the multiplication operator. Because the asterisk is used in both instances, you will have to determine whether it is being used for multiplication or indirection by its context. As a style convention, if you put the pointer operator right next to the variable, as in *px, but put spaces around mathematical operators, as in x * y, your program will be easier to read and you will be less likely to make mistakes.

To sum up, then, the pointer operator tells the compiler to use the location contained by the pointer for placing or retrieving data; the pointer operator does nothing else. Listing 6.1 contains simple pointer expressions. Examine the program and write down what you believe will be printed by the printf statements. Then check Figure 6.1 to see what actually is displayed. Since the values of the pointers themselves will vary from compiler to compiler, we will simply assume that some values will be shown, the exact contents of which are unimportant and probably meaningless.

Notice that the program uses direct and indirect methods to change the values of variables x, y, and z. If you correctly predicted the

```
/*****************************************************
      list601    Pointer manipulation sampler
 *****************************************************/

#include "stdio.h"

main()
{
int     x, *px,                 /* this grouping of variables   */
        y, *py,                 /* is for readability and has   */
        z, *pz;                 /* no effect on the declaration */

    px = &x; py = &y; pz = &z;  /* address assignements         */

    *px = 5;                    /* initialization               */
    *py = 11;
    z = 19;

    display(x, y, z);           /* a display function           */

    /* this next statement just show what the pointers actually
       contain based upon your compiler's implementation        */

    printf("The values of the pointers themselves are:\n");
    printf("px = %ld, py = %ld, pz = %ld\n", px, py, pz);

    (*pz)++;                    /* parentheses required due      */
                                /* to operator precedence        */
    *px += 5;
    *py = *px;
    display(x, y, z);

    py = pz;
    x = *py + y;

    display(x, y, *pz);

    scanf("%*s");
}                               /* end main                     */
/*****************************************************
      display    display values of three integer variables
 *****************************************************/
display(i, j, k)
int     i, j, k;
{
    printf("x = %d, y = %d, z = %d\n", i, j, k);
    return;
}                               /* end display                  */
```

Listing 6.1

```
x = 5, y = 11, z = 19

The values of the pointers themselves are:
x = ??, y = ??, z = ??
x = 10, y = 10, z = 20
x = 30, y = 10, z = 20
```

Figure 6.1: Results from Listing 6.1

results of the program, then you understand the mechanism of indirection. If not, you should continue to study the program, the previous section, and the section on memory until you can easily manipulate pointers and feel comfortable with indirection. To further test your understanding, change or add assignment statements in the pointer program and predict the new results.

A WARNING ABOUT POINTERS

Using pointers has both benefits and drawbacks. Before we demonstrate the uses of pointers, you should note some of the drawbacks that can cause problems while you are writing a program.

First, pointers can be difficult for the uninitiated to understand. The pointer itself is a very simple concept: a pointer contains an address of a memory location. Using a pointer can be tricky, however, because you need to keep track of two things: the fact that you are using a pointer and what the pointer points to. This brings up the next drawback in using pointers.

Indiscriminate use of pointers can lead to unreadable and possibly dangerous code. Because pointers provide one level of distance between you and the data (you need to get the address from the pointer, and then get the data), you may forget what the pointer actually points to. Therefore, whenever you use pointers, you should make sure that the pointer names are distinctive and descriptive, and you should use comments to make clear the intent and use of the pointer.

If you use pointers without care, moreover, you may wind up pointing to some unknown address, as we described earlier in regard to using multiplication and division on pointers. Take your time with this topic, do the examples, and understand them before moving on.

FUNCTIONS AND POINTERS

At this point, it may be useful to quickly review the role of the parameters to a function. The parameters, or arguments, to a function are those values passed to the function at the time the function is called. The parameters appear in the parentheses following the function name. The parameters used when the function is called are said to be the actual parameters because these are the actual values used by the function. The parameters listed in the function definition are said to be formal parameters. They are used within the function body and are local to the function. When the function is called, the actual parameter values are placed into the formal parameters and the function is executed. This is an important point. Only the values of the actual parameters are given to the function. Thus, the function has no way of affecting the actual parameters themselves; it can only work with the formal parameters which are local to the function.

This method of parameter transfer is termed *call-by-value*. The other way to pass parameters to a function is called *call-by-reference*, which uses the addresses of the parameters. We will see how this is used in a moment. For the call-by-value method of parameter passing, the value of the actual parameter is passed to the formal parameters of the function, which reside in a physically different location in memory. In the program shown in Listing 6.1, the statement

```
display(x, y, *pz);
```

passes the *value* of x, the *value* of y, and the *value* pointed to by **pz** to the function **display()**. The call-by-value concept upholds the black box principle by preventing changes made to the values of the variables from affecting the original contents of the variables. This allows a programmer to use the parameters in statements and expressions inside the function without having to worry about how these changes will affect the rest of the program. A function, by design, will not affect any external values used in the program unless it is explicitly told to do so. From what we know about C so far, a function can only change external values by referencing a global variable or returning a value that is used by the calling routine.

Functions can only return a single value in the **return()** statement. What do we do when multiple values need to be returned?

One example is a function that asks the program operator for the date. Such a program will need to return three values: the day, month, and year. Another example is when the values of two variables must be exchanged, requiring the return of the new value for each variable. Normally, the way to exchange the values of two variables is by using three variables, as follows:

```
temp = x;
x = y;
y = temp;
```

The variable temp holds the original value of x in the first line. The second line puts the original value of y into x, which replaces the original value of x. Finally, the original value of x held in temp is placed into y. This exchanges the contents of variables x and y.

If a program required this procedure frequently, we might want to call a function instead of rewriting the code every time. If we write the function swap() shown in Figure 6.2 and call swap(x,y), however, we would simply succeed in wasting computer time because the local variables a and b would be exchanged, while the actual parameters, x and y, remain unchanged.

Technically, we want to return two values: the new value for x and the new value for y. Since call-by-value copies the values of the actual parameters to the formal parameters and then removes the formal parameters when the function returns, we cannot use this type of function call. We can, however, achieve the exchange by giving the function the addresses of the data we want exchanged. Figure 6.3 contains our new function. Now when we call swap(), we will pass the addresses of the variables whose values we want to be swapped:

```
swap(&x, &y);
```

```
swap(a, b)
int  a, b;
{
int  temp;

     temp = a;
     a = b;
     b = temp;
     return();
}
```

Figure 6.2: Ineffective Use of a swap() Function

The function exchanges the contents of the memory locations instead of just the values of temporary variables. This method of parameter passing is called *call-by-reference* because the parameter passed refers to the location of the data required. We will use this method quite frequently when passing more complex data types because this is the only way in which C will pass a complex data type.

What we have done with the function **swap()** is to explicitly create a call-by-reference mechanism. We have not changed the way C calls the function; we merely interpret the data received by the function in a different manner. The data passed when our new version of **swap()** is called is the values of the addresses of the variables to be exchanged. Through the use of pointers, we indirectly exchange the values.

WORKING WITH ARRAYS

The implementation of arrays in C is very much like the implementation of pointers. Let's now examine the concept of arrays, some of their uses, and the relationship between arrays and pointers.

WHAT IS AN ARRAY?

An *array* is a collection of items of the same data type. This book is an example of an array of characters as well as, on a larger scale, an

```
swap(pa, pb)
int  *pa, *pb;
{
int  temp;

     temp = *pa;
     *pa = *pb;
     *pb = temp;
     return();
}
```

Figure 6.3: Proper Use of the **swap()** Function

array of pages. An array provides a means of referring to a single element of a large set of similar items and processing the single element without affecting any other items within the array.

The terminology used with arrays requires discussion. Most arrays consist of a row of elements. A line on this page, for example, could be considered an array of characters. The dimension of an array indicates the number of directions in which these rows lie. A one-dimensional, or linear, array is analogous to a straight line; a two-dimensional, or rectangular, array is analogous to a region or area. Three-dimensional arrays are analogous to volume, and so on. Few programming applications require nonlinear arrays (see Figure 6.4).

The *subscript* of an array designates a specific element within the array. There are always as many subscripts as there are dimensions in the array. For example, a three-dimensional array has three subscripts.

USING ARRAYS

In C an array declaration states the type of the elements and the number of elements to be allocated for the array. For example:

```
int a[5];
```

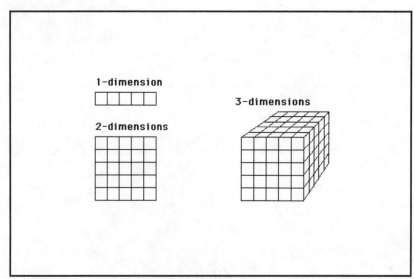

Figure 6.4: Visual Conceptions of One-, Two-, and Three-Dimensional Arrays

The number within the brackets ([]) indicates the total number of elements in the array. The preceding declaration allocates a one-dimensional array (only one subscript) with five elements numbered from 0 through 4. Whenever an individual array element is used in a program statement, the subscript of that element will appear within brackets following the variable name. The five individual elements of this array are referenced within the program code as a[0], a[1], a[2], a[3], and a[4]. Thus, the number used in the declaration statement indicates the total number of elements in the array, and the individual elements are numbered from 0 through *one less than* the number used in the declaration.

The array is our first example of a data structure because it provides us with a way to reference all or some of the items in the array with the same programming statements. For example, assume you have ten integers you want to print (see Figure 6.5). Without the array, you would need to write a statement explicitly printing each of the ten integers. With an array, on the other hand, you can use a **for** loop and a single **printf** statement to list all ten integers.

The second algorithm is more efficient than the first for many reasons. The first algorithm requires the declaration of ten individual variables, whereas the second algorithm needs only the declaration of the array i[10] and the variable j. With the array, if the number of elements needs changing, you need only change the array declaration and the loop itself to reflect the new value. In contrast, the first algorithm would need new variables. The **printf** output format would also need to be changed, and the new variables would have to be inserted

```
        /* without an array */
printf("%d %d %d %d %d %d %d %d %d %d\n",
    i0, i1, i2, i3, i4, i5, i6, i7, i8, i9);

        /* with an appropriately-defined array */
for (j = 1; j < 10; j++)
        printf("%d ", i[j]);
printf("\n");
```

Figure 6.5: Two Methods of Printing Ten Integers

at the end of the printf statement. These seemingly insignificant differences in the work needed to make changes on this short example grow tremendously as program size increases. Simply making a small change, such as increasing the number of data items used in a program, will have widespread effects, as we have seen in the preceeding example. By using the proper data structure—in this case an array— you can minimize the effects of such changes. All in all, using the proper data structure allows for faster program creation and alteration.

Listing 6.2 converts decimal numbers into binary numbers using the algorithm introduced in Chapter 1. Because the algorithm produces the digits in reverse order, we will store each digit in an array

```
/********************************************************
     list602     Convert decimal integers into binary numbers
 ********************************************************/

#include "stdio.h"

main()
{
int     b[32],                   /* allow for 32 binary digits   */
        num, i;

                                 /* convert numbers 0 to 15      */
    for (num = 0; num <= 16; num++) {
        printf("%d in binary = ", num);
        dectobin(num, &b[0]);    /* call conversion function     */
                                 /* output digits in reverse     */
        for (i = 31; i >= 0; i--)
            printf("%d", b[i]);
        printf("\n");            /* move to next line            */
    }                            /* end for(num)                 */
    scanf("%*s");
}                                /* end main                     */

/********************************************************
     dectobin     convert decimal number into binary
        d     =    integer to convert
        a     =    array to store binary digits in. Digits are
                   stored in reverse order.
 ********************************************************/
dectobin(d, a)
int     d, a[];
{
int     count;

    for (count = 0; count < 32; count++)
        a[count] = 0;            /* initialize array to 0        */

                                 /* loop through conversion      */
    count = 0;
    while (d > 0) {
        a[count++] = d % 2;      /* digit =1 if remainder        */
        d /= 2;                  /* divide number by 2           */

    }

    return;
}                                /* end dectobin                 */
```

Listing 6.2

until the entire binary number has been created, and then print the array in reverse order.

As you study this program, notice that we have again used the principle of call-by-reference, passing the address of the first element in array **b** to our function. We can pass an entire array by passing the address of the first element because when the array is declared, a set of contiguous memory locations is allocated. The first element in the array occupies the first space of this segment of memory, the second element occupies the second space, and so on. The term "space" refers to a sufficient amount of memory for the data type of that element. In Figure 6.6, for example, each memory location is represented by an x. Each element in the array occupies a set number of memory locations, which is determined by the data type. Elements of the same array will always be found in consecutive memory locations.

When the address of the first element of array **a** is passed to function **dectobin()** in Listing 6.2, the function can use this address for access to the remainder of the array. The declaration of the parameter as an array does not create a new array; it merely creates a variable for the function to use when accessing the array. Since the call to **dectobin()** is a call-by-reference, the original array will be affected by all changes made to the array during the function's processing. Notice that the **dectobin()**'s parameter declaration for array **a** does not contain any information about the number of elements. This information is dependent upon the original array declaration. In C, using call-by-reference is the only way to pass an entire array to a function.

One final comment about this program. The initialization section of the function **dectobin()** clears the array (that is, all elements must be set to 0). This must be done because we are using the same array each time the function is accessed. On the first function call, each element in the array contains an undefined value; therefore, we

```
Memory location: x x x x x x x x x x x x ...
     Array element: 0        1        2        3 ...
```

Figure 6.6: How Memory Is Allocated for Arrays

assign each element the known value of 0. On the next call to dectobin(), the array contains the values from the previous call. The initialization statement clears these old values. In any case, whenever you must be sure that a variable has a particular value, you should use an initialization statement before using the variable.

ARRAYS AND POINTERS

Listing 6.2 demonstrates similarities between arrays and pointers. In fact, the effect of using a reference to an array element is exactly the same as using a pointer to indirectly reference a memory location. Looking more closely at our figurative representation of an array in memory (see Figure 6.7), let's let each x represent a single byte of memory, and assume that the array is a sequence of the fictitious byte variable, which is one byte in length. For the example, we have the declaration

    byte array[10], *ptr;

We can now make the assignment

    ptr = &array[0];

which sets ptr to point to the first element of our array, or array[0]. If we increment ptr, it then points to the second element of our array, namely array[1]. This means that

    *(ptr + 1)

and

    array[1]

point to exactly the same place. Going one step further, C allows you to construct the expression

    *(array + 1)

which also points to exactly the same place as the two previous expressions.

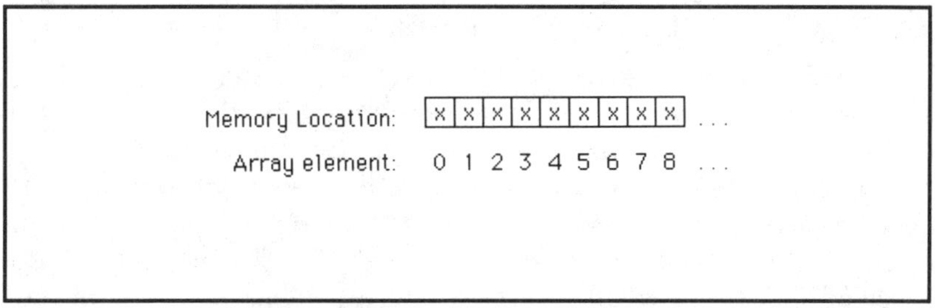

Figure 6.7: Array of **byte** Variables

Thus, we can use an array name as a pointer whenever it is clearer or more convenient. We can now change the call to function **dectobin()** in the Listing 6.2 to

dectobin(num, b);

Similarly, since the array name is an address, we need not use an array in the function. A function parameter containing an address can be declared within the function as a pointer or an array. The parameter declarations

function(addr)
*data-type *addr;*

and

function(addr)
data-type addr[];

both require that an address be passed in the parameter, yet they utilize the address in slightly different ways. Both constructions are valid. The choice of which one to use depends upon how the data is to be accessed.

What exactly is the difference between an array name and a pointer? An array name is semantically defined as a constant, which means that it cannot be assigned a value (an address). For example, all of these constructs are invalid:

array = ptr
ptr = &array
array+ +

Pointers, on the other hand, can have values assigned to them. Except for this difference, an array name can be used in the same way a pointer can.

Array and Pointer Arithmetic

If we can write *(array + 1) to access the second element of an array, array[1], then we can also write *(array + 2) to access the third element, array[2], and *(array + n) to access the nth element, array[n]. This is quite straightforward when we are dealing with an array of data types that require only a single byte each. But what about an array of integers or floating point numbers? The designers of C have specified that this method of access will work with an array of any data type.

One of the advantages of using C is its consistency in its operators and expressions. The expression *(array + n) will always access element array[n], regardless of the declaration type of the array, because the integer n in the *(array + n) expression (n must be an integer) will be *scaled* to the proper size according to the data type of the pointer. The expression array + n takes n and multiplies it by the size of the data type associated with the variable array. This new value is then added to the starting address held by array to give the location of the data being referenced. Likewise, the expression *(p + n) performs exactly the same as p[n]. In either of these expressions, p can be declared as an array or as a pointer, since they are both equivalent and the compiler does not care which form you use. You may also subtract an integer from a pointer and obtain similar results, although this usage is rare.

It should now be apparent why a pointer must be declared to point to a particular data type. The declaration indicates the amount of scaling that needs to be done during pointer arithmetic. Other arithmetic operations that may be performed on pointers are pointer subtraction and pointer comparison. Pointer subtraction gives you the distance, in number of elements, between two locations in memory. For example, if we have an array n and p points to n[5] and q points to n[3], then the expression p − q will yield the value 2. The pointers must be pointing to the same data type for the results to be meaningful; in most cases, they will point to elements of the same array.

Pointer comparison allows you to compare relative pointer positions in memory using the relational or equality operators, which are as follows: >, <, > =, < =, = =, and ! =. The use of these expressions is limited to specialized instances—for example, if you wanted to know whether the ranking of one element was greater than another (that is, which element occurs first in the array). The most frequent use of pointer comparison is in comparing a pointer to the value 0. C guarantees that any pointer with a value of 0 does not point to any data.

ARRAY INITIALIZATION

Initializing a variable or data item in a declaration statement is a common practice among C programmers. Using the declaration statement as an initialization statement allows the compiler to produce more efficient code. It also makes the program easier to read by saving you the work of reading through individual initialization statements.

Listing 6.3 introduces a new method of initialization that is characteristic of arrays. Notice that the array declaration resides outside of main(). C only allows external and static arrays to be initialized in the declaration statement. An array initializer will follow the array declaration with an assignment symbol (=), an opening brace, ({}, and a value for each element. The elements are separated by commas, with a closing brace (}) and a semicolon (;) to indicate the end of the declaration statement, like this:

```
char array[10] = { 'A', 'B', 'C', 'D', 'E',
                   'F', 'G', 'H', 'I', 'J' };
```

You need not supply all of the values for the elements. However, the assignment of the values will always start with the first element of the array, array[0].

```
/********************************************************
    list603      Pointer usage and constructions
********************************************************/
#include "stdio.h"

/*  This array initialization puts each character constant
    into an array element in order starting with 0       */
char    array[10] = { 'A', 'B', 'C', 'D', 'E',
                      'F', 'G', 'H', 'I', 'J' };

main()
{
char    *ptr;
int     i;

    ptr = array;                     /* same as ptr = &array[0]  */

    for (i = 0; i < 10; i++) {
        printf("Array[%d] = %c, ", i, array[i]);
        printf("*(ptr+%d) = %c, ", i, *(ptr+i));
        printf("*(array+%d)=%c\n", i, *(array+i));
    }                                /* end for             */
    scanf("%*s");
}                                    /* end main            */
```

Listing 6.3

If an initialization statement does not state the number of elements in the array, some, but not all, compilers will count the number of initializers. This causes the compiler to determine the maximum number of array elements. Consult you compiler's manual for the exact description of how array initialization is handled.

STRINGS

C uses arrays to manipulate text. The term *string* simply refers to a linear set (array) of characters. Just as a string of bits forms a byte, so a string of characters forms text.

By convention, a string is an array of characters, the last of which is always the \0 character, the termination character, signifying the end of the string. Although you can create strings without the \0 character, most of the standard functions that handle strings expect this character to signal the end of the string.

String constants are created by enclosing a set of characters within quotation marks (" "). For example:

"This is a string constant."

Because a string is an array, the compiler will always equate the string variable name to a pointer. Thus, if you have the declaration

    char *heading;

you can designate this pointer to point to a string constant:

    heading = "DATATECH – Quintessential Publications";

You can also access any single character within the array by adding the appropriate integer, as illustrated previously. For example, to retrieve the "Q" from the word "Quintessential," you can use **heading + 11** because the "Q" is the twelfth character in the string (recall that arrays start with element number 0). This string actually contains 39 characters when the program is compiled: the 38 characters within the quotation marks plus the \0 termination character.

You can also declare and assign **heading** within the same statement, like this:

    char heading = "DATATECH – Quintessential Publications";

Again, the \0 character is automatically supplied by the compiler.

By design, the C programming language does not contain any operators to process strings as a whole. In most development systems, a set of such functions will be provided in the standard function library.

MULTIDIMENSIONAL ARRAYS

Multidimensional arrays are declared and initialized in the same manner as one-dimensional arrays, with the addition of the extra subscripts:

```
int multi[2][5] = {
    { 1, 1, 1, 1, 1 },
    { 5, 4, 3, 2, 1 }
};
```

You may use more than two subscripts if your application requires it. We will be using two-dimensional arrays for simplicity, but any general remarks made about two-dimensional arrays may be extended to arrays of higher dimensions. The maximum number of subscripts you may declare for an array is limited only by memory size and the compiler's characteristics.

The elements in the array are organized in row order so that the first subscript indicates the number of rows and the second subscript indicates the number of items in a row. Figure 6.8 shows the order of the elements from the initialization example for array multi shown a moment ago.

	0	1	2	3	4
0	1	1	1	1	1
1	5	4	3	2	1

Figure 6.8: Row Order of an Array

Overall, multidimensional arrays are used less frequently than one-dimensional arrays. Their main application is to represent tables of information, such as price lists, insurance rates, tax rates, and so on.

ARRAYS OF POINTERS

Combinations of arrays and pointers can be used in many ways. To illustrate this point, we will combine multidimensional arrays, strings, and pointers in the following example:

```
char *day[7] = {
    "Sunday",
    "Monday",
    "Tuesday",
    "Wednesday",
    "Thursday",
    "Friday",
    "Saturday"
};
```

Each array element, day[n], points to a string containing the name of a day of the week. By definition, since each string itself is an array, the day array can be considered a multidimensional array. To access the third letter of each day, we write day[n][2].

Along the same lines, one might have declared the following:

```
char day[7][10] = {
    "Sunday    ",              /*equivalent to 'S', 'u', etc */
    "Monday    ",
    "Tuesday   ",
    "Wednesday ",
    "Thursday  ",
    "Friday    ",
    "Saturday  "
};
```

As you can see, this declaration requires the completion of all ten elements (including the \0 character) in each row. The ability to point to arrays of differing sizes comes in quite handy when the array sizes to be input to the program are not known in advance or can change from execution to execution. For example, sorting algorithms, word processors, and data analysis programs utilize this data storage and access method. As a programmer, you may want an array to contain pointer information, storing addresses to other variables used in the program. This is analogous to maintaining a "map" of addresses to other variables for accessing purposes.

POINTERS TO FUNCTIONS

We already know how to declare a function to return a data type other than an int. For a function to return a pointer requires the same procedure. Within the calling function, we declare the function to be called with the data type to be returned:

```
char *funptr();
```

Function funptr() is expected to return a pointer that points to a character.

We can also declare a pointer to a function. Certain programming situations require execution of particular functions, depending upon specified criteria. An example of this is a comparison routine used by a sorting function. If the sorting function is to sort a set of numbers, a numeric comparison routine must be used. If it is sorting a set of strings, a string comparison routine must be used.

Let's assume we have a program that will perform one of two tasks depending on the input to the program. If the input matches criterion A, function funa() will be performed; otherwise, function funb() will be performed. Let us also assume that these two functions will be called at various points throughout the program. For efficiency, we would not want to continually repeat the test of the input data to see which function we should execute. Instead, we will set a pointer to the function to be used.

When we use pointers to functions, function processing is at least one step removed from the evaluation of the criteria. In Figure 6.9, the function main() evaluates the criteria and passes the appropriate function pointer to process(), which, in turn, uses this information during its execution to call the appropriate function.

The function main() declares funa() and funb() as type int. When main() calls process(), it passes the address of the function which process() is to use. This is very similar to the use of array names as pointers. The function process() declares its parameter to be a

```
/******************************************************************
      FUNPTR     Example of pointer to functions
****************************************|*************************/

#include <stdio.h>

main()
{
int  funa(), funb(), criterion, getcrit();

     while ( (criterion = getcrit()) != EOF) {
          if (criterion == 1)
               process(funa);
          else
               process(funb);
     }                              /* end while(criterion)   */

}                                  /* end main               */

/******************************************************************
      process   process functions example
****************************************|*************************/
process(funptr)
int  (*funptr)();
{
int  result, parameter1, parameter2;

                                   /* do processing          */

                                   /* call special function  */
     result = (*funptr)(parameter1, parameter2);

                                   /* continue processing     */
}                                  /* end process            */

/******************************************************************
      funa       criterion 1 function
****************************************|*************************/
funa(par1, par2)
int  par1, par2;

{ /* body */ }

/******************************************************************
      funb       criterion 2 function
****************************************|*************************/
funb(v1, v2)
int  v1, v2;

{ /* body */ }
```

Figure 6.9: Sample Program Demonstrating Pointers to Functions

pointer to a function signified by the empty parentheses in the statement

```
int (*funptr)();
```

The parentheses surrounding *funptr must be present in order to associate the operators correctly. If they were not present, we would have

```
int *funptr();
```

which declares funptr() as a function returning a pointer to an int. We call the function using the same parenthetical method, where (*funptr)(parameter1, parameter2) calls the function pointed to by (*funptr). Of course, funa() and funb() must be able to accept the same parameters; otherwise, they would not be interchangeable.

Applications using pointers to functions fall into the realm of more advanced programs. We have introduced this concept to familiarize you with its existence. The examples we would need to use to fully demonstrate the usefulness of pointers to functions would be quite lengthy and are beyond the scope of this book.

DATA STRUCTURES

At several earlier points in this book, we have discussed structured programming, emphasizing the importance of outlining the algorithm and dividing the algorithm into single processing tasks. This philosophy continues to apply as we discuss the creation of data structures.

When we begin to code a task, we abstract that task into terms which the computer can understand. This abstraction also applies to the data that the program uses during processing. For example, a check contains different types of data grouped together: the check number, the check date, the amount, and the payee. Some of this data can be divided further: for example, the date contains a month, a day, and a year, and the payee is an array of characters.

We could declare all of these variables independently:

```
int check_no,
    check_date_month, check_date_day, check_date_year;

double check_amount;
char check_payee[30];
```

But this would be extremely awkward later on when we need to process our check as a whole unit. This simple operation alone would require the declaration of six more variables and six assignment statements. Besides being tedious, all of this extra code would make the flow of our program confusing to readers, decrease available storage space, and reduce the efficiency of program execution.

CREATING DATA STRUCTURES: **STRUCT**

Fortunately C allows us to define a new data type based upon our program's requirements. The keyword for building a new data type is struct, for "structure"; it defines a data type built from the existing data types available (int, char, pointers, and so on). We can easily define a data type called date, for example, with the structure declaration:

```
struct date {
    unsigned mon, day, yr;
};
```

Be sure to include the semicolon (;) following the closing brace since this definition is a C statement and all C statements are terminated with the semicolon.

There are a few terms associated with structures that you should know about. First of all, the structure name itself—**date** in the preceding example—is called a *tag*. This simply provides a convenient name for the structure being defined. After you have defined the structure, you can declare a variable as having the structured data type by using the keyword struct and the structure tag followed by the variable name(s). For example:

```
struct date birth_date;
```

The tag itself is optional. However, if the tag is not present, you will have to declare the variables that use the structure in the same statement as the structure definition. For example:

```
struct {
    unsigned mon, day, yr;
} birth_date, another_date;
```

Here, birth_date and another_date are the only two variables using the date structure. If any more variables need the date structure, the structure definition must be supplied again followed by the new variable names because there is no way to reference this data structure. Using the tag makes data declaration much easier.

Next, each of the variables declared inside the structure definition (that is, **mon, day, yr**) is called a *member* of the structure. Members of a structure are accessed using the *member operator,* the period (.). This allows us to assign values to the individual members, just as we assign values to individual elements within an array, as follows:

```
birth_date.mon  =  3;
birth_date.day  =  8;
birth_date.yr  =  1984;
```

A variable may have the same name as the member of a structure elsewhere in the program. For example, a variable named **day** could be used by itself in normal processing, and another variable called **day** could be used within the **date** structure, in which case they are considered to be two different variables. Tag names and member names, on the other hand, must be distinct from each other. You may not have a tag name of **date** and a member of the structure with the name of **date**.

Note that we can use previously defined structures to create other structures. For example:

```
struct check {
     unsigned number;
     struct date written;
     double amount;
     char payee[30];
} paid1, paid2;
```

To access the member of a structure declared within a structure, we simply string the member operators together:

```
paid1.written.mon  =  3;
paid1.written.day  =  8;
paid1.written.yr  =  1984;
```

Assignment of members within structures operates in exactly the same manner as assignment with simple variables. A member of a structure can be assigned any value from any other variable that matches its data type. For example,

```
paid2.written.day  =  paid1.written.day;
```

assigns the member of the date structure value in paid1.written.day to paid2.written.day. Unfortunately, however, C does not allow the transfer of a structure as a whole unit. Thus

```
paid2 = paid1;
```

is an illegal operation. Note that some of the latest versions of C have implemented this capability. The Mac C compiler, for instance, does support structure assignment. Check your compiler's manual to see if it supports this added feature of the C language. If not, then members of structures must be assigned individually.

The important thing about structures is their ability to create precise data types that structure the data as efficently as the programming language structures the code.

POINTERS TO STRUCTURES

Structures simply expand the number of data types available to the programmer: anything you can do with a predefined data type (such as int, char, and so on) you can also do with a structure. C's consistency allows a pointer to a structure to be constructed similarly to all other pointers. For example:

```
struct check *chkptr1, *chkptr2;
```

Now if we assign values to these pointers, we can make assignments of structure members:

```
chkptr1 = &paid1;
chkptr2 = &paid2;

(*chkptr2).number = 8;
```

The parentheses are required in this statement because the member operator has a higher precedence than the pointer operator. Without the parentheses, the compiler would think that chkptr2 was a structure with a member called number. This is not the case, and you would receive an error message during compilation.

Although this statement can be difficult to read, it is perfectly valid. To facilitate the task of reading a program, however, a specialized operator exists for just such occasions—the *structure pointer operator,*

->, created with the hyphen and greater-than symbol:

chkptr2 –>number = 8;

This operator tells the reader that chkptr2 is a pointer to a structure and that the member being accessed is number. Notice that no asterisk (*) is used. The structure pointer implies that its left expression evaluates to a pointer, and the right expression is a member of the structure data type associated with the pointer. If you try to access a variable name that is not a member of the structure associated with the pointer, the compiler will detect this situation and give you an error message.

Before we present the program to demonstrate the use of structures, you should know about one final operator called the sizeof operator. The sizeof operator returns the size of the data type listed in the parentheses following it. For example,

sizeof (struct date);

returns the size of our date structure. The value returned is the number of storage units required to store the structure named. In C, the size of one storage unit is equal to the size used by one char data type. The statement

sizeof (char);

should always return the value 1 (that is, one storage unit). As you can see from this example, the sizeof operator is not restricted to having structures as its operand. Any C data type or structure that you have defined may be operated on by sizeof.

STRUCTURES AND FUNCTIONS

Because a structure cannot be manipulated as a whole unit, it cannot be used as a parameter for a function. Its location can be passed to the function by means of a pointer, however, much as an entire array is passed to a function through a pointer. Under these circumstances, the function will receive the pointer to the structure and use the structure pointer operator to access the members. Thus, in this program fragment the function declaration sets the variable parm to be a pointer to the structure **check**, defined earlier:

```
struct date {
    unsigned mon, day, yr;
};

struct check {
    unsigned number;
    struct date written;
    double amount;
    char payee[30];
};

main()
{
struct check paid1;
...code for main()...
funptr(&paid1);                    /* call to funptr */
...more code for main()...
}

funptr(parm)
struct check *parm;
{
...function body...
}
```

Remember that passing a pointer to a function implies a call-by-reference method of parameter passing. In this case, any changes you make to the structure using the pointer will cause changes in the actual parameter. You should be careful when using this method of parameter passing.

The Consulair Mac C Compiler contains a glimpse of things to come. This compiler does support the C extension of passing structures by value. This is a very convenient mechanism, but it is also very unportable. Passing structures by value is not supported by most C compilers, although it is expected that this and other extensions to the language will become standard in the near future.

Notice that in the example the structure definitions occur external to any function block. This allows variables to be declared by using just the structure name because the structure definition is global to the source code file. If the structure were placed inside of a function block, then that structure definition would only be available within that function. If you wanted to use the structure in another function, you would have to redefine the structure in that other function, and that can add up to a lot of typing.

DATA STRUCTURING TECHNIQUES: A SAMPLE PROGRAM

At the beginning of this chapter we looked at the reasons for structuring your data and mentioned that data structuring occurs at two levels. We have already seen the first level, which was the creation of new data types called structures. The second level of data structuring has to do with the organization and relationship of individual data objects so that, for example, you can quickly search a list of items for the one you want or tabulate columns of information.

For our programming example, assume that you are writing an accounting program. In this program you have a list of account numbers that you want to keep in ascending numerical order. One way to keep the list in order is to have an array that holds the numbers. When you add a new number, your program will start at the beginning of the list and find the two numbers between which the new number will be inserted. For example, if you have the list of numbers 1, 5, 6, 9, 13, 16, and 21, and you want to insert the number 7, your program will start at array element 0 (which holds the number 1) and check each successive array element until it reaches the number 9. Now, in order to make space for the new number, all following numbers are moved up one position in the array, and the new number is inserted.

Although this algorithm will work, it has two problems. The first problem is that the program must move all numbers following the inserted number. If the array contained several thousand numbers and you wanted to add a new number at the beginning of the list, this operation could take quite some time to complete. The second problem has to do with allocating space for the array: how much space should we allow for? If you know the maximum number of accounts that you will have, then you can write the code to allocate this amount of space. But what if the number of accounts may range from 100 to 5000? It would be wasteful to allocate all 5000 array elements if only a few hundred are going to be used. To solve this second problem, you need to be able to allocate each array item as you add a number.

So far we have only briefly mentioned the ability to explicitly allocate memory for direct use by the program. In most cases—for example, entry to the program, entry to a block of statements, and entry to a function—the variables you declare are provided for by the compiler. In other cases, such as creating new variables (usually structures) "on the fly," we need some method of requesting and receiving unused blocks of memory for our newly created variables.

C does not specify an operator to perform this function, because the allocation process depends heavily on the hardware in use; however, the standard library supplied with your compiler should have a function called malloc() or calloc() or both. These functions allow you to gain access to your computer's memory without interfering with the program's data. The function malloc() is passed the size of the data space requested and returns a pointer to the space if it is available; otherwise, a 0 is returned. The function calloc() operates on a similar principle: its parameters are the number of elements to be allocated and the size of each element. It returns a pointer to enough space to hold all of the elements requested. The whole technique of allocating memory in this fashion is called *dynamic memory allocation*.

The difference between malloc() and calloc() is that calloc() will initialize all the elements in the memory segment to 0, whereas malloc() may or may not, depending on how it is implemented. In keeping with the black box principle, we do not need to worry about how the memory allocation is done, so long as we are given the memory requested. For the following example, we will use the malloc() function to allocate our memory as we need it.

To solve the first problem in our original program (the problem of having to move all of the numbers after the number we wish to insert), we will use a data structure called a *linked list*. A linked list consists of individual structures, called *links*, that are all of the same data type structure. This structure contains the data that we want to store (in our case, the account number) and a pointer, called the *link pointer*, to the next structure item in the list. The data structure for each element in our list looks like this:

```
struct link {
    int value;
    struct link *next;
};
```

The member value will contain the number we enter, while the member next points to the next structure in the list.

This is called a *self-referential data structure*, by which we mean that it makes references to itself. In most cases, the self-reference will be a pointer to a structure of itself (it could not logically contain itself exactly). With this data structure, we can start at the first link in the list (which is just like starting at the first array element) and continue through the list until we find the first number that is greater than the number we want to add. Now we can make the previous link point to the added link; the added link will point to the next link (the one containing the next greater number). The technical term for this procedure is an *insertion sort* because we are, in effect, inserting the new link between the next lower and next higher links.

In Figure 6.10, we already have a small list of numbers, and we want to insert the number 15. By linearly searching from the beginning of the list, we eventually find the first link greater than 15. We must conclude that the number before is less than 15 (we will ignore duplicate numbers for this program). Our main algorithm looks like this:

> Get an integer.
> Create a link.
> Insert link into list.

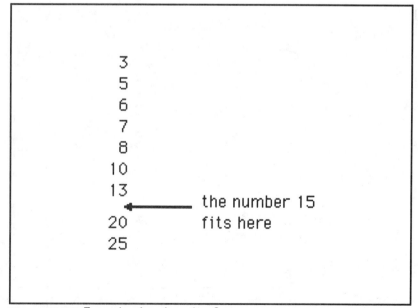

Figure 6.10: Example of an Insertion Sort

Figure 6.11 shows function **main()** for the insertion sort program in Listing 6.4. (We show Listing 6.4 here for your reference. Don't be alarmed by the length of the program. We will examine the individual functions that comprise the structure of the Linear List program in the following pages.) You will notice the uppercase words EOF and NULL. These two words are called *tokens* and are defined by using the compiler directive statement **#define** within the header file **stdio.h**. The **#define** statement has the following format:

> **#define** *token value*

```
/****************************************************************
    list604       Create an ordered linear list
*****************************************************************/

#include "stdio.h"

/**** Use only if your system cannot generate a standard EOF signal ***/
#undef      EOF
#define     EOF 4
/*******************************************************************/

struct link {                   /* link in list              */
    int     value;
    struct link *next;
};

char    *malloc();              /* use base size type        */

main()
{
int     num;                    /* temporary variable        */
struct link *i,                 /* loop control variable     */
        *linkptr,               /* pointer to current link   */
        *firstlink,             /* first link in list        */
        *make_link(),           /* create a new link         */
        *insert();              /* insert link into list     */

    firstlink = NULL;           /* clear list                */

                                /* get numbers for list      */
    printf("Enter integers for list, EOF to stop: ");
                                /* for each number, create   */
                                /* a link. Check if link     */
                                /* was created. Then insert  */
                                /* link into list.           */
    while (getint(&num) != EOF) {   /* cannot use 4 again    */
        if ((linkptr = make_link(num)) != NULL)
            firstlink = insert(linkptr, firstlink);

                                /* display list              */
    printf("\nOrdered List:\n");
    for (i = firstlink; i != NULL; i = i->next)
        printf("%d ", i->value);
    printf("\n\nNext number: ");
    }                           /* end while(getint)         */
}                               /* end main                  */
```

Figure 6.11: Program to Create an Ordered Linear List Through Function **main()**

```
/*************************************************************
    list604      Create an ordered linear list
*************************************************************/

#include "stdio.h"

/**** Use only if your system cannot generate a standard EOF signal ***/
#undef     EOF
#define    EOF 4
/*********************************************************************/

struct link {                    /* link in list            */
     int    value;
     struct link *next;
};

char    *malloc();               /* use base size type      */

main()
{
int    num;                      /* temporary variable      */
struct link *i,                  /* loop control variable   */
        *linkptr,                /* pointer to current link */
        *firstlink,              /* first link in list      */
        *make_link(),            /* create a new link       */
        *insert();               /* insert link into list   */

     firstlink = NULL;           /* clear list              */

                                 /* get numbers for list    */
     printf("Enter integers for list, EOF to stop: ");
                                 /* for each number, create */
                                 /* a link. Check if link   */
                                 /* was created. Then insert */
                                 /* link into list.         */
     while (getint(&num) != EOF) {   /* cannot use 4 again  */
        if ((linkptr = make_link(num)) != NULL)
            firstlink = insert(linkptr, firstlink);

                                 /* display list            */
        printf("\nOrdered List:\n");
        for (i = firstlink; i != NULL; i = i->next)
            printf("%d ", i->value);
        printf("\n\nNext number: ");
     }                           /* end while(getint)       */
}                                /* end main                */


/*************************************************************
    getint      retrieve an integer from the console
    pnum        =   pointer to an integer
    Returned values: the integer is returned through pnum.
            The function returns the termination character.
    Notes: the sign character must appear in the first position.
            Any non-digit characters are ignored.
            Termination must be with \n or EOF.
*************************************************************/
getint(pnum)
int    *pnum;
{
int    c, sign = 1;
```

Listing 6.4

```
        *pnum = 0;               /* initialize values       */
        c = getchar();           /* get first character     */

        if (c == '+' || c == '-') { /* check for sign character */
            if (c == '-')
                sign = -1;
            putchar(c);
            c = getchar();       /* get next character      */
        }                        /* end if                  */

        while (c != '\n' && c != EOF) {
            if (c >= '0' && c <= '9') { /* check if numeric    */
                *pnum = (*pnum * 10) + (c - '0');
                putchar(c);
            }
            c = getchar();
        }                        /* end while(c)            */

        *pnum *= sign;           /* adjust for sign         */
        return(c);               /* return termination char */
}                                /* end getint              */
/***************************************************************
        make_link   create and initial a link
           v    =    value to initialize link with
        Returned values: returns a pointer to the link if allocation
                   was successful. Otherwise NULL is returned.
***************************************************************/
struct link *make_link(v)
int     v;
{
struct link *temp;               /* temporary pointer       */

        temp = (struct link *) malloc(sizeof(struct link));

        if (temp == NULL) {      /* check if allocatedOK    */
            printf("Memory allocation error");
            return(NULL);
        }                        /* end if(temp)            */

        temp->value = v;
        temp->next = NULL;
        return(temp);
}                                /* end make_link           */

/***************************************************************
        insert      insert a link into the list
           lprt  =   pointer to link to insert
           firstptr= pointer to first link in list
        Returned values: updates links as required.
                   Returns pointer to new first link if changed.
***************************************************************/
struct link *insert(lptr, firstptr)
struct link *lptr,
            *firstptr;
{
struct link *loopptr,            /* loop control variable   */
            *lastptr;            /* previous link checked   */

        lastptr = NULL;          /* no previous links yet   */
        loopptr = firstptr;      /* start with first link   */
```

Listing 6.4 [continued]

```
      while (loopptr != NULL) {    /* continue until no more  */
                                   /* links in list           */
  /*  In this section, when a current list value is found
      that is greater than the value to be inserted, then
      the insert link is placed before the current link.
      Then, if no previous link existed, insert link becomes
      the new first link, otherwise the previous link is
      set to point to the insert link.                     */

      if (loopptr->value > lptr->value) {
          lptr->next = loopptr;
          if (lastptr == NULL)
              return(lptr);
          else {
              lastptr->next = lptr;
              return(firstptr);
          }                        /* end if-else           */
      }                            /* end if(loopptr)       */

                                   /* ignore duplicate entries */
      if (loopptr->value == lptr->value)
          return(firstptr);

      lastptr = loopptr;           /* move to next link     */
      loopptr = loopptr->next;
  }                                /* end while(loopptr)    */

  /*  If entire list is passed through, then insert link must
      go at the end of the list. NULL is checked to see if
      insert link is the first link entered.                */

  if (lastptr != NULL) {
      lastptr->next = lptr;
      return(firstptr);
  } else
      return(lptr);
}                                  /* end insert            */
```

Listing 6.4 [continued]

At compilation time, the compiler will replace every token with its associated value. Notice that no semicolon appears after *value*. (We will discuss the #define directive in Chapter 8.) You may also have noticed that the token EOF does not have an associated #define statement in our listing, but the #define statement does exist in the file stdio.h; you may examine this file to be sure of this. (If you do not have this token defined in file stdio.h, look in your compiler manual for its proper value and create a #define statement in your source file. The EOF token is the standard name for the symbol representing the value returned as the end-of-file signal. All C systems have a value for this token (either −1 or 0), and most systems will have the EOF token already defined.)

The while loop in Figure 6.11 calls three functions. In the control statement, the function getint() will get an integer from the console and place its value in variable num. We use the call-by-reference method in this case since there are two possible values that may exist when the function returns: the value entered and the termination character. Because characters are represented as integers, if we had one returned value, we would not know whether it was an EOF character or an integer. The integer entered is placed directly in the parameter variable used (through the call-by-reference technique), and the termination character is the returned value of the function. The other two functions in the while loop create a link in memory and then insert it into the list.

The for loop shown in Figure 6.11 is more interesting. We initialize i to point to the first link in our list. For each link, we print the value contained in that link and move to the next link, until the next link becomes the NULL pointer. Since i is a pointer, we use the structure pointer operator to access the member of each link. This loop could also have been controlled by a while statement, but the for loop places all of the loop control information in one place, making the logic of the program more readily apparent.

Our getint() function will be an improvement over our previous getint() function and will include a new input function called getchar(), which returns a character from the console. The new getint() function shown in Figure 6.12 is more flexible than the original version, but it is not quite a general-purpose function; the entry of a number requires the first character to be a sign character (+ or −) or a digit. This function also ignores any nondigit characters found in the middle of the input and returns only when a newline (carriage return) or EOF character has been entered. If the EOF character is entered, it is returned, causing termination of our program, regardless of whether or not a number was entered. (As an exercise, you may want to develop a general numeric input routine that overcomes these limitations.)

In the figures for the Linear List program, the comments preceding the function are more elaborate than before. This is necessary because our sample programs are getting larger, making it crucial to explain the purpose of the various portions in relation to the whole program. We suggest you likewise begin more extensive commenting as you write larger programs.

As a rule for writing comments for functions, you should list the function's purpose, its parameters, returned values, and any special notes you deem necessary. We have presented one possible format for commenting. You should select a commenting format that is easy to read, very noticeable, and easy to write. When commenting a function, because the parameters of a function must be declared, you may write a comment for each parameter in its declaration statement instead of in the function comment heading.

Looking more closely at the memory allocation statement in Figure 6.13, we see some rather interesting constructs. We know that malloc() will allocate the amount of memory specified by its parameter. Since we require enough memory to hold one link structure, we need to know the amount of space used by the link structure. To get this value, we use the sizeof operator on the link structure, and then use the expression sizeof(struct link) as the parameter for malloc().

```
/**************************************************************
      getint        retrieve an integer from the console
        pnum     =    pointer to an integer
      Returned values: the integer is returned through pnum.
                    The function returns the termination character.
      Notes: the sign character must appear in the first position.
             Any non-digit characters are ignored.
             Termination must be with \n or EOF.
      **************************************************************/
getint(pnum)
int     *pnum;
{
int     c, sign = 1;

    *pnum = 0;                    /* initialize values        */
    c = getchar();                /* get first character      */

    if (c == '+' || c == '-') {   /* check for sign character */
        if (c == '-')
            sign = -1;
        putchar(c);
        c = getchar();            /* get next character       */
    }                             /* end if                   */

    while (c != '\n' && c != EOF) {
        if (c >= '0' && c <= '9') {   /* check if numeric     */
            *pnum = (*pnum * 10) + (c - '0');
            putchar(c);
        }
        c = getchar();
    }                             /* end while(c)             */

    *pnum *= sign;                /* adjust for sign          */
    return(c);                    /* return termination char  */
}                                 /* end getint               */
```

Figure 6.12: The New getint() Function from the Linear List Program

But what about the (struct link *) preceding the malloc() portion of the statement? The parentheses surrounding a data type indicate a cast operator. The cast operator will convert the format of its operand into the data type defined within the parentheses. We declared malloc() to be a function returning a pointer to a character. In most cases, the default declaration from the library is that malloc() returns a pointer to the smallest data type, which can then be cast (expanded) into a larger data type. If you do not use the cast operator, this program may or may not work on your computer. To be on the safe side, use the cast operator to ensure that your program will work on your computer and any other computer you might need to use.

If you have the calloc() function instead of malloc(), change the allocation statement to

temp = (struct link*) calloc(1, sizeof(struct link));

If you do not have either of these memory allocation functions, you will have to skip this program example.

Figure 6.14 lists our program's last function, insert(), whose purpose is to insert the newly created node into the list. In Figure 6.15, we can see a graphic representation of the links in the list. Each new link will have a link pointing at it (link A), and it will point to a link following it (link B). In function insert(), the variable lastptr holds the

```
/**************************************************************
    make_link    create and initial a link
        v        =    value to initialize link with
    Returned values: returns a pointer to the link if allocation
                was successful. Otherwise NULL is returned.
 **************************************************************/
struct link *make_link(v)
int     v;
{
struct link *temp;              /* temporary pointer        */

    temp = (struct link *) malloc(sizeof(struct link));

    if (temp == NULL) {         /* check if allocatedOK     */
        printf("Memory allocation error");
        return(NULL);
    }                           /* end if(temp)             */

    temp->value = v;
    temp->next = NULL;
    return(temp);
}                               /* end make_link            */
```

Figure 6.13: Function **make_link** from the Linear Link Program

previously accessed link, indicated by A; and the variable **loopptr** is the link we are currently examining, indicated by B. As we move through the list, we keep track of the previous and current links until we find two links with values surrounding the link to be inserted. In

```
/***************************************************************
       insert         insert a link into the list
          lprt   =    pointer to link to insert
          firstptr=   pointer to first link in list
       Returned values: updates links as required.
                       Returns pointer to new first link if changed.
       ****************************************************************/
struct link *insert(lptr, firstptr)
struct link *lptr,
            *firstptr;
{
struct link *loopptr,          /* loop control variable    */
            *lastptr;          /* previous link checked     */

    lastptr = NULL;            /* no previous links yet     */
    loopptr = firstptr;        /* start with first link     */

    while (loopptr != NULL) {  /* continue until no more    */
                               /* links in list             */

    /*  In this section, when a current list value is found
        that is greater than the value to be inserted, then
        the insert link is placed before the current link.
        Then, if no previous link existed, insert link becomes
        the new first link, otherwise the previous link is
        set to point to the insert link.                   */

        if (loopptr->value > lptr->value) {
            lptr->next = loopptr;
            if (lastptr == NULL)
                return(lptr);
            else {
                lastptr->next = lptr;
                return(firstptr);
            }                      /* end if-else            */
        }                          /* end if(loopptr)        */

                                   /* ignore duplicate entries */
        if (loopptr->value == lptr->value)
            return(firstptr);

        lastptr = loopptr;         /* move to next link      */
        loopptr = loopptr->next;
    }                              /* end while(loopptr)     */

    /*  If entire list is passed through, then insert link must
        go at the end of the list. NULL is checked to see if
        insert link is the first link entered.             */
    if (lastptr != NULL) {
        lastptr->next = lptr;
        return(firstptr);
    } else
        return(lptr);
}                                  /* end insert             */
```

Figure 6.14: The Function **insert()** from the Linear List Program

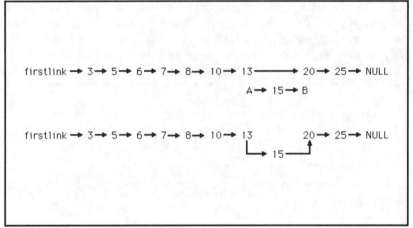

Figure 6.15: Inserting a New Link into the List

this case, the link containing 13 becomes link A and the link containing 20 becomes B. Before running the program, trace through the function and determine what happens when (1) the first link is put in; (2) a new lowest link is inserted; and (3) a new highest link is inserted.

The sample program we have been studying incorporates most of the tools and techniques introduced in this chapter. It also includes an introduction into the realm of more complex data structures, which is a subject by itself. At this point, we have completed our survey of most of the specified utilities available within the C programming language. The rest of this chapter deals with a few more extensions to the flexibility of C structures.

Because so much information has been incorporated into Listing 6.4, take some time to study it and make sure you understand the use of structures in programming. One of the benefits of the C programming language is that it allows the programmer to define new data types.

FIELDS AND UNIONS

We will now go from the macrocosm to the microcosm of data structures. Listing 6.4 presented one of the many global data structures that programmers use to organize the data used by a program. Because C has the ability to use pointers and create structures, these global data structures can be implemented and utilized by a C programmer. But C also allows the programmer to determine how data is stored in memory. When using a structure, the programmer can define the size of a member down to a single bit by using a *field*. The programmer can also place different data types into the same variable by using a variation on the structure called a *union*. Both of these data organization concepts are very powerful, as you will see in a moment.

FIELD STRUCTURES

The programmer can define an *n*-bit variable within a structure called a *field*. To indicate that a member is a field, the member name is followed by a colon and the number of bits within the field.

The most common use for a field is for switches or flags, especially when controlling hardware components. Since the hardware of the computer only works with the binary values of on and off, a field is ideal when you need to access a piece of the hardware. Another use for a flag is in determining what options are currently active. For example, in the MacPaint program, the Style menu consists of several options. When you select an option, a check appears next to the option. We could write a structure for this purpose as follows:

```
struct {
    unsigned plain : 1;
    unsigned bold : 1;
    unsigned italic : 1;
    unsigned underline: 1;
    unsigned outline : 1;
    unsigned shadow : 1;
} attribute;
```

We can access the fields just as we would any other member of a structure and perform operations on them as if they were of the int data type. In this example, we can assume that when the field contains a 1, the option is selected.

Fields are always stored in the space required by an int data type and are always taken to be unsigned quantities. The use of the declaration **unsigned** reminds us of this fact. All members of a structure are stored sequentially in memory. The structure

```
struct {
    char c;
    unsigned f1 : 1;
```

```
        double x;
        unsigned f2 : 2;
        unsigned f3 : 2;
        int i;
    } sample;
```

will contain a char, an int, a double, an int, and another int. Although fields allow access only to the specified set of bits, they require a full int space to be stored (assume an int requires 16 bits). In this example, f1 wastes fifteen bits, and f2 and f3 will be combined to use only four bits of an int space. If you are using fields to save memory space, you should place all fields sequentially within the structure to save the maximum amount of storage.

A field will not straddle an int boundary. For example, in the structure

```
    struct {
        unsigned f1 : 9;
        unsigned f2 : 4;
        unsigned f3 : 6;
    } sample;
```

f1 and f2 will be placed in the same int space and a second int will be created to hold f3. The bits can be placed within the int itself in left-to-right or right-to-left order, depending upon your compiler.

Use a field when you require a minimum of wasted space or when you will be manipulating data or hardware at the bit level. Remember: fields are always unsigned quantities and will always be stored in an int space.

Unions

The final structured data storage type is called a *union*. A union is a type of data structure allowing a variable to hold different data types within the same data space. Of course, only one data type may be stored at a time, but this method of storage allows a great deal of flexibility in programming.

On the other hand, the programmer has an increased responsibility to remember what data type was last stored in the union. If you should mismatch the data type being stored and the type required for the operation, your program will produce meaningless results.

A union is constructed in the same manner as a structure. A union has a tag and a list of possible data types it may contain. For example:

```
union sample {
    int i;
    double x;
} ux;
```

This union can take on an int data type or a **double** data type by assigning the associated member a value, as follows:

```
ux.i = 6;
```

or

```
ux.x = 8.345;
```

In the first case, the member i is assigned a value and the union contains an integer value. In the second case, the member x is assigned a value and the union contains a floating point value. The union will hold only one of these values at any given time. The same set of operations can be used on a union as can be used on a structure: that is, referring to a member and taking its address.

Unions, like fields, are among the more esoteric concepts of the C programming language. We have presented them here to let you know that they exist, in case you should come across either of them in someone's source code. As your programming experience increases, you will discover applications for these tools.

THE TYPEDEF FACILITY

The **typedef** facility provides a convenient method for creating pseudonyms for already existing data types. It reduces the amount of typing the programmer needs to do and increases the readability of the program.

To create an alternative name, use the **typedef** statement as in this example:

```
typedef double SALARY;
SALARY check_amount;
```

The first statement declares **SALARY** to be a synonym for the data type **double**. Now, whenever **SALARY** appears, it declares the variables following it to be of type **double**.

Use of the **typedef** facility can be quite convenient and much easier to read, especially when you have several long or complicated structures in use within your program. For example:

```
typedef struct emp {
      int emp_no;
      char last_name[20];
      char first_name[10];
      long ss_no;
      SALARY payrate;
      struct date birthdate;
} EMPREC, *EMPPTR;
```

This **typedef** statement declares **EMPREC** to be the data type name for structure **emp**, and **EMPPTR** to be the data type name for a pointer to the structure emp. The **typedef** statement also contains the definition for the **emp** structure. Now, instead of writing

```
struct emp employee1, employee2, employee3;
struct emp *emp1, *emp2, *emp3;
```

we can use the new data type names, like this:

```
EMPREC employee1, employee2, employee3;
EMPPTR emp1, emp2, emp3;
```

If a pointer is declared as part of a **typedef** name, then when the new data type name is later used to declare variables, the pointer reference is automatically distributed throughout the listed variables. In the preceeding example, the variables **emp1**, **emp2**, and **emp3** are pointers to an **emp** structure. This latter format is much easier to type and easier to read than the explicit declaration.

Essentially, a **typedef** statement is similar to a data declaration statement. The differences are that the **typedef** statement starts with the keyword **typedef**, and ends with the new data type names instead of variable names. The use of the uppercase characters for the **typedef** name is a standard formatting convention to emphasize the fact that the word has been defined by the programmer.

BIT MANIPULATION OPERATORS

We still have a few *bits* and pieces to mention before we complete our coverage on the C language operators. To finish the C operators, we return to the bit—the smallest informational unit in the computer. The bit can communicate one of only two pieces of information. Under most circumstances this will be a Boolean value (true or false). To make it easier for the programmer to manipulate bits, C provides a number of bitwise operators, a topic that we discussed briefly in Chapter 3.

Floating point numbers are stored as a series of bits within the computer's memory. Because of the variations in floating point representations, however, using bitwise operations on a floating point number provides no useful information. Thus, bitwise operators only work with integer operands. Each of C's logical operators have associated bitwise operators.

The bitwise AND operator is a single ampersand, (&). All bitwise operators act, as their name implies, bit-by-bit. This means that the first bit of one operand will be ANDed with the first bit of the second operand, the second bit with the second bit, and so on.

The bitwise inclusive-OR operator is the vertical bar, (|), and the exclusive-OR operator is the caret (^). These two ORs both work in the same bitwise manner as the bitwise AND.

The programmer can also shift bits within an integer. The left-shift operator

A << B

shifts the bits in A to a new position B units to the left (see Figure 6.16).

```
             The Left-Shift Operator:

                 5 << 10    takes 00000000,00000101
                    and shifts to 00010100,00000000


             The Right-Shift Operator:

                 193 >> 5   takes 00000000,11000001
                    and shifts to 00000000,00000110
```

Figure 6.16: Example of Left-Shift and Right-Shift Operators

The right shift operator, $>>$, performs the reverse operation of the left-shift operator. If B is negative or larger than the number of bits within the object A, the result is undefined. When shifting left, zeroes are used to fill the empty bits at the right end. When shifting right, the emptied bits will be *zero-filled* if A is an **unsigned** data type. In other cases, filling may be done with the value of the sign bit (the leftmost bit). As for the bits being shifted out of the other end of the word, they are simply discarded.

Because bit operations work with much greater speed than full-byte operations, we will rewrite our binary conversion routine using bitwise operators in Listing 6.5.

The number of elements in the array must be equal to the number of bits in an integer. The initialization routine has been removed because as **pos** moves through the variable **d**, the element in array **a**

```
/*********************************************************
     list605     Convert decimal integers into binary numbers #2
*********************************************************/

#include "stdio.h"

main()
{
int     b[32],                  /* allow for 32 binary digits   */
        num, i;

                                /* convert numbers 0 to 15      */
     for (num = 0; num <= 16; num++) {
        printf("%d in binary = ", num);
        dectobin(num, b);       /* call conversion function     */
                                /* output digits in reverse     */
        for (i = 31; i >= 0; i--)
             printf("%d", b[i]);
        printf("\n");           /* move to next line            */
     }                          /* end for(num)                 */
     scanf("%*s");
}                               /* end main                     */

/*********************************************************
     dectobin    convert decimal number into binary
        d   =   integer to convert
        a   =   array to store binary digits in. Digits are
                stored in reverse order.
*********************************************************/
dectobin(d, a)
int     d, a[];
{
int     count = 0, pos = 1;

                                /* loop through conversion      */
     while (pos != 0) {
        a[count++] = ((d & pos) && 1);
        pos <<= 1;              /* shift left 1 bit             */
     }                          /* end while(pos)               */

     return;
}                               /* end dectobin                 */
```

Listing 6.5

will be forced to either 0 or 1. The loop will stop when **pos** has its single bit shifted off the left end. At this point, **pos** will equal zero because left-shifting guarantees zero fill, and the bit is discarded once it is shifted out of the integer.

The last bitwise operator is the bitwise NOT, represented by the tilde, (~), and sometimes referred to as the *one's-complement operator*. This operator changes all ones to zeroes and zeroes to ones within an integer, so that, for example, ~11100011 equals 00011100.

This operator is particularly useful in creating *masks*. A mask is a bit string used in bitwise operators to examine specific bits. The **pos** in the function **dectobin()** of Listing 6.5 is a mask. In this case, the mask contains a single bit. The mask is then ANDed with the number being converted. Because all other bit positions in the mask are 0, the AND operator forces these bit positions to become 0. If the number has a bit set to 1 in the same position as the single bit set to 1 in the mask, then the resulting value is true (that is, nonzero). A result of true sets the array entry to 1.

In general, bitwise operators will be found in hardware-related processes or in special circumstances like the example program presented a moment ago.

SUMMING UP

Chapter 6 has covered the advanced and complex topic of data structuring. Starting with pointers and addresses, we saw how to access and manipulate data in memory. Pointers were used when passing parameters to functions using call-by-reference instead of the normal parameter passing method, call-by-value. We also saw that pointers are an integral part of how arrays are stored and manipulated. We saw, in fact, that we could access an array element through either a reference using the array name and a subscript, or through pointer arithmetic. From the array, we moved into the general subject of data structuring in C.

Structures are quite a powerful tool in a programming language. With a structure, you can group together data objects of differing data types. This group can then be manipulated as a single unit, which means that you do not need to worry about keeping track of all the individual pieces. Now that most compilers are including the ability to assign structures as a whole, to pass structures as parameters, and to return them from a function, using a structure has become much easier.

Through the use of structures, we created a data structure called the linked list. The linked list program encompassed many concepts including self-referential structures, dynamic memory allocation, and an application for pointers.

The final topics in our discussion of data structures were fields and unions. Fields specified a set number of bits to be used for storage. A field is generally used for keeping track of flags or switches. Unions allow the programmer to store data of more than one type into the same variable. A union is used when differing data types might be used, depending upon the operations you are performing.

Finally, bit manipulation operators completed our discussion of the C programming language in this chapter. These operators performed logical operations on integers or shifted the bits within an integer either to the left or the right.

As you write more and more programs, you will become more familiar with structures and data structures in general. As you begin to program, you will probably be using the array most often. It is a very useful data structure. When you begin to write more complex programs that handle large amounts of data, you may want to do further research into the topic of data structures.

Chapter 7 continues our discussion of C by describing some of the functions supplied in the standard input/output library. As you will see, these functions make C a much easier programming language to use.

SEVEN

THE
STANDARD
LIBRARY

The C programming language does not include any commands or keywords for handling data input or output, or for the handling character strings. The designers of C, Brian Kernighan and Dennis Ritchie, chose not to include these capabilities because, as we will see in a moment, these routines would make the language hardware-specific. Yet because most programming applications require a means of communicating with the external environment, most implementations of the C programming language will include a set of predefined routines, called the *standard I/O library*. The term *library* refers to a file containing precompiled functions. When the linker is used to create an executable program, your program object file is linked together with the standard I/O library file so that your program will have access to the standard I/O functions.

The library consists of a set of functions (like **getchar()**, **putchar()**, and **printf()**) that provide input and output facilities. The reason that this file is called the "standard" I/O library is that the names and parameters of these functions, and their results, if any, will be the same from compiler to compiler. In effect, the designers of C realized that each person who writes a C compiler would probably come up with a different set of I/O functions. To maintain consistency, Kernighan and Ritchie produced a set of functions to provide for some basic I/O applications. The two designers listed the function name, its purpose, what its parameters are, and what values are returned.

The development of the standard library is, by the way, an ideal example of the black-box principle in action. The author of a compiler (a programmer) has the specification for a single element of the program—the I/O function specified in the standard library. Now, the programmer can implement the function in any manner that he or she sees fit, as long as it performs the task specified.

The purpose of defining a standardized set of input/output functions is to provide portability among various computers. We will discuss the issue of portability when we discuss the UNIX interface in a moment. Following the discussion of UNIX, we will look at the standard library routines that deal with the console. We will also look at some of the functions used in text processing. The chapter goes on to present the functions used for manipulating input and output disk files from within a program, giving several examples of how the file facilities can be used. Finally, the chapter concludes with a brief comparison of the advantages of developing programs on the Mac or under UNIX.

C AND UNIX

UNIX is an *operating system* developed in the early 1970s by researchers at Bell Laboratories. An operating system is a program that controls the various actions that a computer must perform in order to make all of the different components work together as a single system. For example, on the Macintosh the Finder is the operating system.

You may be wondering why we are discussing UNIX in a book relating to the Macintosh. There are two reasons for this. First of all, some C compilers available for the Macintosh provide a programming environment that is very similar to the UNIX environment (the Aztec C68K compiler from Manx Software Systems is one example). Secondly, many of the I/O features of C were written specifically with UNIX in mind. There are many features of UNIX that we could discuss, but we will limit our view to the I/O interface and the issue of portability.

THE STANDARD INPUT AND OUTPUT

In UNIX, all I/O is handled as if the data is going to or coming from a file. Thus, to the operating system, a disk file, the printer, the data communications to other computers, and even the user's terminal all appear as files. In fact, the terminal keyboard is called the *standard input* and the terminal screen is called the *standard output*. Whenever a program makes a request for input or output without specifying a file, UNIX assumes that the request is for the standard input or output "file."

A secondary feature of this file-oriented operating system is that the user can redefine the standard input and output files. For example, let's say that you are testing a program that requires a long list of numbers as its input. Instead of entering these numbers in each time you test the program, you can place the numbers into a file on the disk. Then, when you run the program, you tell UNIX to get the input data from that disk file instead of from the keyboard. You can also apply this process to have a program send its output to a file instead of to the terminal screen. The process of redefining the standard input and output files is called *I/O redirection*.

PORTABILITY

Our second reason for discussing UNIX is to get at the issue of portability. This is where C comes in. While working on UNIX, Dennis Ritchie developed a programming language for the operating system called C. As we saw in Chapter 1, it is easier to work with a higher level language than with an assembly language, which is what UNIX was originally written in. Therefore, after a few enhancements to the programming language, almost all of UNIX was rewritten in C.

C was written to be as hardware independent as possible, which means that its operations do not require any special hardware to be included in the computer. So if a C compiler exists for two different machines, say Machine A and Machine B, then a program written in C will compile and run exactly the same on both machines, regardless of how different the two machines may be. This is quite an ideal situation, because if you write a program in C on one machine, you only need to recompile the program for it to work on a second machine. Unfortunately, total hardware independence in a programming language is not always practical. A case in point is the standard I/O library functions.

Input and output is one of the most hardware-dependent activities that a computer does. As we have already discussed, the way Kernighan and Ritchie solved this problem was to supply an external set of functions to handle these tasks. How does this relate to UNIX? Because Ritchie was involved with both UNIX and C and because C was designed under a UNIX system, many of the I/O routines in the attended library developed by Kernighan and Ritchie work with the standard input and output. We will use the standard input and output as we explore some of the standard library functions later in the chapter. Those of you who are programming the Macintosh without a UNIX environment will not have access to the redirection of the standard input and output used in some of the programming examples given later in this chapter.

Overall, UNIX and C have a common history and together they work extremely well. If you remove C from the UNIX environment, however, you lose some of its hardware independence, and once you start writing hardware-dependent programs, you lose portability. Because the basic operations of C are not affected by the hardware, the functionality of the language remains intact. Thus if you are not concerned about having your program run on several different computer systems, this loss of hardware independence should not be a problem. On the other hand, if you do need to have your program running on several different computers and you also need hardware-dependent code, you should place the hardware-dependent sections into individual functions. This will make changing the program for a new machine very quick and easy.

USING THE STANDARD I/O LIBRARY

C does not have built-in functions to handle strings or other tasks that make a language hardware-dependent, even though most programming situations require the same types of functions: string comparison, math functions, memory allocation, and so on. To make the programming process quicker and easier, a representative set of string and other functions has been provided in C's standard I/O library.

The functions of the standard I/O library that we will be looking at can be broken into five categories: console routines, string and character routines, math functions, memory allocation routines, and file accessing routines. We will discuss each of these categories in turn.

When you write a C program that uses one of the standard I/O library routines, you need to have this statement at the start of your program:

```
#include <stdio.h>
```

This line tells the compiler to include the file stdio.h into your program source code. The stdio.h file contains a some #define statements and external function declarations to tell the program what data type the functions will return. Tokens such as EOF, and in some cases, TRUE and FALSE, are defined within this file. Take a look at this file to see what it contains.

CONSOLE ROUTINES

The first set of standard I/O library routines we will look at have to do with the console. The *console* is the keyboard and display where the user works.

We have already encountered the **getchar()** and **putchar()** functions. As single-purpose functions, they provide a convenient starting point for writing your own more elaborate console input and output functions. For example, most C packages also have two other functions called **gets()** and **puts()** that input and output strings. The function **gets()** uses **getchar()** to get a character from the keyboard and place it in the string. It may work like this:

```
gets(s)
char *s;                                    /* pointer to string to fill */
{
int c;
char *pos;

    pos = s;
    while ((c = getchar()) != EOF) {
                                    /* carriage return ends input */
        if (c == 13) return(c);
                                    /* backspace deletes last char */
        else if (c == 8) *(-pos) = '\0';
        else {
                    *pos++ = c;    /* put char in string */
                    pos = '\0';    /* set new end of string */
        }
    }
    return(EOF);
}
```

This is just one possible implementation of **gets()**. More features can be added—for example, you can add a special character to erase all of the input entered so far and start over. The **puts()** function uses **putchar()** in much the same manner.

THE **PRINTF()** FUNCTION

The **printf()** function is by far the most frequently used output function in the standard I/O library. This function formats your output regardless of the data type or mix of data types. We have casually introduced the use of the **printf()** function earlier through its appearance in our programming examples. Now we will examine the full range of capabilities this function offers.

Formatted printing, also called "pretty printing," provides easily read and understood data output. Look at Figure 7.1 and decide which format would you rather read. Clearly, the table format provides a better presentation. In the unformatted example, the numbers have varying lengths (number of digits). The formatting function gives the programmer a way to specify a constant size and format of each variable to be output.

Formatting output, for the most part, involves the conversion of an object of a particular data type into its formatted character representation. Take a look, for example, at the print() function's parameters:

printf("*control string*", *output data list*);

The *control string*, first of all, contains the output format of the *output data list*. Two types of fields can be used in the control string: literal characters and format fields. Literal characters will be printed as they appear within the control string. The statement

printf("This is a literal string.");

will print

This is a literal string.

Format fields perform the conversion of the output data list into its formatted character representation. There must be a one-to-one correspondence between data items in the output data list and format

```
x = 1, square root of x = 1, square of x = 1
x = 2, square root of x = 1.414214, square of x = 4
x = 3, square root of x = 1.732051, square of x = 9
x = 4, square root of x = 2, square of x = 16
x = 5, square root of x = 2.236068, square of x = 25
x = 6, square root of x = 2.44949, square of x = 36
x = 7, square root of x = 2.645751, square of x = 49
x = 8, square root of x = 2.828427, square of x = 64
x = 9, square root of x = 3, square of x = 81
x = 10, square root of x = 3.162278, square of x = 100


    x    square root of x    square of x

    1       1.000000              1
    2       1.414214              4
    3       1.732051              9
    4       2.000000             16
    5       2.236068             25
    6       2.449490             36
    7       2.645751             49
    8       2.828427             64
    9       3.000000             81
   10       3.162278            100
```

Figure 7.1: Formatted and Unformatted Display

fields, and the format field must specify the data type of its matching data item. For example, we have used the %d format field when we wanted to print an integer variable.

Each format field consists of the following:

%(−)(width)(.precision)(l)(conversion character)

The percent symbol (%) and the *conversion character* must be included in a format field; all the other zones of the format field are optional. The percent symbol indicates to the function that the following characters signify information for a conversion process as opposed to a literal string. The conversion character indicates the data type of the data to be output. Let's take a look at each of these fields.

The hyphen (−) produces left justification of the characters within the field. By default, all fields will have the rightmost character of their output placed in the rightmost position of the field (this is called right justification). Using the hyphen will cause left justification instead: the first character of the output will be placed in the leftmost character position of the field.

The *width* zone specifies the minimum width of the field in number of characters. When the length of the data item is shorter than the width value, the field will be filled with blank spaces on the right or left, depending upon whether the field is to be left- or right-justified, respectively. If the first character of the width zone is the digit 0 (like 04), then zeroes (instead of blanks) are used to fill on either the left or right. If the length of the data item exceeds the minimum width, then all characters of the data item are output and no further spacing (using blanks or zeroes) is provided. If no width is specified, the minimum width will be 0, and there will be no minimum width formatting of the field.

The *precision* zone, which requires a leading period (.), can have either of two meanings, depending upon whether the output is a string or a floating point number. For a string, the precision indicates the maximum number of characters to be printed. If no precision is given, all of the characters in the string up to but not including the \0 character, which signals the end of all strings, will be printed. If the data item to be output is a **float** or **double**, the precision specifies the maximum number of digits to print following the decimal point. The default value for this case is 6 digits.

The character l indicates that the associated data object is of type **long**. This is used for formatting **long** integers or **double** data types.

The conversion character tells the printf() function what data type to expect. The conversion characters are as follows:

c The data object is a character.

s The data object is a string. All characters of a string will be printed until the function reaches the \0 character, or until the precision has been filled.

d The data object is to be converted to decimal notation. This applies to integer objects: int, long int, unsigned int, and short int.

u The data object is of type unsigned and is printed in decimal format.

e The data object is a float or double and is printed in the scientific format [−]m.nnnnnnE[+ −]xx as a decimal value, where m.nnnnnn represents a number between 0 and 9.999999 and x is an exponent of the power of 10. The number of n's is limited by the value of the precision zone (the default value is 6).

f This code is similar to the conversion character "e," except the output format is [−]mmm.nnnnnn as a decimal value, where mmm.nnnnnn represents the value of the data object. Again, the number of n's is limited by the precision zone (the default value is 6). Note that the precision does not indicate the total number of digits printed.

g This tells the printf() function to use the "d," "e," or "f" conversion character format, whichever is shorter. This format will print only significant digits; insignificant zeroes, like zeroes following the decimal point, are not printed.

o The data object, an integer type, is converted to unsigned octal notation. No leading zero is printed.

x The data object, an integer type, is converted to unsigned hexadecimal notation. No leading "0x" is printed. (The "0x" is used to create a program constant in hexadecimal.)

It's important to remember that there must be format field for each item in the output data list, and the format field type must match the data object type. If either of these conditions is not met—for example, if you try to print an integer with a %f format field—unexpected results will occur.

If the characters following the percent symbol (%) cannot be interpreted as a format field, they will be printed as a literal character. A pair of percent symbols (%%), for example, will be printed as a single percent symbol.

Listing 7.1 utilizes some of the formatting possibilities we have listed. After entering and running this program, make some changes to test other formatting combinations, like printing integers in octal and hexadecimal format. This program purposely crosses the use of floating point variables with the **d** conversion character to demonstrate the results of such actions. You may try other invalid type matching; however, we strongly advise you not to leave out either a formatting field or a data object. If you do, your program may halt the computer.

```
/****************************************************************
        list701      Formatted printing example
 ****************************************************************/

#include "stdio.h"

char    s[] = "abcdefghi";

main()
{
int     i = 5432;
float   f = (float) 123.321;
double  d = 987654.123456789;
char    c = 'C';

    printf("Integer Test\n");
    printf("%%d |%d| |%d| |%d|\n", i, f, d);
    printf("%%-d |%-d| |%-d| |%-d|\n", i, f, d);
    printf("%%8d |%8d| |%8d| |%8d|\n", i, f, d);
    printf("%%-8d |%-8d| |%-8d| |%-8d|\n", i, f, d);
    printf("%%3.4d |%3.4d| |%3.4d| |%3.4d|\n", i, f, d);
    printf("%%ld |%ld| |%ld| |%ld|\n", i, f, d);
    printf("%%x |%x|\n", i);
    printf("%%o |%o|\n", i);

    printf("Press Return");
    scanf("%*s");

    printf("\nFloating Point Test\n");
    printf("%%e |%e| |%e|\n", f, d);
    printf("%%20.9e |%20.9e| |%20.9e|\n", f, d);
    printf("%%020.9e |%020.9e| |%020.9e|\n", f, d);
    printf("%%-20.9e |%-20.9e| |%-20.9e|\n", f, d);
    printf("%%-020.9e |%-020.9e| |%-020.9e|\n", f, d);

    printf("\n%%f |%f| |%f|\n", f, d);
    printf("%%20.9f |%20.9f| |%20.9f|\n", f, d);
    printf("%%020.9f |%020.9f| |%020.9f|\n", f, d);
    printf("%%-20.9f |%-20.9f| |%-20.9f|\n", f, d);
    printf("%%-020.9f |%-020.9f| |%-020.9f|\n", f, d);
```

Listing 7.1

```
        printf("\n%%g |%g|  |%g|\n", f, d);
        printf("%%20.9g |%20.9g|  |%20.9g|\n", f, d);
        printf("%%020.9g |%020.9g|  |%020.9g|\n", f, d);
        printf("%%-20.9g |%-20.9g|  |%-20.9g|\n", f, d);
        printf("%%-020.9g |%-020.9g|  |%-020.9g|\n", f, d);

        printf("Press Return");
        scanf("%*s");

        printf("\nCharacter Test\n");
        printf("%%c |%c|\n", c);
        printf("%%20c |%20c|\n", c);
        printf("%%-20c |%-20c|\n", c);
        printf("%%20.20c |%20.20c|\n", c);
        printf("%%-20.20 |%-20.20c|\n", c);
        printf("%%020.20c |%020.20c|\n", c);

        printf("Press Return");
        scanf("%*s");

        printf("\nString Test\n");
        printf("%%s |%s|\n", s);
        printf("%%20s |%20s|\n", s);
        printf("%%-20s |%-20s|\n", s);
        printf("%%20.5s |%20.5|\n", s);
        printf("%%-20.5s |%-20.5|\n", s);
        printf("%%020s |%020s|\n", s);
        printf("%%.5s |%.5s|\n", s);

        scanf("%*s");
}                                   /* end main              */
```

Listing 7.1 [continued]

Depending upon the precision available for **float** and **double** data types with your compiler, and the accuracy of number-to-character conversion, you may get results that vary slightly from what you expect when you run this program. Also notice the use of the zero preceding the width value. The zero changes the character used for filling the extra space (this filling process is also known as *padding*) and applies to both numeric and character output.

THE SCANF() FUNCTION

The input counterpart to the printf() function is the **scanf()** function. The **scanf()** function reads data from the standard input (the keyboard), and places the data into program variables based upon matching the input data with the fields in the control string. The control string may contain any number of format fields. For each format field there must be an address to the appropriate data type. This is the address in memory where the **scanf()** function will store the data.

The format field for scanf() consists of

%(*)(*width*)(l)(*conversion character*)

As with printf(), the percent symbol (%) and the conversion character must be present. The asterisk (*) indicates that the sequence of characters matching this format field specification is to be ignored. In other words, the character sequence will be read and no assignment to a variable will be made. We have used this type of format field in our programs already to stop the display at various points so that we are able to read it. The width indicates the maximum number of characters that scanf() is to read from the input sequence. The letter l tells the function that the input will be of type long int or long float (that is, double), depending upon the conversion character.

When the scanf() function reads the input, it processes the input character by character. Assignment to the associated variable in the data list stops when the number of characters specified by the width is reached, or when the scanf() function finds a character unacceptable for the expected data type, such as a newline or a blank.

The conversion characters represent input types as follows:

d A decimal integer.

h A short integer.

o An octal integer (with or without the leading zero).

x A hexadecimal integer (with or without the leading "0x").

f A floating point number. The conversion character "e" may be used synonymously with the "f." The format of the input should be the same as a floating point constant.

c A single character. This control character will read the very next character in the input sequence.

s A string of characters. The string will be placed in the character array being pointed to by the pointer in the data list. The termination character \0 will automatically be placed at the end of the string. It is the programmer's responsibility to insure that the character array has been allocated in such a way that it is large enough to hold all of the characters of the input string.

The control string may contain any number of format fields, literal characters, and blank spaces. The blank spaces are ignored in both the control string and the input stream (that is, the sequence of input characters). The literal characters in the control string, however, must be matched exactly in the input sequence.

Listing 7.2 reads the input required to calculate an employee's paycheck. The input is expected to contain the employee's number, name, total hours worked, hourly pay rate, and a department code. The program does not perform any calculations; it simply demonstrates the **scanf()** function.

Notice that each format field has an address corresponding to a variable of the appropriate type. The array name does not need the address operator (&) before it, since an array name is also an address.

Here are some sample inputs to try with Listing 7.2 and their associated variable assignments. The three sample inputs all have the

```
/***************************************************************
      list702      Formatted input test
****************************************************************/

#include "stdio.h"

main()
{
long      empno = 0;
char      empname[11];
double    hours = 0.0, payrate = 0.0;
int       dept = 0, c;

    empname[0] = '\0';               /* initialize for safety   */

    for (;;) {
        c = scanf("%6ld%10s%lf%lf%2d",
            &empno, empname, &hours, &payrate, &dept);

        if (c == EOF)
            break;

        if (c == 0) {                /* no valid entries        */
            scanf("%*s");
            continue;
        }                            /* end if(c)               */

        printf("\nempno   = %ld\n", empno);
        printf("empname = %s\n", empname);
        printf("hours   = %f\n", hours);
        printf("payrate = %f\n", payrate);
        printf("dept    = %d\n", dept);

    }                                /* end for                 */
}                                    /* end main                */
```

Listing 7.2

same variable assignments:

```
102032Smith 52.00 12.50 14

102032 Smith 52.00 12.50 14

102032Smith
52.00 12.50 14
```

All three provide the same output:

```
empno = 102032
empname = Smith
hours = 52
payrate = 12.5
dept = 14
```

In the third example, the input spans across two lines. From the definition of the input field, we can see that the **scanf()** function stops assigning data to a field when it reaches the number of characters specified by the width. It also stops when it finds either a character that is invalid with respect to the data type or a whitespace character (that is, a newline, blank, or tab).

Technically, the newline character (also called linefeed and equivalent to decimal ASCII value 10) is a whitespace character. Generally, the newline character causes **scanf()** to continue to the next input field just as if a blank space had been entered. Because the **scanf()** function is part of the "standard" I/O library, however, it can vary from one compiler to the next. For example, in some cases, the newline character (which is usually produced simply by a press of the Return key) will simply be ignored, causing the characters "52" to be placed in the employee name field. In other implementations of the **scanf()** function, such as the Consulair's, the newline terminates the entry for the **scanf()** function so that the next line restarts the assignment of data to variables with the first field of the **scanf()** control string.

When the **scanf()** function is called in Listing 7.2, it remains in control of the system until all of the input fields have been filled or until it cannot match the input data to the input type expected. The **scanf()** function returns the number of items that it was able to match. It should return an EOF if an EOF character was entered. Because the **scanf()** function deals with a stream of input, when it stops reading the input stream the very next character on the input stream will be the first character used on the next call to scanf(). The program in Listing 7.2 checks first for an EOF that would signal the end of the program. Then the program checks to see if what is on the input stream is valid data. If not—that is, if scanf() could not match any fields—then the variable c will contain 0 and the program reads the input stream up to the next whitespace delimitation.

While this is not the ideal error-handling algorithm, because it allows incomplete data to be accepted, it is quite safe for you to experiment with as you practice using scanf(). Try various entries and note the results. Remember: the input stream remains intact from the point at which the scanf() function stops reading.

If you are using the Consulair system, the scanf() function works as follows. The newline character terminates the input line, and scanf() will fill as many fields as it can with the data up to the newline character. If there is extra data on the line, it is discarded. The value that the Consulair scanf() function returns is the position of the last field that it was able to fill. For example, the employee number is position one, the name is position two, and the department is position five. If a blank line is entered, a −1 is returned that acts like the EOF. (Notice that the alteration from the previous programs of defining EOF to have the value 4 was not included in this program.)

By this time, you may be wondering why the Consulair Mac C Compiler has so many variations from other systems? Actually, it doesn't. Remember that C does not specify any input or output functions for the language because of the variations in hardware and operating environments. The implementations that Consulair has chosen for their standard I/O library are most appropriate for the Macintosh environment. This allows (and also forces) the programmer to write more standardized and user-friendly Macintosh applications instead of programmer utilities, which are quick little programs that only the programmer knows how to use.

As a final sample input for scanf(), use the following:

```
6666Smithsonian 34.00 18.50 1594
```

The following output will be generated:

```
empno = 6666
empname = Smithsonia
hours = NAN(17)
payrate = 34.000000
dept = 18
```

The employee name field will be truncated since its length exceeds the specified width. Thus, **scanf()** tries to assign the final "n" in "Smithsonian" to the **hours** variable, which cannot be done because "n" is not a number. The remainder of the line may still be processed depending upon the implementation of the **scanf()** function you are using. In most instances, **scanf()** returns without changing the values of **hours, payrate,** or **dept.** For the Consulair system, the character "n" is assigned to **hours,** which in turn causes a special value to be assigned to the variable **hours** indicating an invalid entry. The **scanf()** function continues to assign as many values as it can.

THE SPRINTF() AND SSCANF() FUNCTIONS

The **printf()** and **scanf()** functions have counterparts that can be used to create or dissect a string. These functions are **sprintf()** and **sscanf(),** and they are constructed as follows:

> **sprintf(***output string, control string, data list***);**

> **sscanf(***input string, control string, data list***);**

These functions perform exactly as the previous two functions do, except that the location of the input or output will be the string specified by the first parameter. When using the **sprintf()** function, it is the programmer's responsibility to insure that the size of the output string is large enough to hold the output.

The **sprintf()** and **sscanf()** functions are handy when generating printouts. For example, on an accounts payable check, the check portion may come before the check stub. When your program finds an item to be paid, it uses **sprintf()** to create a formatted string, which will later by printed on the stub. After all items of detail have been found, a total is calculated and the check is printed. Now, the program prints on the check stub each of the preformatted strings it created earlier. The **sprintf()** function would be used in a similar situation in which you get a string and want to dissect it later.

CHARACTER AND STRING FUNCTIONS

Programming tasks demand the ability to handle character strings as whole units (for example, when you want to use an employee's name). String functions and certain character functions are not part of the C programming language because character codes and processing methods vary with hardware. The Macintosh uses ASCII characters and contains a microprocessor capable of a wide variety of string functions, which makes for extremely rapid execution. Here are a few of the functions for string and character manipulations found in a C's standard I/O library:

isalpha(c)
: Returns true (nonzero) if the character is between (and including) "A" through "Z" or "a" through "z"; otherwise returns false (0).

islower(c)
: Returns true if the character is lowercase; otherwise returns false.

isupper(c)
: Returns true if the character is uppercase; otherwise returns false.

tolower(c)
: Converts the character to lowercase if it is between "A" and "Z."

toupper(c)
: Converts the character to uppercase if it is between "a" and "z."

atoi(s)
: Converts the contents of a string s (actually a pointer to a string) and returns the integer value contained by the string; for example, atoi("123") returns integer value 123.

atof(s)
: Converts the contents of the string s and returns a floating-point value.

index(s, c)
: Returns the index (position) of the character c within the string s.

strcmp(s1, s2)
: Compares string s1 to string s2 through the standard alphabetical comparison and returns the following:

> −1 if s1 is less than s2.
>
> 0 if s1 is equal to s2.
>
> 1 if s2 is greater than s1.

All of these string and character functions can be written using the operators available in the C programming language. While on larger machines these functions are usually written in C, on microcomputers these functions are usually written in assembly language to maximize the capabilities of the microprocessor and make the functions work faster. Either way they are written, the functions still work in the same manner.

MATHEMATICAL FUNCTIONS

Another set of functions provided in a library are dedicated to performing common mathematical operations. These functions may be supplied in the standard I/O library or in a separate library of mathematical functions. Most math functions return a **double** type value. The declarations exist in a math header file which is like the **stdio.h** file. The math header file is usually called **math.h** and is used in the same manner as the **stdio.h** file.

The math functions include the trigonometric functions, like sine, cosine, tangent, and the inverses to sine, cosine, and tangent; exponent and logarithmic functions; and square roots and powers.

MEMORY ALLOCATION AND SYSTEM INTERFACE FUNCTIONS

Two other function categories in the standard I/O library are memory management functions and operating system interface functions. We have already seen the use of the functions **malloc()** and **calloc()** to allocate memory. If your compiler has either of these functions, then you probably have the inverse of these functions, which release or "free" memory from use and which are called **free()** or **cfree()**. Memory is a limited resource and one must manage it wisely.

System interface functions allow you to access the operating system and its unique internal capabilities. This category of functions is extremely machine- and operating system-specific; these functions will therefore vary greatly from compiler to compiler. If you decide to use a system interface function, you will reduce the portability of your program. To maintain portability, however, you can write your own enclosing function to call the system function. For example:

```
interface(parameters)
parameter declarations
{
set-up
call system function
return values
}
```

If program speed is less important than portability, you may choose to use this method of system interface. Writing such an **interface()** function makes it possible to have a standardized function for your program to call. Within **interface()**, you can embed the routines that communicate with the specific operating system, and if you must transport programs, only this section, instead of each occurrence of the operating system function, will require modification. You can even create your own operating system function library. In this way, function **interface()** provides a black box to the operating system function call.

Check your compiler manual for the functions available in your library. Chapter 8 will explain the process of and reasons for creating your own libraries and will expand upon the processing capabilities of the compiler itself.

ACCESSING FILES FROM WITHIN YOUR PROGRAM

The final category of standard I/O library routines consists of the file accessing routines. Because the use of files from within a program requires some preliminary explanation, we will postpone the introduction of the file functions until after we have briefly explained the overall need for data files and how they are used.

Earlier we discussed the use of files as a way of extending the computer's primary storage unit (that is, main memory) onto a secondary storage device (a disk drive). The foremost reason for using an external storage device is so that your program can maintain a nonvolatile set of the data it is using. It would be extremely time-consuming to have to reenter several thousand employee names and their financial information just to run the week's payroll. Instead, the data is stored in an external device (usually a disk or tape drive) that the program can access and update as needed.

Another reason for using an external storage device is that the computer's memory has a limited amount of space. The size of the computer's memory is usually small compared to the possible size of an external storage device. Therefore, much more data can be stored and manipulated by a program using an external storage device as opposed to a program that just uses the computer's main memory.

USING DISK FILES FOR INPUT AND OUTPUT

As we explained at the outset of this chapter, C views all input and output facilities as "files" just as UNIX does. C also supports the redirection of the standard input and output. This means that C allows you to specify where you want data to come from and where you want data to go. In other words, C only recognizes the standard input or output stream as somewhere to receive or place data. Whether the standard input or output comes from or goes to a file, the keyboard, a video screen, or a printer makes no difference to the functions using the input or output file.

For the purposes of this discussion, we will concentrate on disk files as the standard input and output since they have the most attributes. You can read from, write to, create, delete, and search disk files. Other devices, like printers, can be thought of as a place to put or get data, but they do not have all of the attributes that a disk file has. A printer, for example, is a file that can only be written to because it does not produce or store any data.

If you write a program that uses particular files, then when your program is executed, it will only use the data that is located in the files that have been specified.

A disk file can be thought of as a segment of memory with one byte after another. Each byte in the file has an address relative to the first byte, which is located at position 0. Thus, if a file contains 1,000 bytes, they will be numbered consecutively from 0 through 999.

TYPES OF FILE ACCESS

Files may be accessed in two ways: sequentially and randomly. *Sequential files* act very much like a standard input or output stream, where characters are processed one after another. *Random-access files* allow the programmer to indicate where (that is, at which specific byte) within the file to begin reading (input) or writing (output). In this case, the programmer places a *position pointer*, which is internally maintained by the functions accessing the file, at a particular place in the file. From here sequential reading or writing begins until the indicated number of characters has been processed.

Reading and writing are always done sequentially inside the computer, whether a sequential or random-access file is used. The programmer can place the file pointer at any position in the file (beginning, end, or somewhere in between), and processing begins from there. There is no difference in the storage properties of randomly placed data and sequentially placed data.

FILE FUNCTIONS

The standard operating procedure for manipulating files is closely linked to the operating system. For the most part, the interface to the operating system is hidden by the black box principle incorporated into the file access functions, but we still need to appease the operating system with some required protocol (in addition to common sense practices, such as valid file names and not exceeding the maximum allowable size for a file).

FUNCTIONS FOR ACCESSING A FILE

To be accessed, a file must exist. If it does not exist, then it must be created before it can be accessed. The function **open()** opens a file and the function **creat()** will create one.

The **creat(***filename***)** function makes a file specified by the string *filename* contained within the parentheses. If a file with this name already exists, it will be erased and a new file of the same name will be made. **Creat()** returns a number called a *file descriptor,* which is merely an **int** that uniquely identifies the file to the operating system for subsequent file access. If the file descriptor returned is −1, then an error has occurred in creating the file. After file creation, the file will be in either write or read/write mode (depending upon the compiler's implementation of the function).

The function **open(***filename, accessmode***)** opens an already existing file, and it too returns a file descriptor, or −1 if an error occurred. The *accessmode* specifies how the file will be accessed. In most cases, a value of 0 indicates read-only; 1 indicates write-only; and 2 indicates read/write access. For the most part, you will be using the read/write mode to give your programs unrestricted access to the files in question.

FUNCTIONS FOR CLOSING AND DELETING A FILE

When processing of a file has been completed, the file should be closed. Closing a file involves two procedures. First, the file is flushed from memory. Many operating systems will hold portions of a file in memory (to increase performance efficiency), and closing the file sends these memory portions to the disk. If the program does not officially close the file, the portions of the file held in memory can be lost.

The second task performed by the close operation is to remove the file reference from a table of files maintained by the operating system in order to keep track of which files are open. The operating system or your compiler may limit you to a maximum number of files that may be open at any one time. Thus, when you have completed processing on a file, it should be closed to insure that the data will be saved in the file completely and to allow room to open another file.

To close a file, use close(*filedescriptor*), where *filedescriptor* is the file descriptor number of the file to be closed. Remember that all files should be closed prior the program's completion. It is considered a poor programming practice, as well as dangerous, to leave files unclosed when exiting the program.

The final function you can perform on files as a whole is to delete a file from the disk. The function unlink(*filename*) deletes the file named by the string *filename*. If the file named by the filename string does not exist or is currently open, then unlink() will return a − 1 error.

FUNCTIONS FOR ACCESSING DATA WITHIN A FILE

Once a program has opened or created a file, it can access the data within the file. There are two types of file access—read access and write access—which are accomplished by the read() and write() functions, respectively.

```
read(filedescriptor, buffer, numchar);
write(filedescriptor, buffer, numchar);
```

The first parameter of both the read() and the write() functions is the file descriptor of a previously opened or created file. The second parameter is a pointer to a *buffer*, which is a portion of memory that has been allocated to hold the data that will be input or output (for example, an array of characters). The size of the buffer is somewhat arbitrary; however, it must be of a size greater than or equal to the *numchar* (number of characters) parameter of the function being called.

For the read() function, the *numchar* parameter specifies the maximum number of characters to be read. The read() function returns the number of characters actually read, or a − 1 if an error occurred. Under most circumstances, the value returned will be equal to *numchar* until the EOF character is reached. At this point, **read()** will return the number of characters read (which will probably be less than *numchar*), and on the next call **read()** will return 0, indicating that the end of the file has been reached.

For the **write()** function, the *numchar* parameter limits the number of characters written from the buffer to the file. The returned value is the number of characters written, which should equal *numchar*. If the returned value is − 1 or some other value that does not equal *numchar*, then an error has occurred. Your programs should check for this condition and respond to it appropriately.

The **read()** and **write()** functions operate sequentially, so that after each character is input or output, the file position pointer will be incremented by 1, thereby facilitating sequential processing of the file. For random access to a file, the functions **lseek()** and **seek()** allow the programmer to move the file position pointer to a specified location. The function call to position the pointer is **lseek(***filedescriptor, offset, origin***)**. The **lseek()** function moves the position pointer within the file specified by *filedescriptor*. The position pointer is moved by the number of characters specified by *offset* relative to *origin*. The offset must be of type **long**. The origin is an integer with a value of 0, 1, or 2: 0 starts counting the offset from the beginning of the file, 1 starts counting the offset from the current position, and 2 starts counting the offset from the end of the file. Moving the position pointer past the beginning of the file will place the position pointer at the beginning of the file, while moving past the end of the file will have varying results based upon the implementation of the **lseek()** function.

The **seek()** function is an older version of **lseek()**, in which *offset* is of type **int**, which means that it cannot access as large a data space as **lseek()** without performing some special techniques.

Stream vs File I/O

The term "file" has acquired a number of potentially confusing definitions. With respect to the C programming language, we will define a file as "a set of data with an established ordering." For example, a source code file consists of a set of characters organized into program statements. The term "file" does not imply a specific type of ordering; ordering is merely an attribute of how the data is stored in the file. In other words, all files will have a sequential ordering of data regardless of whether the order has any meaning or not. Thus, if a file exists and is not altered, a program can access that file over and over and expect the same sequence of data.

Given the notion of an ordered set of data, we can think of this ordered set as either as a stream of data or a file. Both a stream and a file have a beginning, an end, and zero or more data items in between. The conceptual difference, however, is that the file presents the set of data as a whole, and each data item has a position within the file that can be accessed randomly. The stream, on the other hand, should be thought of as presenting only one data item at a time in the sequential order of the data set.

The access functions we have discussed so far give us the ability to process a file in either a sequential or random-access manner. These functions fall into the category of *file I/O*; they operate on a data collection as a whole. The following functions perform *stream I/O*. For the most part, stream I/O functions imitate the file I/O functions but use sequential access only.

FUNCTIONS FOR OPENING AND CLOSING A STREAM

The primary difference between stream and file I/O in C is the method of referencing the file. The file I/O functions refer to the file to be accessed through a file descriptor, whereas stream I/O functions use a pointer to a structure describing the file for the operating system. We do not know (nor should we care about) what this structure actually contains; we only need a pointer to perform the stream I/O.

To declare a pointer, use the following statement:

```
FILE *fp;
```

The word **FILE** is a type declarator, like the words **int** and **double**, and it appears in the same position. It is not, however, a data type like other data types that are part of the C programming language. The word **FILE** is defined using a **typedef** statement in the file **stdio.h**, thereby allowing the user to define the proper structure for the operating system and the hardware.

To open a file for stream access, use

```
FILE *fopen(), *fp;
fp = fopen(filename, accesstype);
```

The fopen() function will open the file named by the string *filename*. The *accesstype* is a string indicating how the stream will be accessed. It will be either r for "read" access, w for "write" access, or a for "append" access. Read access causes the position pointer to be placed at the beginning of the stream and restricts access to reading only. Write access discards the current contents of the file and treats the file as if it had just been created. In fact, if the file named does not exist, it will be created automatically. Append access allows the user to add to the end of the file, which is very useful in most programming applications. (For example, if your program is keeping a list of expenses, it can simply append today's expenses onto a list of total expenses entered so far.) The fopen() function returns a pointer to a FILE structure, or NULL if an error has occurred.

To close a stream file, use the function fclose(*filepointer*) to insure that the contents of the file will be saved properly.

FUNCTIONS FOR CHARACTER STREAM I/O

Two functions perform character I/O in this mode:

```
getc(filepointer);
putc(c, filepointer);
```

The function getc() will retrieve one character from the file pointed at by *filepointer*; it returns an integer, an EOF code at the end of the file, or a read error. An integer is returned, not a character, because a character may not be able to represent EOF if a character is implemented as an unsigned value and EOF is set at -1. The putc() function outputs character c (as a parameter) to file *filepointer* and returns -1 if an error has occurred.

FORMATTED STREAM I/O

You may also use the stream output counterparts to the formatted input and output functions printf() and scanf():

```
fprintf(filepointer, control string, data list);
fscanf(filepointer, control string, data list);
```

These two functions operate in exactly the same manner as the printf() and scanf() functions, respectively, with the addition of the *filepointer* parameter in the first position. Instead of using the standard input or output, these functions will input or output to the file indicated by *filepointer*.

FUNCTIONS FOR STRING STREAM I/O

Finally, two functions expand **getc()** and **putc()** by making it possible to input or output whole strings in a stream:

> **fgets**(*stringpointer, buffersize, filepointer*);
> **fputs**(*stringpointer, filepointer*);

The **fgets()** function will read in a string from the file specified by *filepointer*, up to and including the next newline (\n) character. The resulting string, including the termination character (\0), is placed where *stringpointer* indicates. The number of characters read is limited by the parameter *buffersize*, where the maximum number of characters read will be at most *buffersize* − 1. The **fgets()** function returns *stringpointer* on normal termination; otherwise, a NULL is returned (for end-of-file or error).

The **fputs()** function places the string located at *stringpointer* into the file specified by *filepointer*. The string need not contain a newline character, but it must have a termination character (\0). A − 1 is returned if an error occurs.

USING STANDARD I/O FILES

We mentioned the use of I/O redirection of the standard input and output earlier. Now we will discuss its implementation within a C program.

When a C program is executed, three files are automatically opened: the standard input, the standard output, and the standard error files. These files are assigned to the pointers **stdin**, **stdout**, and **stderr**, respectively. These pointers are constants and cannot be reassigned.

Making a program's input and output independent of a specific data file (like the keyboard or display) is accomplished by using the **stdin** and **stdout** pointers. Whatever the user redirects as input will be assigned to the **stdin** pointer, and all output will be assigned to the **stdout** pointer. This redirection of input and output is only available if your operating environment will support it. If you do not have this facility, you should still read through this section as it will culminate in a general file copying program.

When you use the standard I/O functions, all input functions refer to stdin, and all output functions refer to stdout. By using stream I/O functions, we can define the functions getchar() and putchar() in terms of getc() and putc().

```
getchar()          /* get a character from the standard input */
{
     return(getc(stdin));
}

putchar(c)              /* put a character to standard output */
int c;
{
     putc(c, stdout);
}
```

Listing 7.3 is a utility program (similar to the cp command in UNIX) that uses the standard input and output files. The object of

```
/*************************************************************
     list703      Copyfile Version #1:
                  Copy standard input to standard output
*****************************************************************/

#include "stdio.h"

/**** Use only if your system cannot generate a standard EOF signal ***/
#undef      EOF
#define     EOF 4
/*****************************************************************/

main()
{
int    c;

    while((c = getc(stdin)) != EOF)
        putc(c, stdout);
}   /* end main */


PROGRAMMING THE MACINTOSH IN C  Chapter 7  Listings  11/10/85


Listing 7.4 (cont.):

    while((c = getc(inp)) != EOF)
        putc(c, outp);
}                                   /* end copyfile          */
```

Listing 7.3

this first program is to copy the standard input to the standard output. If you do not have I/O redirection, you should be able to type characters at the keyboard and see them echoed on the display screen.

In this program, most of the housekeeping required for file manipulation (that is, opening, reading, and closing) is done by the operating system through I/O redirection when the program first starts. Therefore, because we don't need functions to open, close, and read the file, this program shrinks to a mere two lines of code. Unfortunately, Listing 7.3 will only copy one file at a time, and your operating environment must have the I/O redirection capability if you are to use the program to actually copy files.

A more sophisticated program would allow us to concatenate several files. We can write such a program so that it would ask for the file to copy to (that is, for the destination) and then for each file to be copied. Listing 7.4 first asks for an output file; if the file name is blank, the standard output is assumed. Then, the program continually asks for a file to be copied to the output file. If the file exists, it is copied; otherwise, the program gives an error message and requests another file name. Copying stops when a blank file name is encountered. You can practice using this program by copying some of the code files you created while reading this book into one file. Then use the editor to check the contents of the new file.

The program in Listing 7.4 is considered to be an *interactive* program because it requires operator intervention periodically. It also does not use I/O redirection. Generally, utilities should be able to get all of their information from the command that starts the program and require little attention from the operator. To make our utility self-sufficient in this way, let's rewrite this latest version so that it works like the commands found in the UNIX operating system. We will want our utility program to resemble an operating system command in being able to retrieve *arguments* (a synonym for parameters) from the *command line* instead of through operator input. (The command line of an operating system command consists of the command name, followed by the arguments to be used by the command. For example, when compiling a program, you enter in the compiler's name, followed by the file to compile and any options you want the compiler to perform.)

Listing 7.5 shows the revised version of our copy utility program. Note that the **stderr** file should be used for outputting error messages. This file is not affected by the I/O redirection of the standard output, so all error messages will be output to the current error file. In general, the video display is used for all error messages.

```
/************************************************************
    list704     Copyfile Version #2:
                Copy multiple files to one file
 ************************************************************/

#include "stdio.h"
#define MAXNAME 64              /* set a length maximum    */

main()
{
char    inname[MAXNAME], outname[MAXNAME];
FILE    *outfile, *infile, *fopen();

                            /* get output file name    */
    printf("Enter file to copy to: ");
    scanf("%64s", outname);
    printf("\n");               /* move to next line       */
    if (outname[0] != '\0')     /* not a blank input       */
        outfile = fopen(outname, "w");
    else
        outfile = stdout;

    printf("Enter first file name to copy: ");
    while (scanf("%64s", inname) != EOF) {
        printf("\n");

                            /* open file               */
        if ((infile = fopen(inname, "r")) == NULL)
            printf("***> Cannot open file %s\n", inname);
        else {
            copyfile(infile, outfile);
            fclose(infile);
        }                       /* end if(infile)...else   */

        printf("Enter next file name to copy: ");
    }                           /* end while scanf         */


    if (outfile != stdout)      /* do not close if stdout  */
        fclose(outfile);
}                               /* end main                */

/************************************************************
    copyfile    copies stream files
        inp     =   pointer to input stream
        outp    =   pointer to output stream
    Returned values: no values returned.
 ************************************************************/
copyfile(inp, outp)
FILE *inp, *outp;
{
int c;
```

Listing 7.4

Listing 7.5 introduces another UNIX concept that is available through C: command line arguments. The command line arguments supply the specific data that the program will use.

COMMAND LINE ARGUMENTS

A command line argument can consist of any sequence of characters following the command name. The argument list is created by

```
/*****************************************************************
    list705      Copyfile Version #3:
                 Copy multiple files to one file
 *****************************************************************/

#include "stdio.h"
#define MAXNAME 64                  /* set a length maximum    */

main(argc, argv)
int     argc;
char    *argv[];
{
FILE    *outfile, *infile, *fopen();
int     i;

                                    /* set argc to index of    */
    argc--;                         /* last argument           */

    if (argc < 1) {                 /* check for proper format */
        printf("Format: prog705 infile1 infile2 ... -Ooutfile\n\n");
        exit(1);
    }                               /*end if(argc)             */

                                    /* check to see if last arg */
                                    /* is output file          */
    if (argv[argc][0] == '-' && argv[argc][0] == 'O') {
                                    /* open output file        */
        if ((outfile = fopen(argv[argc]+2, "w")) == NULL) {
            printf("***> Cannot open file: %s\n", argv[argc]+2);
            exit(1);
        }                           /* end if(outfile)         */
    } else {                        /* assume no output file   */
        outfile = stdout;
        argc++;                     /* reset argc to include   */
                                    /* this last file          */
    }                               /* end if(argv)...else     */

    if (argc == 1 && outfile != stdout) {
                                    /* output file, no input   */
        copyfile(stdin, outfile);
    } else {                        /* copy each argument      */
        for (i = 1; i < argc; i++) {
            if ((infile = fopen(argv[i], "r")) == NULL) {
                printf("***> Cannot open file: %s\n", argv[i]);
                exit(1);
            } else {
                copyfile(infile, outfile);
                fclose(infile);
            }                       /* end if(infile)...else   */
        }                           /* end for(i)              */
    }                               /* end if(argc)...else     */
    if (outfile != stdout)          /* do not close if stdout  */
        fclose(outfile);
    exit(0);
}                                   /* end main                */

/*****************************************************************
    copyfile     copies stream files
        inp      =    pointer to input stream
        outp     =    pointer to output stream
    Returned values: no values returned.
 *****************************************************************/
copyfile(inp, outp)
FILE *inp, *outp;
{
int c;

    while((c = getc(inp)) != EOF)
        putc(c, outp);
}                                   /* end copyfile            */
```

Listing 7.5

placing blank spaces between sets of characters. For example:

COMMAND arg1 arg2 arg3 . . .

Any number of arguments may appear on the command line as long as the number of characters does not exceed the maximum command line length specified by the operating system (usually 128 characters).

C provides a convenient mechanism for retrieving the command line arguments. As you know, all C programs must have a function called main(). Since main() is a function, it too can have parameters passed to it. Here are the parameters to function main():

```
main(argc, argv)
int argc;
char *argv[];
```

The variable argc is an integer containing the number of arguments on the command line. The variable argv is an array of pointers, each containing the string of characters that make up the command line argument. The arguments are kept in order, and the first argument, *argv[0], contains the name of the command that initiated the program (usually the name of the program).

C maintains strings as arrays of characters. Because the string of characters composing the command line is an array, we can examine any element within the command line by using the appropriate subscript. For example, many UNIX- and C-related programs (compilers, utilities, and so on) use the command line arguments for program control. Control arguments can be distinguished from file names because the control arguments will be preceded by a hyphen. The program can check the first character of the argument to see if it is to be used for program control or not.

Here is an application of an array of pointers in which each element points to an array of characters. We can access the first character array by using *argv[0], the second character array with *argv[1], and so on up to character array *argv[argc − 1] because we have argc elements in the array of pointers. We have many options in accessing the first element of the first character array. The most straightforward method is

```
(argv[0])[0]
```

This expression is usually written without the parentheses; however, the parentheses explicitly indicate that this is not a two-dimensional array. Because it is a pointer, the variable argv[0] contains an address.

This address is then used as the pointer to an array of characters. Thus, the expression accesses the first element of the first argument (the command name itself). The second element of this character array is argv[0][1]. The first element of the next character array is argv[1][0]. All argument strings—that is, character arrays—are terminated by the \0 termination character.

In rewriting our copy program, we have listed all the file names in the command line. The output file name must be the last argument on the command line and must be preceded by a −O (uppercase letter "O") character pair to indicate output. In English, in effect, we say "Copy these files to that file"; hence, we make the name of the output file the last argument in the command line. If we write our program to imitate this thought pattern, it will be easy to learn and remember how the program works. If the −O flag is not found, the standard output is to be used. If no input files are given, the standard input is to be used.

Let's look more specifically at Listing 7.5 now. The program first determines where to output the data. We decrement argc to equal the index of the last argument instead of repeatedly writing argc − 1. The program checks the last argument to see if it is specified as the output file. If no −O is found, then the standard output is used. Otherwise, the file named is created as the output file.

After determining what the output file is, the program checks to see if the first argument was the output file. If so, then the first argument is also the last argument, meaning that no input files were specified. In this case the standard input is used. If input files were specified, the program loops through each argument as an input file.

Those readers who are using a compiler that does not offer a UNIX interface will not be able to use Listing 7.5 unless you have some facility that allows you to access the C command line. Even if you can't run the program, however, you should study it to familiarize yourself with using the command line argument.

In Listing 7.5, we have introduced a new function called exit(), which causes immediate termination of the program. The parameter of the function is the return value of the program, as if the program were one big function itself. UNIX uses this returned value, especially when batch processing several programs. By convention, a value of 0 indicates normal termination, and any nonzero value indicates that an error has occurred. The range of values would depend upon the operating system and the compiler. You should generally use the exit(0) statement as the final line of function main() to indicate that the program has completed execution successfully.

At this point we have covered most of the file facilities generally provided with a C compiler and a few examples of how they can be used. This survey of file manipulation in C should provide you with a broad enough basis from which to create functional utilities and applications for your computer system.

THE MACINTOSH ENVIRONMENT VS THE UNIX ENVIRONMENT

The C programming language and the UNIX operating system are closely linked. Most C implementations on UNIX-based computer systems will have a set of functions through which the C programmer may determine and change system attributes. For example, under UNIX, the C program may activate other programs for subordinate or parallel processing; determine the current terminal type that the user is running; stop subordinate programs; determine the name of the other users on the system (UNIX is a multiuser system); and perform a number of other functions.

Unfortunately, after C is removed from the UNIX environment, the access to this data becomes difficult, if not impossible. In the previous sections, we have seen that the command line arguments are located by the pointers of array **argv**. More specifically, the first pointer of this array, **argv[0]**, points to a character array containing the program's name. While access to the command line is possible under UNIX, however, under CP/M-80, CP/M-86, PC-DOS, MS-DOS, and several other operating systems, the first pointer of the array points to an empty character string. These operating systems simply do not retain the name of the program once the program has been activated.

This example clearly shows the difficulties in making a program independent of its execution environment. Because the Macintosh does not use a command line, no Macintosh applications can have access to any command line information.

The C programming language is now available on many different computers using quite a variety of operating systems. If you are working under the UNIX system or a similar environment, then you will probably not find any greater difficulty or difference in working with standard I/O routines than in working with the rest of the language (the rest of the language is strictly defined and cannot be altered if it is indeed a full implementation of C). On the other hand, if you are reading this book, you undoubtedly plan to use a Macintosh to develop your own C programs. You most likely want to develop your programs to run under this environment for a variety of reasons. One of the strongest reasons is to be able to use the full capabilities of the Macintosh in creating a program that is extremely easy to use.

In particular, the User Interface Toolbox in ROM contains routines to manipulate windows, get information from the mouse and keyboard, create and display menus, access Macintosh files, access the printer, and design complex graphic displays, to name just a few of the routines that support Macintosh programmers in their efforts to create applications that can be intuitively learned and that present a consistent, Mac-like interface to the user.

Essentially, you are faced with a trade-off of features. If you use the desktop as your development environment, your programs will look like Macintosh applications from the very start. The compiler is more likely to give you access to the Macintosh utilities. However, the standard I/O routines provided with your compiler will most likely vary from the what we have discussed in this chapter and you won't have access to the command line nor to I/O redirection. If you use a UNIX environment on the Macintosh, on the other hand, you give up the desktop but gain utilities, such as programs that automate the program development process and I/O redirection, that are very useful to a programmer during development. It is not an easy choice if you have used both systems. There are advantages and disadvantages. The decision about which environment you want to develop under should be based on whether you want access to the Toolbox or to I/O redirection and also on your overall style of programming.

A NOTE ABOUT USING TOOLBOX ROUTINES

This book will not detail any of the routines available within the Toolbox. Because most Macintosh C compilers, including the Consulair, provide access to the Toolbox, we should caution you about one central problem involved in using the Toolbox from C.

The problem is simply this: the ROM routines in the Toolbox were written in Pascal, which means that you will have to do some translation from C to Pascal when you pass parameters. For the most part, using a Toolbox function from C will be similar to a Pascal function call. Most of the problems occur as a result of differences in data types. Pascal has a Boolean data type that equates more or less to a short int in C. Also, Pascal uses the first byte of a string as a count byte to hold the number of characters in the string.

If your compiler provides routines for accessing the Toolbox, it most likely also includes a header file and library routines to handle the conversion between C and Pascal. Read your compiler manual carefully. If you don't know Pascal, you will need to get a Pascal reference book as well.

If you do decide to delve into the depths of your Macintosh, we wish you the best of success. The routines are relatively easy to use, but require a fairly high degree of sophistication to be used properly. Good luck!

EIGHT

COMPILING
YOUR
PROGRAM

In Chapter 1 we briefly introduced the process of writing and compiling your program. Chapter 2 covered some of the advantages and disadvantages of writing a program in a language that needs to be compiled. In this chapter, we will explore in more detail some of the advantages and benefits of a compiled language.

We will begin with a look at the steps needed to translate an idea into a working program, explaining why the step is necessary and how it is executed. Next, the C compiler's preprocessor and its features will be explained. It is most likely that as you start to write your own programs, you will come across errors that the compiler detects in your programs. We will cover some of the errors encountered and how you can go about locating and correcting these errors. We will also explain how you can increase your productivity as a programmer by writing functions in separate files, compiling these files separately, and then linking them together. The chapter concludes with a description of one of the most powerful capabilities provided by a compiled language—the use and creation of libraries.

COMPILING YOUR PROGRAM

By now you should be familiar with the process of creating an executable program. Basically, the process consists of four steps. You first design the program. Next, you use an editing program to create a file that contains the appropriate programming statements to implement your design. This file is then given as input to the compiler, which generates a file that is used by the linker. Finally, the linker produces a file that can be executed by the computer. Because we looked at the first two of these steps in Chapter 2, we will concentrate on the second two here, focusing particularly on what the compiler actually does.

The purpose of the compiler is quite simple: it takes the file in which you have entered program statements and generates a new file. Your program file is called the *source code* because it is the source of the compiler's input. The compiler's output file is called the *relocatable* file; it contains an intermediate translation of your program. (The term "relocatable file" comes from the fact that different operating systems and environments have certain protocols about where the program is to be located within the computer's memory as well as certain initiation procedures when the program is executed.)

This is where the linker comes in. The linker takes the relocatable file as its input and locates the program's parts so that the program knows where it will reside in memory. The linker also inserts the necessary initiation and termination procedures that are required by the operating system.

Now you may be wondering why the compiler doesn't do all of this in one step. Actually, it could, but this would prevent us from performing *separate compilation*, which is an important technique used in creating very large programs. Separate compilation is a process in which a programmer can write a relatively small section of a large program (like an operating system), and then compile and test this section without having to write the entire program. When all of the individual sections have been written and tested, the linker is used to combine all the pieces into one program. For example, the UNIX operating system consists of about 100,000 lines or so of source code, of which a few hundred lines of code are written in assembly language instead of C. It would take a compiler quite a long time to compile all of that code. Plus, once the program has been compiled it needs to be tested, and if a problem is found (which is almost guaranteed in a program of that size), then it needs to be fixed and the entire program must be recompiled. To avoid the long delays between each test of the program, the program is divided into sections that perform a specific task for the program. Now, when a problem is found with the program, only the section that is affected needs to be recompiled.

Another benefit of separate compilation relates to the fact that part of UNIX is written in assembly language. These sections of the program are assembled by the assembler program, which also generates a relocatable file. The resulting relocatable file can then be linked with the relocatable files from the C compiler. This can be done because the compiler and the assembler generate an intermediate form of their respective programs, and this intermediate form is understood by the linker. In fact, you can write sections of a program in any compiled programming language (for example, C, assembly, Pascal, FORTRAN, Ada, and so on) as long as the compiler is able to produce a relocatable file in the format that can be used by the linker. Note that the compiler must be able to generate a format acceptable to the linker; otherwise, this process will not work.

The other purpose of using the linker is being able to utilize library files. But, before we discuss the advanced features of the linker, let's look at some of the features available in a C compiler.

USING COMPILER DIRECTIVES

Compiler directives give explicit instructions to the compiler from within your source file. These instructions have no effect after the program has been compiled, but they can affect the program's compilation. The compiler contains a preprocessor that translates various commands before compilation begins. The C preprocessor is designed to intercept any line beginning with the number symbol (#).

THE #DEFINE DIRECTIVE

We have already seen one use for the **#define** directive in the following form:

    #define *identifier constant-expression*

The *identifier*, called a token, can be used throughout the rest of the program wherever the *constant-expression* would have been used. This symbolic replacement facilitates quick program alteration since any required changes will affect only this line of code and not an untold number of lines, which may be forgotten or missed when the change needs to be made. For example, when we write programs that use fixed arrays for storage, the size of the array will be limited by the amount of memory the computer has available. If we use the definition and declaration

```
#define MAXSIZE 999
        . . .
char array[MAXSIZE + 1]
```

any number of lines may separate the definition and its use. We can even use **MAXSIZE** in a loop control statement like

```
for (i = o; i < = MAXSIZE; i + +)
```

Now, wherever the number of elements in the array needs to be changed, we can just change the number in the **#define** statement. For a programmer interested in programs that are easy to maintain, this can be quite convenient.

Also take note of the value used in the **#define** directive. C creates arrays containing the number of elements specified in the declaration, and the elements are numbered from 0 through one less than the size of the array. Defining MAXSIZE as the highest index in the array and declaring the size of the array as MAXSIZE + 1 allows MAXSIZE to be used as a limit value in loops instead of writing MAX-SIZE − 1. (In a loop using MAXSIZE − 1 as its limit value, the compiler will generate the code for the subtraction, and this code will be executed each time the loop is encountered. This is extra work for your computer and will make your program slower.)

The #define statement can do more than just define symbolic constants, however. It can be used to define segments of source code called *macros*. A macro, or macro-instruction, is an identifier that represents a series of one or more instructions. In short, a macro is an abbreviation for source code. The macro definition can take either of two forms. The first form is

    #define *identifier replacement-code*

And the second form is

    #define *identifier(token list) replacement-code*

The first form simply names a set of instructions. For example, in many systems the function getchar() is defined as a macro in terms of the function getc(), as follows:

    #define getchar() getc(stdin)

When the compiler encounters the name getchar(), it substitutes the name getchar() with its definition, so that

    while((c = getchar()) != EOF) {

literally becomes

    while((c = getc(stdin)) != EOF) {

The second form of the macro allows tokens to be used within the macro code. The putchar() function can be defined like this:

    #define putchar(c) putc(c, stdout)

Now the statement

    putchar(x)

becomes

    putc(x, stdout)

The tokens of a macro replacement list need not be declared like variables because they are not variables, only placeholders to be filled when the macro is used. For this reason, when the macro is used, the number of arguments within the parentheses must equal the number of tokens in the macro definition.

Long definitions may be continued on the next line by placing a backslash (\) character at the end of the line to be continued. The definition is considered complete when a new line character without a backslash is encountered. A **#define** statement may reference a previous **#define** statement.

A **#define** statement remains in effect from the point of definition until the end of the source file. A token may be undefined by using

 #undef *identifier*

causing the preprocessor to forget the definition.

One last comment about macro definitions: the characters following the identifier name of the macro will be substituted for the macro name exactly as listed, and all replacement tokens will be substituted before compilation. Therefore, do not use a semicolon (;) in the macro, as in the cases of **getchar()** and **putchar()**, unless you wish to designate the end of a source code line.

If you use an identifier within a set of macro instructions and the identifier is not a replacement token, then the identifier is taken to be a variable and must be declared prior to using the macro. For example:

```
#define SWAP(P, Q) { temp = P;\
                P = Q;\
                Q = temp; }
```

The macro **SWAP()** defines a statement block for exchanging the replacement tokens P and Q. The variables used to replace P and Q and the variable **temp** must all be declared as the same type before the macro **SWAP()** is used. This allows the same macro definition to be used in many different situations. The following two function segments use the same **SWAP()** macro with different variable types.

```
f1()
{
int x, y, temp;
     . . . statements which set x and y . . .
     if (x > y) SWAP(x, y)            /* note no {} or    ; */
```

```
            . . . finish function . . .
    }
    f2()
    {
    double x, y, temp;
            . . . statements which set x and y . . .
            if (x > y) SWAP(x, y)
            . . . finish function . . .
    }
```

Remember that structured data may not be copied using the assignment operator. Therefore, **SWAP()** will not work with structures.

While macros are most frequently used for constant definitions and repetitive statements like **SWAP()**, there are no restrictions regarding their use.

THE #INCLUDE DIRECTIVE

Frequently, the same source code can be used in many different programs. A standard set of macros used for generalized functions such as sorting arrays and input verification can be used this way. To avoid rewriting this code for each new program, you can place the macros in a file of their own, and then include them into the program through the #include directive. You have already used this directive with the stdio.h file.

The #include directive has two formats, First,

   #include "filename"

And second:

   #include <filename>

The first format, in which *filename* is enclosed in quotation marks (''), causes the compiler to search for the file in the current directory first, and then perform default searches in other directories if the file was not found. The second format—enclosing *filename* between < and >— causes the compiler to search only the directory containing standard inclusion files. These two formats are used specifically with the UNIX operating system, but they can be extended into some other operating systems that use subdirectories. Otherwise, like the Mac's desktop, these two formats will have the same effect: that is, both will cause the compiler to search the current directory or disk.

The #include directive causes the compiler to search for the file name listed and to replace the directive line with the entire contents of that file. After the file has been completely included, the compiler continues to the next line of the original source file. Files included in the source program may contain other #include directives; however, the compiler may place a limit upon the depth of this nesting (that is, on the number of included files open simultaneously). Most compilers produce an error if an attempt is made to include a file that does not exist.

CONDITIONAL COMPILATION DIRECTIVES

The preprocessor also allows you to include or exclude certain programming statements based upon a specified condition. These preprocessor commands are called, naturally, conditional compiler directives.

THE #IF AND #ENDIF DIRECTIVES

The directive statements

```
#if constant-expression
     statement list
#endif
```

will compile the statements contained in the statement list between the #if and #endif directives, if *constant-expression* evaluates to true (nonzero). For example,

```
#define    TRUE      1
#define    FALSE     0

#define    MAC       TRUE
#define    MSDOS     FALSE
#define    CPM       FALSE
#define    UNIX      FALSE

#if MAC
. . .
#endif

#if MSDOS
. . .
```

```
#endif

#if CPM

. . .

#endif

#if UNIX

. . .

#endif
```

will compile the statements beginning with #if MAC because the identifier **MAC** has been defined as true. This type of set-up procedure saves a tremendous amount of time by defining the operating system through the use of macro identifiers, which can then be used to implement functions for that operating system. Each #if statement must be followed by its own **#endif** statement.

THE #IFDEF AND #IFNDEF DIRECTIVES

Two alternative forms of the #if directive are #ifdef and #ifndef. The #ifdef directive

```
#ifdef identifier
```

evaluates to true and compiles the lines of code that follow if the identifier has been defined to the preprocessor in a **#define** statement. The #ifndef directive

```
#ifndef identifier
```

evaluates to true on the opposite condition—that is, if the identifier has not yet been defined. Using these alternative forms, we can rewrite the preceeding #if example as

```
#define MAC TRUE

#ifdef MAC

    . . .

#endif

#ifdef MSDOS

    . . .

#endif

#ifdef CPM

    . . .
```

```
#endif

#ifdef UNIX
        . . .
#endif
```

The outcome is the same as before because only the identifier **MAC** has been defined within the file. Since the **#ifdef** and **#ifndef** are just alternative forms of **#if**, they must also be followed by a matching **#endif** statement.

THE #ELSE DIRECTIVE

The preprocessor has a conditional alternative construct, the **#else** directive. It is used in the same manner as any other **else** construct and has the same effects.

```
#if constant-expression
    statement list 1
#else
    statement list 2
#endif
```

The **#else** can be used with any of the conditional directives: **#if**, **#ifdef**, or **#ifndef**. All of these constructs may be nested as long as each **#if** is followed by a corresponding **#endif** statement.

MISCELLANEOUS DIRECTIVES

Your compiler may have some additional directives, the most common of which is the **#asm** directive. This indicates to the compiler that the following lines consist of assembly language instructions and should be treated as such (that is, either assembled or left for an assembler program). While the directive to terminate assembly language handling varies from compiler to compiler, usually it is called **#endasm**.

Two other directives you should know about are **#fortran** and **#line**. The **#fortran** directive has the same effect as the **#asm** directive, except that it indicates that the following lines are treated as FORTRAN statements. This will generally not be available on smaller computer systems because of memory limitations.

The #line directive is used by the programmer for determining the cause and position of compilation errors and for counting the number of lines (terminated by a newline) the compiler reads in. Here's how #line is used. When the compiler finds an error, it will usually print the line number, the line, and a diagnostine) the compiler reads in. When the compiler finds an error it will usually print the line number, the line, and a diagnostic message about the error found. The compiler may also print the name of the source code file used to initiate the compilation procedure. When other files have been included in the source code through the #include directive, however, the information disclosed by the compiler about the location of the error can become confusing.

For example, program SAMPLE starts with 10 source lines, includes a file INC1 containing 20 source lines, and then continues with 50 more source lines. The #include statement counts as line number 11 within file SAMPLE, with the result that the remaining lines begin at the number 12.

```
/* SAMPLE */
Source lines numbered 1 through 10
#include "INC1"
Source lines numbered 12 through 61

/* INC1 */
Include lines numbered 1 through 20
```

If, for instance, an error occurs on line 4 within INC1, the compiler would normally indicate an error on line 14 of program SAMPLE, which is not very accurate. By changing file INC1 to begin with the statement

```
#line    1    INC1
```

we make the compiler believe, when it encounters this directive, that it is beginning at line 1 of file INC1 (which it is); in effect, the compiler temporarily forgets that this is a file included into another program. Now the error message will accurately locate the error as being on line 4 of file INC1. When returning to the original file, SAMPLE, we use the statement

```
#line    12    SAMPLE
```

to tell the compiler it has returned from the included file. Essentially, this is the only use for the **#line** directive, since it does not affect the compilation of the program.

Formally,

> **#line** constant identifier

causes the preprocessor to change the current source code line number maintained by the compiler to the value of *constant* and to change the name used by the compiler for the current source file to *identifier*. None of these changes alter the compilation process in any way; they merely change the values displayed within error messages. Some compilers will keep track of included file names and line numbers automatically.

To a great extent, the preprocessor implementation in the compiler determines the directives available on your particular computer system. Read your compiler manual carefully to determine which directives are available and how they work.

Dealing with Compiler Errors

A compiler error occurs when the programmer has violated command syntax in writing a line of source code. This section will provide a compendium of errors derived from the authors' experience with programming and with compilers. This brief overview of probable causes and solutions of compiler errors should cover most of the situations you will encounter during the period in which you are learning C.

First of all, it's important to note that the error message a compiler produces communicates very little. Only large and complex compilers can determine the error that has actually occurred. For the most part, the error message you receive is merely a guideline for determining what action should be taken to correct the situation. In our experience, only 50 percent of all the varied error messages received correctly identify the erroneous construction. Because of the general unhelpfulness of compiler error messages, when tracing an error you must first interpret the general category of the error message, and then search out the indicated line and the surrounding lines for the actual cause of the error.

By far the most common cause of compilation errors is improper syntax. A single typographical error can cause numerous error messages to cross your console. For example, if you mistype a variable name in a declaration statement (using cuont instead of count, for example), then for every place you used the correctly spelled variable name, the compiler will remind you that it is undefined. The most frequent typographical error is omission of a closing punctuation mark: for example, a parenthesis, a quotation mark, a semicolon, and so on. Both of these kinds of typographical errors are usually identified properly by the compiler.

On the other hand, you may get an error message that does not match the context of the line, such as "missing operand," when you know that all of the operands exist. The first plan of attack in this situation is to look for syntactical errors in surrounding lines. Perhaps you forgot to use a closing brace to finish the previous function. Or maybe you forgot the opening apostrophe for a character constant. These types of errors are very difficult for a compiler to decipher. The best it can do is determine that an error exists and make an educated guess about the error type and location.

Error messages also occur as a result of the programmer's forgetfulness. For instance, a programmer will write a section of code, use a new variable, and forget to go back to declare the new variable. Usually, error messages that occur under these circumstances accurately reflect their causes: for example, "undefined variable," "missing . . .," and "need . . . ." This category of errors also includes nonexistent #include source files.

Moving into more context-dependent situations, there are errors for illegal constructs or semantics that may inadvertently be caused by syntactical errors. These errors include taking the address of constant expressions (&44), declaring an auto type variable outside of a function (only extern or static variable types may be declared in this situation), and invalid assignment (assigning a char to an entire structure, for example). These sorts of errors are easily recognized when you look at your source code.

The hardware can also cause compiler errors. On a full disk, for example, the compiler will not be able to write the relocatable file; a bad disk may make some source files unreadable; and bad RAM has extremely varied and unpredictable effects. The first two causes are relatively easy to determine. Most compilers will be able to indicate if the disk is full or if it cannot read a file. Bad or damaged memory, on the other hand, can cause various symptoms, and it may take some time to diagnose whether or not your computer's memory is at fault, although the problem should be consistent within various programs.

The compiler itself has limitations that cannot be exceeded. These limitations, enumerated in your compiler manual, usually concern the number of #include directives or #define directives that may be nested. Exceeding the maximum source file size or using an overly complex expression can also stretch some compilers beyond their capabilities. Error messages given under these circumstances are also generally accurate in indicating their cause.

The final category of compiler errors derives from how well the compiler can handle source code errors. In other words, how easily does the compiler get "confused" or tricked? Most compilers (even those on large computer systems) can become confused after the first six to ten errors, depending upon what the errors are. This "compiler confusion" will result in many error messages being displayed throughout the rest of the compilation process, whether or not an actual error condition exists. For example, if you place one too many closing braces within a block, the compiler will think that you have ended the function and will give you an error for all of the statements following the extraneous brace. If you get numerous errors on a first compilation of a program, correcting the first few errors and recompiling the program may significantly reduce the number of error messages displayed the next time through.

With some experience at writing and compiling programs, you will begin to categorize error messages. Frequently, an error will be obvious once it is pointed out to you by the compiler. In other instances, you may need to do some code simplification to insure that your code is correct and that the compiler has not reached its limit with code that is too complex. Furthermore, large source files have a tendency to be error-ridden on an initial compilation, which, of course, is a good reason to use segmented coding.

Generating smaller source files makes compiling programs and correcting errors much faster. You will not have to wait for a large source code file to compile, only to have an error detected near the end. A little practice and a good compiler manual will provide you with enough tools for avoiding and correcting errors.

LINKING YOUR RELOCATABLE FILES

The linking process, as we mentioned earlier, converts the relocatable file into an executable file. We will now further discuss the topic of linking files.

In case you have not already noticed, functions such as printf(), scanf(), open(), atoi() and so on, are neither defined nor declared in the source code file (unless they are macros in the stdio.h file). When you compile your program, the compiler takes note of all references to functions that do not exist within the source file. The notes that the compiler makes concerning these undefined functions are called *unresolved references*.

When linking the relocatable file, the linker accesses a file called a library, attempting to resolve these references. When resolving the standard library functions listed above, for example, the linker looks through a file called the standard library, which has been catalogued and indexed with the names of the functions it contains. (In the Consulair system, the library does not exist as a separate file; instead, it is contained in the compiler.) Library files are really a form of relocatable files.

In some cases, you may wish to supply your own set of functions. One way of providing your own functions is to write a #include file to be included and recompiled each time you compile a program. The disadvantage of this approach is that it lengthens the compilation process and decreases a programmer's productivity. To avoid this inefficiency, the linker allows you to compile this function file separately and then link the two files together. This way you need to compile the function file only once, and you can use it over and over for each program you write.

How does the compiler know whether to expect a function (or variable) reference to be external to the source file? Generally, all references will be expected to be resolved within the same source file, so C uses the extern storage class declarator to inform the compiler not to look for the definition but instead to let the linker handle it.

To accommodate programming large systems, many programming teams use the black box principle that we first described in Chapter 4. This approach is applicable not only within a single source file, but across an entire system of source files, which can then be linked together into one or more programs. Applying the back box principle, there will be functions used locally (that is, they are only used by other functions within the file), analogous to the use of local variables within a function. We hide these local functions from other source files by declaring their storage class as static.

A data storage program that creates, deletes, edits, and retrieves data from a data file is an excellent application for separate files and local functions. Through our structured programming method, we divide the program into two sections— one section deals with the user (to accept commands, and receive and display data), and the other section performs the data file manipulation. The system as a whole needs to be able to perform each of these functions, but one section of the program does not need to know how the other section works.

The second source file must contain functions to create, retrieve, store, and delete data from the file (an edit function is the combination of retrieving and storing functions). This file may also contain other functions to support these four interface functions, but the first source file need not know about any of the supporting functions.

We now have two source files. The first file references the functions for creating, retrieving, storing, and deleting, which it declares as **extern** and does not define. The second file contains the definition of these four functions (without any storage class declared), and other supporting functions (declared as **static** to hide them from the first file). These two files, compiled separately, generate two relocatable files to be linked into a single program.

Now we need to combine the two files into a single program using the linker. The linking process for this example will contain both file names on the command line. The linker will look through these files in addition to the standard library to resolve all external references. If all external references have one (and only one) associated definition, the linker will create an executable file and we will now have a program ready for use.

The segmentation methodology we have just used also makes program changes easier. To change the user interface portion of the program, you need only edit and recompile the first source file. After any changes, though, the whole system needs relinking.

The linker takes all relocatable files and links the system into one program file. When we use the **extern** declaration, the linker allows functions and variables to be defined in one place within the source files and utilized by any other source file. The linking process, although quite short, enables the black box principle and program segmentation methodology to be employed on large program systems.

CREATING YOUR OWN LIBRARIES

In the preceding section, we discussed linking multiple source files together into one file. While the multiple source files are not libraries, they are similar to an actual library.

To create your own libraries, you must have a program known as a *librarian*. At the least, the librarian will have the capability of creating library files; however, it may also be able to remove or replace existing *library modules.*

What is a library module? A library file consists of a relocatable file, called a module in librarian terminology, and created either by a compiler or by another program such as an assembler. A library may contain any number of modules, and each module may contain any number of valid source code lines (within limits). To create a library file, you give the librarian a list all of the modules to be included in the library file, an operation that is similar to the process of linking files into a program. Check your manual for the exact details of the librarian process.

Libraries work like the #include directive to reduce the amount of redundant programming. The advantage of using a library rather than #include files is that the library file has already been compiled and may be linked immediately; this reduces the amount of time required for program development. The advantage of library files over the multiple source file method is the modularity of the library approach.

If the library file consists of more than one function, these functions usually have a common purpose and are likely to be needed with some degree of frequency. For example, one library may contain functions to do screen formatting, another may have mathematical functions, and still another may have file accessing functions. You may have as many library files as needed. The libraries' contents will depend upon your programming needs.

A library file, originating from one or more relocatable files, has the names of the externally available functions (and variables, if any) listed in some manner. You can use a library file just as you would any other relocatable file during the linking process. If your linker can use library files, it will search the library files named (more than one library can be included during the linking process) for any unresolved references. The linker will search all of the listed files in a specific order. Note that the search order depends upon the linker, and it may affect the outcome of the resulting program.

The efficiency of the librarian and linking programs will determine the efficiency of the resulting program. To examine this relationship, we will look at an example. Suppose that a library contains three functions a(), b(), and c(), but the program being linked only references function b(). What happens to functions a() and c()?

A library can be broken into three levels: the library file as a whole, a module file within the library file, and a particular function within a module. In order to resolve external references, the linker will search the library for the function name.

The least efficient linker would use the entire library regardless of whether or not function a() or c() was used within the program. The next step toward efficiency would have the linker use only the module in which the function is defined. If each of our functions resided in a separate module before being placed into the library, then they could be used separately so that only function b() would be extracted from the library.

Making our example more complex, if function b() referenced function a(), then a very efficient linker would extract both functions b() and a(). This level of efficiency provides the greatest advantage over simply linking separate relocatable files together. If all three functions were defined within the same module, then the entire module would be used with the result that in all three functions would be incuded in the format program. The most efficient linker would extract just the functions referenced and used from a library, regardless of how the library was created.

Librarian programs provide a convenient method of efficiently storing segments of frequently required code, which in turn results in decreased programming time. The use of the librarian is by no means a prerequisite to programming. On the other hand, when you become proficient at programming skills, you will find the librarian's role beneficial. You should learn to use this helpful tool.

NINE

REFERENCE

GUIDE

This chapter provides rapid-access answers to questions that may arise while you are first learning the C language. It deals exclusively with syntax and semantics. It does not go into detail or discuss the philosophy of using the constructs available, nor explore the inner-workings of the language itself. For a deeper analysis of the elements of C, you should, of course, read Chapters 3 through 7 of this book. If you require greater depth and explanation in the process of using this chapter, consult the table of contents or the index to determine which section of this book will best answer your question.

DEFINITIONS

For the sake of concision and consistency, we will begin by defining the set of terms we will use in this reference guide. Their actual counterparts (for example, variable names, operators, and so on) rather than the shorthand have to be used during programming, of course.

The following definitions represent only those words and phrases directly associated with the C programming language. Additional programming terminology can be found in the Glossary. In providing these definitions, we assume you have a basic knowledge of programming terms and philosophy.

1. *Newline:* A character indicating the end of a line of characters. In UNIX, this character corresponds to a linefeed (ASCII decimal value of 10), whereas MS-DOS and CP/M require a carriage return and linefeed pair (ASCII values 13 and 10). For the Macintosh, the newline character is usually a linefeed, although it may vary from compiler to compiler. This requirement may vary with other compilers and operating systems.

2. *Whitespace:* Collectively refers to the newline, blank space, tab, and comments.

3. *Data type:* Determines the size and format of the data to be stored.

4. *Storage class:* Determines where in memory the data will be stored and its range of scope.

5. *Scope:* The range of source lines in which an object is accessible.

6. *Object:* A region of memory that can be manipulated.

7. *Expression:* Any combination of objects and operators that evaluate to a single data object of the appropriate type.

8. *Identifier:* Any sequence of letters, numbers, and the underscore character (_), beginning with a letter. The compiler defines what constitutes uniqueness between identifiers. The C programming language states that no more than the first eight characters are significant; the Consulair compiler differentiates between . . . ; upper- and lowercase characters may or may not be distinguished. Check your compiler manual for exact details regarding the construction of an identifier.

9. *Token:* Categorizes identifiers, keywords, constants, strings, operators, and other separators.

STATEMENT CONSTRUCTION

The programming statement is the basic unit of operation in C. A statement consists of either whitespace, a comment, a statement block, or a series of one or more valid expressions terminated by a semicolon.

WHITESPACE

Whitespace is ignored by the compiler except when it is used to separate tokens. An input line will be parsed between whitespaces, and each token is assumed to be the next longest string of characters that could possibly form a token. In some cases, whitespace may be necessary to separate adjacent identifiers, keywords, and constants.

COMMENTS

Comments, considered by the compiler to be whitespace, begin with the first occurrence of the /* character pair, and end with the first */ character pair. Comments may not be nested.

STATEMENT BLOCKS: {}

By surrounding statement blocks, braces ({}) delimit a basic structural element in C. A statement block begins with the left brace ({) and ends with the right brace (}). Block statements may be nested.

To the surrounding source code, a statement block appears to be a single statement, and a statement block may be used anywhere a single statement can be used. C is not a completely block-structured language, however, because it does not allow a function to be defined within another function.

STATEMENT TERMINATION: THE SEMICOLON

All source code line statements must be terminated by a semicolon (;). A source line may be extended across multiple lines (the newline is treated as whitespace) and will be considered terminated upon the first occurrence of a semicolon. (A newline may not appear within a string constant or in the middle of a token.)

DATA DECLARATION

All data objects used in a C program must be defined before being referenced in a source line. A data object has two related attributes: a data type and a storage class.

DATA TYPES

C has three distinct data type classifications: character, integer, and floating point. Character variables (type **char**) will be large enough to contain any member of the character set in use (ASCII for most implementations). A character variable stores the character's integer equivalent based on the character set in use.

Integers come in three sizes—**short**, regular (**int**), and **long**—to accommodate different usages within a program. The actual range of values represented by each integer size depends upon the implementation. To use the full range of positive integer values based upon the size of the data type ($2^n - 1$, where n is the number of bits used in the representation), you may declare all three sizes as **unsigned**.

Floating point values may be represented in single- or double-precision depending upon the implementation.

Here is a list of all the data types:

char	A single character.
int	An integer value.
short int	An integer value whose range depends upon implementation. The word **int** is not required.
long int	An integer value whose range depends upon implementation. The word **int** is not required.
unsigned int	An unsigned integer value. May be combined with a **long** or **short** data type, and with **char** in some implementations.
float	A single-precision floating point value.
double	A double-precision floating point value.

STORAGE CLASSES

Based upon scoping rules (see the section on scoping rules later in this reference guide), the variable's storage class determines where the data object is stored and how it is accessed. The default storage class of all variables declared within a statement block or function is **auto**. Although it is not necessary, you may want to include the **auto** storage class as part of a data declaration statement. Storage is allocated to an **auto** variable upon entry to the statement block or function and is relinquished upon exit.

The **static** declaration causes storage to be allocated at the time of compilation instead of at execution time. A **static** variable will retain its value even after program flow leaves the statement block or function that defined it, although it will not be accessible outside that block or function.

An **extern** declaration indicates that the declared variable has been defined outside the enclosing block. A variable is implicitly declared as being external by the location of its declaration statement. A declaration outside a function declares its variables to be externally available.

Register, the final storage class provided by C, allows placement of the variable's data directly into the extremely fast and efficient registers of the computer's central processing unit. The existence of the **register** variable and how many you can use depends again on your compiler.

Here is a summary of the four storage classes available in C:

auto	The default storage class. These variables are active only while their enclosing statement block is active.
extern	The variable has been declared in another portion of the program.
static	The variable will become active when the enclosing statement block is first activated. The variable will remain after the block is exited and will retain its last value. The variable will not be accessible from outside of the statement block.
register	Specifies use of the internal storage registers of the central processing unit as the storage location for the data.

DATA DECLARATION

A data declaration statement informs the compiler what data type is to be associated with a particular token. The data type determines the amount of storage space required and what operations are valid for the specified token. All data objects must be declared and defined prior to their use.

DECLARATION AND DEFINITION

While defining a data object causes space to be allocated for the data, data declaration does not necessarily allocate storage space for the data. The **extern** declaration does not allocate any storage space; it defers this allocation to another point in the program. An **extern** declaration must have a corresponding data definition.

The data declaration format is

storage-class data-type variable-list;

The *storage-class* and *data-type* may be any of the valid keywords we have listed. The *variable list* consists of identifiers separated by commas (,); all of the identifiers contained in the *variable-list* will have the storage class indicated by *storage-class* and the data type indicated by *data-type*. *Storage-class* may be omitted if it is to be **auto**. If *data-type* is omitted, the named variables generate a compiler warning message and are assumed to be of type **int** for the remainder of the statement block.

EXTERNAL DECLARATIONS

A definition that allocates storage space occurring outside a function block makes that identifier external and is called a *global variable*. All subsequent **extern** declarations naming the identifier will refer to this declaration.

A global variable can be used in any function from the point of definition to the end of the source file without an explicit declaration. For example, if no declaration is made within the function, the variable is assumed to have been defined within the same source file. An explicit **extern** declaration within the function may also be used. An external variable defined in another source file must be explicitly declared **extern**.

INITIALIZATION

A declaration statement may contain an assignment operator to designate an initial value for the variable being declared. The variable is followed by the assignment operator (=), which is followed by the initial value for the variable. Certain restrictions apply to initialization statements depending on the data type and storage class of the variable.

Static and **extern** variables will always be initialized to 0 if no explicit intialization value is given. **auto** and **register** variables, however, start with some undefined value. For example:

```
static int i;               /* initializes i = 0 */
auto int i;                 /* initializes i = ?? */
```

Pointers and variables may be initialized with any single expression, which may be enclosed within braces to give it the appearance of a single expression. The expression must evaluate to a single value of the proper data type after all normal type conversions have been applied (see Appendix E). For example:

```
static int i = 10;          /* initializes i = 10 */
auto int i = 10;            /* initializes i = 10 */
auto int i = 5, j = 6;      /* multiple initialization */
```

Other data types, collectively called *aggregates*, include structures and arrays. These types use an initializer consisting of a list of values separated by commas and enclosed within braces. When an aggregate contains another aggregate as its member, the initialization procedure is applied recursively to the member (see the following two-dimensional array example). Providing more initializing values than members causes a compilation error; providing too few initializing values will cause the uninitialized members to be filled with zeroes.

Here are two examples of initialization:

```
int a[5] = { 6, 5, 4, 3, 2 };
int b[4][4] = {
        { 9, 8, 7 },
        { 6, 5 },
        { 4 },
    };
```

The first example initializes all the elements of array **a**. The second example initializes a two-dimensional array in which each element is an array. We apply the recursive intialization procedure, where each subset of braces initializes a single line in the two-dimensional array. Graphically, the second array would look like Figure 9.1. Because each line contained fewer initializers than space available, the remaining elements of the array became zero. The fourth row of the array also initialized to zero because no value set was provided.

```
      0  1  2  3
   0  9  8  7  0
   1  6  5  0  0
   2  4  0  0  0
   3  0  0  0  0
```

Figure 9.1: Two-Dimensional Array Initialization

If an initializer list follows, a one-dimensional array does not require a subscript to indicate the number of elements in its declaration. For example:

    char n[] = { 'A', 'B', 'C', '\0' };

This example initializes array n and declares its size to be four elements. Character arrays may also be initialized by a string constant. The termination character (\0) is automatically supplied. The preceding declaration can be shortened to

    char n[] = "ABC";

A variable declared as **extern** may not be initialized because the **extern** storage class does not actually allocate any memory.

SCOPING RULES

The *scope* of a data object defines which portions of the program have access to the object. Data objects declared within a block have a scope over the entire block and all blocks initiated within it. This data object cannot be accessed from outside the block. Data objects declared externally to any block (that is, outside of a function) are available as external data objects through all subsequently defined blocks until the end of the source file.

In Figure 9.2, I defined in function fun4() is accessible only to statements within function fun4(); and g, defined externally in the middle of the source file, can be utilized by all of the functions following the

```
fun4()
{
int l;     /* local to this function */
}

int g;     /* global to all following functions */

fun5() { }
fun6() { }

/* end of file */
```

Figure 9.2: Example of Scoping Rules

declaration until the end of the file. An **extern** declaration will follow the same scoping rules as other declarations, depending upon its position within the file (internal or external to any function).

Statement blocks may appear within functions and data objects may be declared within these blocks. If a data object identifier declared with an **auto** or **static** storage class has the same name as a data object existing in an enclosing block or as an external data object, then the innermost declaration has precedence when that data object name is referenced by a program statement. The outer data objects still exist, but they can no longer be accessed by the current statement block because of the scoping precedence. When the block is exited and the inner data object is discarded, the previously available data object of the same name becomes accessible again.

DATA TYPE OPERATORS

The C programming language contains several operators for use with data types. These operators can obtain the amount of storage space required by a specific data type, altering the data type of a token, and defining new data types.

DATA TYPE SIZE OPERATOR: SIZEOF

As we have seen, C has seven predefined data types. Each data type has an associated size and method of representation. The size of a data type is specified in units, where each unit is the size of the smallest data type, **char**. Most compilers for personal computers will use a single byte to store a **char**, and the size of a data type will be equivalent to its size in bytes. However, for the sake of portability to other machines, do not assume this equality of byte and **char** size.

To determine the size required to store an expression or a particular data type, use the **sizeof** operator, which can be used in the following formats:

    sizeof *expression*
    sizeof (*data type*)

The first form evaluates to the size in **char** units required by *expression*. The size is based upon the declaration of the objects used in the expression. The second form returns the size of the *data type* named in the parentheses.

THE CAST OPERATOR: ()

In the example,

> *(data-type) expression*

the cast operator forces the conversion of *expression* into the data type given by **data-type** named within the parentheses.

THE TYPE DECLARATOR: TYPEDEF

The creation of a data structure or complex data type can sometimes make the source code very difficult to read and understand. To alleviate this problem, C provides a keyword to bind the data structure or complex data type declaration to an identifier:

> **typedef** *declaration identifier;*

The keyword **typedef** equates *identifier* to *declaration* so that in subsequent declarations the identifier may be used in lieu of the actual (usually cumbersome) declaration. For example:

```
typedef char STRING, *LIST;
typedef struct { char last[20], first[10]; } NAME;
```

The following declarations can now be made.

```
STRING input[50]
LIST pc;
NAME emp;
```

The identifiers have been used in the **typedef** statement to replace the conventional declaration statements. In this example, input is an array of 50 characters, **pc** points to a **char**, and **emp** is a structure containing the character arrays **last** and **first**.

The **typedef** statement creates a synonym for the declaration; it does not allocate any storage. As a matter of style and convention, the identifiers of the **typedef** statement use uppercase letters, but this has no bearing on their function.

GENERAL OPERATORS

Operators are used in creating expressions in C. Expressions are used to process the program's data. The operators presented in this section fall into five categories: assignment, arithmetic, bitwise, assignment combinations, and increment and decrement operators.

ASSIGNMENT OPERATOR: =

In the construct

data-object = *expression*;

the assignment operator causes the value of *expression* to be assigned to *data-object*. The assignment should make sense with regard to data types after the standard conversions are applied (see Appendix E).

ARITHMETIC OPERATORS: + − * / %

C contains four basic arithmetic operators, plus a modulo operator.

addition	expr1 + expr2
subtraction	expr1 − expr2
multiplication	expr1 * expr2
division	expr1 / expr2
modulo	expr1 % expr2

In all cases, both *expr1* and *expr2* must be numeric. The modulo operator evaluates the remainder of the division of *expr1* by *expr2*. The modulo operator cannot be used with **float** or **double** expressions.

Integer values may be added to or subtracted from pointers. In this case, the integer value will be scaled to the proper size for the type of the pointer.

The use of the minus as a unary operator,

− *expr1*

results in the arithmetic negative of *expr1*.

Bitwise Operators: & | ^ >> << ~

Bitwise operators perform bit-by-bit manipulations on integer operands.

AND	*expr1* & *expr2*
inclusive-OR	*expr1* | *expr2*
exclusive-OR	*expr1* ^ *expr2*
right-shift	*expr1* >> *expr2*
left-shift	*expr1* << *expr2*
one's complement	~ *expr1*

All of the bitwise operators use integer operands.

The AND (&), inclusive OR (|), and exclusive OR (^) perform their associated bitwise operation on the two operands in a bit-by-bit manner. A table illustrating different bit combinations is located in Appendix F.

The shift operators shift the integral value of *expr1* either left or right by the number of bits specified by *expr2*. If *expr2* is negative or greater than the number of bits in the data type of *expr1*, undefined results can occur.

The left-shift operator (<<) fills the vacated bit positions with zeroes. The right-shift operator (>>) may fill arithmetically (by copying the leftmost bit) or with zeroes. If *expr1* is declared unsigned, then the right-shift operator will always fill with zeroes.

The one's-complement operator (~) performs a bit-by-bit complementing of *expr1*: changing each occurrence of one to zero and zero to one.

Assignment Combinations

For concise source code, C allows any of the preceding binary operators to be combined with the assignment statement in the following form:

data-object op = *expr*

This equates to the longer version:

data-object = *data-object op* (*expr*)

Notice the parentheses surrounding *expr* which indicate that the operand *expr* will be evaluated before the operator is applied. Thus, in the statement

    x += y * 6

the expression y * 6 will be evaluated first, then added to x. All standard data type conversions will be performed.

When += or −= is used, the *data-object* may be a pointer, in which case *expr* must be an integer for the proper scaling to be performed on *expr*.

THE INCREMENT AND DECREMENT OPERATORS: + + AND − −

Because incrementing and decrementing data objects by one unit is a frequently used operation, C has an operator for each of these operations:

increment	*+ + data-object* or *data-object + +*
decrement	*− − data-object* or *data-object − −*

These constructions are the same as writing

    data-object = *data-object* + 1

for the increment operator, and

    data-object = *data-object* − 1

for the decrement operator. The *data-object* may be any arithmetic data type or a pointer. If *data-object* is a pointer, then the proper scaling is applied.

The position (prefix or postfix) of the increment or decrement operator affects the value of the expression. The prefix operator causes *data-object* to be incremented or decremented, and then this new value is used as the value of the expression. The postfix operator causes the current value of *data-object* to be the value of the expression; then the value of *data-object* is incremented or decremented. In all cases, the final value of the data-object will have been incremented or decremented from the original value.

Logical Statements

Logical statements are based upon Boolean algebra. In Boolean algebra, there exist only two possible values—either true or false. In C, there are two types of expressions that result in either true or false. The first kind of expression performs a logical operation such as NOT, AND, OR, equal to, and not equal to. These expressions take two Boolean values, perform the operation, and evaluate to true or false based upon the truth tables given in Appendix F. The second kind of expression evaluates to true or false based upon the relationship of one numeric value to another (for example, through a decision that one value is greater than another).

For purposes of convention, the value of a false expression is taken to be zero and the value of a true expression is nonzero. Through this convention, the programmer can test any data object of an arithmetic type by using a logical test for true or false, a very fast testing capability.

Logical Operators: ! == != && |

The logical operators available in C perform a logical comparison between the operands. A false expression evaluates to 0 and a true expression evaluates to 1; both values are returned as int. All expressions used by the logical operators are taken to be logical values—true (nonzero) or false (zero).

logical NOT	! expr1
equality	expr1 == expr2
inequality	expr1 != expr2
logical AND	expr1 && expr2
logical OR	expr1 | expr2

The logical NOT, a unary operator, returns the converse of expr1: that is, if expr1 is nonzero, then the logical NOT returns 0; if it is zero, then the logical NOT returns 1.

The equality and inequality operators are self-explanatory.

The logical AND and logical OR return true or false. Neither operator will evaluate farther than required in order to determine the truth value of an expression. For example, if expr1 in the logical AND is false, expr2 will not be evaluated.

Relational Operators: < > <= >=

The four relational operators in C yield a truth value of 1 or 0 based upon the truth of the expression. The relational operators provide a method of testing the relationship between two arithmetic operands.

less than	expr1 < expr2
greater than	expr1 > expr2
less than or equal to	expr1 < = expr2
greater than or equal to	expr1 > = expr2

The relative positions of pointers may also be compared. This information is generally not very useful, because it is implementation-dependent. Pointer comparison is meaningful only when the pointers indicate objects in the same array.

Controlling Program Flow

All languages have some ability to control the execution of programming statements depending on given values determined at execution time. All statements in a C source code file will be executed sequentially until a construct is encountered that evaluates an expression to determine the course of action.

Repetition

Almost all programming applications require some form of controlled repetition, or looping. Loops fall into two general categories: those based upon a variable condition and those based upon a predefined number of iterations.

The WHILE Statement

From the first category, the while loop

while (*expression*) *statement*

continues to execute *statement* (which may be a statement block) as long as *expression* remains true. The expression is tested prior to executing the loop statement.

THE FOR STATEMENT

The for loop comes from the second category. The loop

> for (expr1; expr2; expr3) *statement*

begins by executing *expr1* and then testing *expr2*. While *expr2* remains true, the loop repeats: *statement* is executed, and after each execution of *statement*, *expr3* is executed. This construction is functionally equivalent to

```
expr1;
while (expr2) {
statement
expr3;
}
```

In the for construct, any of the expressions may be omitted (the semicolons must remain as placeholders). If *expr2* is omitted, the loop will require an alternative method of termination. The for loop will be used when the number of iterations is known at the start of the loop. If we assume that **max** iterations are to be performed and that the variable **count** is the loop control variable, then the for loop will look like this:

> for (count = 1; count < = max; count + +) { *statement* }

THE DO-WHILE STATEMENT

The do-while construct provides a slightly different execution of the while loop. The construct

> do *statement* while (*expression*);

postpones the termination test until after the statement is executed, guaranteeing statement execution at least once.

Any of these loop constructs may be nested within themselves or within any other construct.

CONDITIONAL EXECUTION

All programming languages have some form of statement that allows a set of statements to be performed or skipped based upon a specified condition. Conditional execution in C is initiated either by the **if** statement or the **switch** statement.

THE **IF** STATEMENT

The most conventional form of a conditional statement uses the if construct:

    if *(expression) statement1*
    if *(expression) statement1* **else** *statement2*

The first construction evaluates *expression*, and if *expression* is true (nonzero), then *statement1* is executed; otherwise, *statement1* is ignored. In either of these circumstances, execution continues with the statement following the **if**.

In the second construction, if *expression* evaluates to true, then *statement1* is executed; otherwise, *statement2* is executed. When either *statement1* or *statement2* has been completed, execution will continue with the code following *statement2*. In any execution of the **if-else** construct, only one of the two statements will be executed.

The **if** and **if-else** constructs may be nested. An **else** will always be matched with the last **if** that is not associated with an **else** within the same block. For example:

```
if (expr) {                              /* 1 */
    if (expr) {                          /* 2 */
    } else {                             /* 2 */
        if (expr) {                      /* 3 */
        }
    }
} else {                                 /* 1 */
}
```

This example shows the matching of **if** to **else** based on the last-unmatched **if** rules. The numbers in the comments indicate which if's and **else**'s form pairs.

THE CONDITIONAL OPERATOR: ?:

This second conditional construct is actually an operator and thus returns a value. The **?:** operator is applied as follows:

    expr1 **?** *expr2* **:** *expr3*

This operator works like an if-else construct: that is, either *expr2* or *expr3* is executed, depending upon the evaluation of *expr1*. If *expr1* evaluates to true, then the result of the operator is *expr2*; otherwise, the result is *expr3*. Only one of the expressions will be evaluated.

Arithmetic conversion will be applied to *expr2* and *expr3* to yield the same data type. If either expression is a pointer, then the other must be a pointer of the same type or the constant 0.

THE SWITCH-CASE-DEFAULT STATEMENT

The final conditional construct causes program flow to be transferred to one of several statements, depending on the value of an expression. The **switch** statement

> switch (expression) *control-statement*

evaluates *expression*; this evaluation must result in an **int** value. Within the *control-statement* (which is usually a statement block), one or more **case** statements may be present. As we will see shortly, it would not make sense to have zero **case** statements.

In the **case** statement

> case *constant-expression*:

the *constant-expression* must evaluate to **int**. The value of expression in the **switch** statement will be compared to the value of the *constant-expression* in all **case** statements within the *control-statement* (from the **switch** construct). When the value of *constant-expression* equals the value of *expression*, execution begins at the first statement following the **case** statement. Execution continues through to the end of *control-statement* or until a **break** statement is encountered (see the next section).

The *control-statement* may contain at most one statement of the form

> default:

Should none of the values of the **case** statement match the value of *expression*, execution continues with the **default** statement. If no statements match the expression and no **default** statement is supplied, then no statements within the *control-statement* will be executed.

Essentially, the **case** and **default** statements supply labels on an expression/value match, so that program execution may jump there. After control has been transferred to a **case** or **default** statement, all subsequent **case** statements will have no effect on the program flow.

Use of the **break** statement will cause the program flow to exit the **switch** statement.

UNCONDITIONAL PROGRAM FLOW

The C programming language also allows program flow to be altered unconditionally. The statements that perform an unconditional change in program flow are **break**, **continue**, and **goto**.

THE BREAK STATEMENT

The **break** statement

    break;

causes immediate termination of the currently enclosing **while**, **do-while**, **for**, or **switch** statement. Execution begins at the first statement following the aborted statement.

THE CONTINUE STATEMENT

The **continue** statement

    continue;

causes immediate termination of the current iteration of the enclosing **while**, **do-while**, or **for** loop. The **continue** statement transfers program control to the statement that performs the loop control.

THE GOTO-LABEL STATEMENT

A *label* is an identifier followed by a colon. The label possesses no processing function; it merely marks a particular position or line in the source file.

    identifier: statement

The statement need not be on the same line as the identifier.

A statement labeled in this manner serves no purpose other than as a target for a **goto** statement. The scope of the label is the current function, excluding any subblocks that have redefined the identifier (for the duration of that block). The **goto** statement

> **goto** *identifier;*

causes unconditional transfer of program execution to the statement labeled by the identifier. The identifier must label a statement within the current function.

FUNCTIONS

C is a procedural language based on functions. Every program must have a function called **main( )**, where program execution begins. Functions have the ability to accept parameters and return a single value of one of the data types defined by C.

FUNCTION DEFINITION

A function definition is similar to a data declaration:

> *storage-class data-type function-name (parameter-list)*
> *parameter declarations;*
> {
> *local-variable-declarations;*
>   *function-statements*
> }

The *storage-class* of a function is limited to **extern** or **static**. If the *storage-class* is omitted, then the function is assumed to be **static**. (An **extern** declaration is discussed in the next section.) The *data-type* of the function determines the data type of the value to be returned by the function; this too may be omitted, and the default is **int**.

The *function-name* can be any valid identifier not yet declared. The *parameter-list* names the formal parameters of the function as identifiers separated by commas. The formal parameters are declared in the *parameter declaration* statements. Each formal parameter must have an associated declaration. A function need not have any formal parameters.

The function body, enclosed in a pair of braces, contains a declaration statement for the local variables, if any, and a group of statements.

EXTERNAL FUNCTION DEFINITION

By design of the language, functions may not be defined within other functions. When you are programming large systems, it is sometimes necessary to divide functions among several different source files. To allow another file to access a function, make an **extern** definition of the function name. If the function is defined with a **static** storage class, then it is available throughout the source file in which it is defined, but not in any other source file. This follows, by analysis, from the explanations of storage classes given earlier.

RETURNING VALUES FROM FUNCTIONS

Although the default data type returned by a function is **int**, functions can be made to return any other C data type. Because of automatic conversion of data types, it becomes pointless to declare a function returning anything other than **int**, **long**, or **double**.

To change the data type returned by a function, two declarations must be made. First, the function definition requires a data type. Second, the calling routine must declare the function as returning the new data type.

The statement

data-type function-name( );

with the empty parentheses, declares that the function *function-name* will return the data type specified. The calling routine must expect the type of the returned value, otherwise, undefined values will result.

PARAMETER PASSING CONVENTIONS

C passes all function parameters by value. Using a data object as a parameter to a function will not change its current value within the calling routine. Pointers to data objects may be passed; this provides call-by-reference. Actual parameters will undergo data type conversions based upon the conventions outlined in Appendix E.

The only data types that may be passed are the data types defined by C and pointers. A program may not pass an entire array or data structure to a function. However, a pointer to any of these objects may be passed as a parameter.

RECURSION

The C programming language supports recursive calls to functions. Upon each invocation of the function, a new set of formal parameters and local variables is created, giving each function call a separate and unique set of data (assuming the default call-by-value is used). External and static variables will not change.

POINTERS AND ADDRESSES

C provides access to the address of any data object in use except a data object with a storage class of **register**. A special data object, called a pointer, may be used to store an address and to access the data contained therein.

THE INDIRECTION OPERATOR: *

By using the indirection operator (*), you can access the data located at the address stored by the pointer. For example, if px contains the address of a data object, then *px will refer to the data at that address.

POINTER DECLARATION

Pointers must be associated with a specific data type. Using the indirection operator, one declares a pointer as follows:

```
int *px, *py, x, y;
char *pc, c;
```

Variables px and py may contain the addresses of int data types, and pc may contain the address of a char data type. The variables x and y are of type int and c is of type char.

A pointer must have a particular data type because the pointer can be altered through integer addition, integer subtraction, incrementation, and decrementation. When the addition or subtraction is executed, the integer is scaled by the size (in char units) of the data type, and then added to or subtracted from the value contained by the pointer. The increment and decrement operators work in a similar manner by shifting the pointer forward or backward one data object. This ties in closely with arrays and dynamic storage allocation, discussed later in this reference guide.

THE ADDRESS OPERATOR: &

To determine the address of a data object, apply the address operator (&):

```
px = &x;
py = &y;
pc = &c;
```

The address operator may be applied to any data objects except those declared with the storage class register.

POINTER RESTRICTIONS AND CONVENTIONS

To a great degree, common sense dictates how pointers are used. The use of pointer comparison, for instance, has no general purpose except when comparing elements within the same array.

There is one important convention concerning a pointer value of 0. This pointer value guarantees that the pointer does not indicate any data object. A pointer of this kind is commonly called a *NULL* or *NIL* pointer.

ARRAYS

An array represents a set of related data objects of the same data type.

ARRAY DECLARATION

An array declaration includes a data storage class, a data type, an identifier, and the number of objects in the array. The number of objects is specified by subscripts enclosed in square brackets. ([ ])

storage-class data-type identifier[subscript1][subscript2]. . .;
storage-class data-type identifier[ ];

The number of subscripts an array may have is limited only by available memory. The second format of the array declaration references an externally defined array that has already allocated appropriate storage; hence, there is no need to specify the size of this array again. In this case, the storage class would either be omitted or listed as **extern**.

Arrays and Pointers

In C, arrays and pointers are very closely related. An array element reference actually converts to a pointer reference during compilation. Assuming the declaration

```
int a[10]
```

has been made, then the array element reference

```
a[i]
```

actually converts to

```
*(a + i)
```

The array name **a**, when used alone, has a data type of pointer to int. Thus, in the addition expression, i is scaled to the size of an **int** and then added to **a**. After the addition, the indirection operator is applied to retrieve the data at the specified location.

In a multidimensional array such as **int b[3][4][5]**, the same conversion procedure applies repetitively. To access element **b[x][y][z]**, the expression becomes

```
*( ( (b + x) + y) + z)
```

where (b + x) is the base address of a two-dimensional array of size 4 × 5; ((b + x) + y) is the base address of a one-dimensional array of size 5; and (((b + x) + y) + z) is the address of an integer. This conversion implies that the arrays are stored in row-major order, meaning that each row is filled before moving to the next (see Figure 9.3).

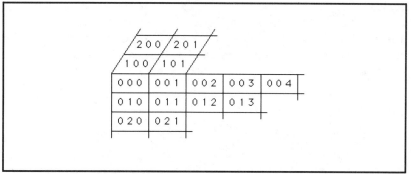

Figure 9.3: Row-Major Ordering of a Three-Dimensional Array

STRINGS

A string consists of an array of characters terminated by the \0 character. Strings are not considered a separate data type in C, and therefore cannot be manipulated as whole units.

STRUCTURES

C allows the programmer to define complex data types called structures. A structure consists of any number of members, where each member is an object of a predefined data type, a field, a union, or another structure.

STRUCTURE DECLARATION

Structures must be declared because the definition of a structure does not allocate any storage. After the structure has been created, identifiers can be associated with the structure type.

A structure declaration

> **struct** *structure-name* {
>   *member list*
>   } *identifiers to have this structure;*

begins with the keyword **struct**, followed by an optional *structure-name*, a statement block containing the *member list*, terminated with any identifiers to have this structure as their data type. Either the *structure-name* or the identifiers may be omitted, but not both. Once the structure is declared, the *structure-name* can be used later to define identifiers.

For example:

struct **test** { *member list* };

struct **test** t1, t2, *t3;

This example defines a structure called **test**. The identifiers t1, t2, and t3 (a pointer to this structure) are declared to have the data type of this structure. Notice the placement of **struct test** in the type declaration position. Generally, the structure definition occurs at the external level of the program, and structure identifiers are declared as needed.

A second format of the structure declaration

struct { *member list* } t1, t2, *t3;

does not associate any name with this structure. It defines the structure and declares the identifiers t1, t2, and t3 as having this structure as their data type. If any other identifiers required this same structure, they would have to be declared here or the structure definition would have to be repeated. From these two examples, one can see that omitting both the structure-name and the identifiers to be defined would cause no effect.

STRUCTURE MEMBER DECLARATION

The member list of a structure declaration

data-type identifier;

closely resembles the declaration of variables.

STANDARD MEMBER TYPES

The members of a structure will be stored sequentially in memory in the order in which they are declared.

The structure

```
struct dates {
    int yr, mon, day;
};
```

contains three integer types. The following structure references structure dates:

```
struct person {
    long codenum;
    char last_name[20], first_name[10];
    long ssnum;
    struct dates dob;
};
```

The names of the members of a structure may be the same as any regularly defined identifier, but they must be distinct from other structure names. With the following restrictions, the same member names may be used in different structures. First, the type of the identifier must be the same in both structures. Second, the identifier must have the same offset (position in memory relative to the start of the structure) in both structures. Third, all previous members of the structure must be the same. Although the compiler is defined only to perform checks for the same type and offset and does not the check for previous members, a structure meeting only two of these criteria may not be portable. Most newer compilers simply ignore the restrictions and just allow duplicate member names.

FIELDS

A *field*, a special member available within a structure, consists of a specified number of bits. A field is defined as follows:

data-type identifier : constant-expression;

Although many compilers will accept various data types, the only sensible data type, and the one used by the compiler regardless of the data type specified, is **unsigned int**.

A field member will accommodate the number of bits specified by *constant-expression*. A field may be as wide as a machine word but must not span a word boundary. If there is no room left in the current machine word to store the field, then the field will be placed at the beginning of the next word boundary.

The identifier for a field may be omitted, causing the number of bits specified to be 0 and inaccessible. If the identifier for a field is omitted, the alignment of following fields will be forced to a required position.

The address operator (&) may not be applied to a field member.

UNIONS

A union can store several different data types using the same identifier, but only one data type may be stored at any given time. The union definition is the same as that of the structure.

```
union union-name {
     member list
} identifiers to have this union;
```

In a union, the members of the *member list* can only be used independently, not simultaneously. The size of the union will be the size of the largest data object it will hold.

Here is an example of a union definition:

```
union utest {
     int iu;
     double du;
     char cu;
} ux, uy, *uz;
```

The union utest can hold either an int, a double, or a char data type. Just as in the structure definition, the identifiers following the definition have the data type created by the union (*uz is a pointer to a union of this type). Like structure definitions, the union definition of utest may be used subsequently to declare more identifiers.

STRUCTURE AND UNION OPERATORS

When you have declared a variable to be of a structured data type, you will need to be able to access the individual members of that structure. C provides two operators to access a structure member: the direct member operator for use with the variable declared to be of that structured type, and the indirect member operator for use with a pointer to that structure type.

The member operator: .

Currently, C does not support the ability to copy an entire structure or union. Only members of structures and unions may be accessed for assignment or for passing as parameters to functions.

Use the member operator (.) to reference a particular member of a structure or union:

> *structure-name.member-name*
> *union-name.member-name*

The member of a structure or union may be used like any other object of the associated data type.

The indirection member operator: ->

When using a pointer to a structure or union, you can access the members of the structure or union through the indirection member operator (->), constructed from a hyphen (-) and a greater-than symbol (>):

> *pointer->member-name*

The *pointer* must indicate a structure or union, and the *member-name* must be a member of that structure or union. This operator has the same result as

> (*pointer).member-name*

Both the indirect (-) and direct (.) member operators may be combined with each other and themselves. For example:

```
struct a {
    int ai;
    struct b *pb;
} sa, *spa;

struct b {
    int bi;
    struct a *pa;
} sb, *spb;

spa = &sa; /* initialize structure pointers */
spb = &sb;
sa.pb = spb; /* set member pointers */
sb.pa = spa;
```

With this program fragment, references to **sa.ai** can be made with any of the following references:

```
spa->ai
b.pa->ai
spb->pa->ai
```

Any combination of member operators may be used if their construction maintains the use of pointers with the indirection member operator and if all member names referenced actually exist. In general, complex constructions should be avoided because they obscure the meaning of the code and increase the chances of syntactical errors.

APPENDIX A

TABLE OF ASCII VALUES

ASCII	Hexadecimal	Decimal	Octal	Binary
^@	00	000	000	00000000
^A	01	001	001	00000001
^B	02	002	002	00000010
^C	03	003	003	00000011
^D	04	004	004	00000100
^E	05	005	005	00000101
^F	06	006	006	00000110
^G	07	007	007	00000111
^H	08	008	010	00001000
^I	09	009	011	00001001
^J	0A	010	012	00001010
^K	0B	011	013	00001011
^L	0C	012	014	00001100
^M	0D	013	015	00001101
^N	0E	014	016	00001110
^O	0F	015	017	00001111
^P	10	016	020	00010000
^Q	11	017	021	00010001
^R	12	018	022	00010010
^S	13	019	023	00010011
^T	14	020	024	00010100
^U	15	021	025	00010101
^V	16	022	026	00010110
^W	17	023	027	00010111
^X	18	024	030	00011000
^Y	19	025	031	00011001
^Z	1A	026	032	00011010
^[	1B	027	033	00011011
^\	1C	028	034	00011100
^]	1D	029	035	00011101
^^	1E	030	036	00011110
^_	1F	031	037	00011111
	20	032	040	00100000
!	21	033	041	00100001
"	22	034	042	00100010
#	23	035	043	00100011
$	24	036	044	00100100
%	25	037	045	00100101
&	26	038	046	00100110
'	27	039	047	00100111
(	28	040	050	00101000
)	29	041	051	00101001
*	2A	042	052	00101010
+	2B	043	053	00101011

ASCII	Hexadecimal	Decimal	Octal	Binary
,	2C	044	054	00101100
-	2D	045	055	00101101
.	2E	046	056	00101110
/	2F	047	057	00101111
0	30	048	060	00110000
1	31	049	061	00110001
2	32	050	062	00110010
3	33	051	063	00110011
4	34	052	064	00110100
5	35	053	065	00110101
6	36	054	066	00110110
7	37	055	067	00110111
8	38	056	070	00111000
9	39	057	071	00111001
:	3A	058	072	00111010
;	3B	059	073	00111011
<	3C	060	074	00111100
=	3D	061	075	00111101
>	3E	062	076	00111110
?	3F	063	077	00111111
@	40	064	100	01000000
A	41	065	101	01000001
B	42	066	102	01000010
C	43	067	103	01000011
D	44	068	104	01000100
E	45	069	105	01000101
F	46	070	106	01000110
G	47	071	107	01000111
H	48	072	110	01001000
I	49	073	111	01001001
J	4A	074	112	01001010
K	4B	075	113	11001011
L	4C	076	114	01001100
M	4D	077	115	01001101
N	4E	078	116	01001110
O	4F	079	117	01001111
P	50	080	120	01010000
Q	51	081	121	01010001
R	52	082	122	01010010
S	53	083	123	01010011
T	54	084	124	01010100
U	55	085	125	01010101
V	56	086	126	01010110
W	57	087	127	01010111

ASCII	Hexadecimal	Decimal	Octal	Binary
X	58	088	130	01011000
Y	59	089	131	01011001
Z	5A	090	132	01011010
[	5B	091	133	01011011
\	5C	092	134	01011100
]	5D	093	135	01011101
^	5E	094	136	01011110
—	5F	095	137	01011111
'	60	096	140	01100000
a	61	097	141	01100001
b	62	098	142	01100010
c	63	099	143	01100011
d	64	100	144	01100100
e	65	101	145	01100101
f	66	102	146	01100110
g	67	103	147	01100111
h	68	104	150	01101000
i	69	105	151	01101001
j	6A	106	152	01101010
k	6B	107	153	01101011
l	6C	108	154	01101100
m	6D	109	155	01101101
n	6E	110	156	01101110
o	6F	111	157	01101111
p	70	112	160	01110000
q	71	113	161	01110001
r	72	114	162	01110010
s	73	115	163	01110011
t	74	116	164	01110100
u	75	117	165	01110101
v	76	118	166	01110110
w	77	119	167	01110111
x	78	120	170	01111000
y	79	121	171	01111001
z	7A	122	172	01111010
{	7B	123	173	01111011
|	7C	124	174	01111100
}	7D	125	175	01111101
~	7E	126	176	01111110
DEL	7F	127	177	01111111
—	80	128	200	10000000
—	81	129	201	10000001
—	82	130	202	10000010

ASCII	Hexadecimal	Decimal	Octal	Binary
–	83	131	203	10000011
–	84	132	204	10000100
–	85	133	205	10000101
–	86	134	206	10000110
–	87	135	207	10000111
–	88	136	210	10001000
–	89	137	211	10001001
–	8A	138	212	10001010
–	8B	139	213	10001011
–	8C	140	214	10001100
–	8D	141	215	10001101
–	8E	142	216	10001110
–	8F	143	217	10001111
–	90	144	220	10010000
–	91	145	221	10010001
–	92	146	222	10010010
–	93	147	223	10010011
–	94	148	224	10010100
–	95	149	225	10010101
–	96	150	226	10010110
–	97	151	227	10010111
–	98	152	230	10011000
–	99	153	231	10011001
–	9A	154	232	10011010
–	9B	155	233	10011011
–	9C	156	234	10011100
–	9D	157	235	10011101
–	9E	158	236	10011110
–	9F	159	237	10011111
–	A0	160	240	10100000
–	A1	161	241	10100001
–	A2	162	242	10100010
–	A3	163	243	10100011
–	A4	164	244	10100100
–	A5	165	245	10100101
–	A6	166	246	10100110
–	A7	167	247	10100111
–	A8	168	250	10101000
–	A9	169	251	10101001
–	AA	170	252	10101010
–	AB	171	253	10101011
–	AC	172	254	10101100
–	AD	173	255	10101101
–	AE	174	256	10101110

ASCII	Hexadecimal	Decimal	Octal	Binary
–	AF	175	257	10101111
–	B0	176	260	10110000
–	B1	177	261	10110001
–	B2	178	262	10110010
–	B3	179	263	10110011
–	B4	180	264	10110100
–	B5	181	265	10110101
–	B6	182	266	10110110
–	B7	183	267	10110111
–	B8	184	270	10111000
–	B9	185	271	10111001
–	BA	186	272	10111010
–	BB	187	273	10111011
–	BC	188	274	10111100
–	BD	189	275	10111101
–	BE	190	276	10111110
–	BF	191	277	10111111
–	C0	192	300	11000000
–	C1	193	301	11000001
–	C2	194	302	11000010
–	C3	195	303	11000011
–	C4	196	304	11000100
–	C5	197	305	11000101
–	C6	198	306	11000110
–	C7	199	307	11000111
–	C8	200	310	11001000
–	C9	201	311	11001001
–	CA	202	312	11001010
–	CB	203	313	11001011
–	CC	204	314	11001100
–	CD	205	315	11001101
–	CE	206	316	11001110
–	CF	207	317	11001111
–	D0	208	320	11010000
–	D1	209	321	11010001
–	D2	210	322	11010010
–	D3	211	323	11010011
–	D4	212	324	11010100
–	D5	213	325	11010101
–	D6	214	326	11010110
–	D7	215	327	11010111
–	D8	216	330	11011000
–	D9	217	331	11011001
–	DA	218	332	11011010

ASCII	Hexadecimal	Decimal	Octal	Binary
–	DB	219	333	11011011
–	DC	220	334	11011100
–	DD	221	335	11011101
–	DE	222	336	11011110
–	DF	223	337	11011111
–	E0	224	340	11100000
–	E1	225	341	11100001
–	E2	226	342	11100010
–	E3	227	343	11100011
–	E4	228	344	11100100
–	E5	229	345	11100101
–	E6	230	346	11100110
–	E7	231	347	11100111
–	E8	232	350	11101000
–	E9	233	351	11101001
–	EA	234	352	11101010
–	EB	235	353	11101011
–	EC	236	354	11101100
–	ED	237	355	11101101
–	EE	238	356	11101110
–	EF	239	357	11101111
–	F0	240	360	11110000
–	F1	241	361	11110001
–	F2	242	362	11110010
–	F3	243	363	11110011
–	F4	244	364	11110100
–	F5	245	365	11110101
–	F6	246	366	11110110
–	F7	247	367	11110111
–	F8	248	370	11111000
–	F9	249	371	11111001
–	FA	250	372	11111010
–	FB	251	373	11111011
–	FC	252	374	11111100
–	FD	253	375	11111101
–	FE	254	376	11111110
–	FF	255	377	11111111

APPENDIX B

KEYWORDS

All of the words in this list are keywords in the C programming language. They have reserved definitions and may not be used for any other purpose (for example, as identifiers).

asm	entry	return
auto	extern	short
break	float	sizeof
case	for	static
char	fortran	struct
continue	goto	switch
default	if	typedef
do	int	union
double	long	unsigned
else	register	while

The keyword **entry** does not have an assigned definition at this time, but it is reserved for future use. The keywords **fortran** and **asm** are available in some, but not all compilers. Your compiler may reserve additional keywords. Check you compiler manual for details.

APPENDIX C

CHARACTER
ESCAPE
SEQUENCES

C provides a special metacharacter, the backslash (\) to make possible the graphic representation of certain nongraphic characters so that these characters can be used within a program.

Character name	Output character	Escape sequence
apostrophe	'	\'
backslash	\	\\
backspace	BS	\b
bit pattern	see below	\ddd
carriage return	CR	\r
form feed	FF	\f
horizontal tab	HT	\t
newline (line feed)	LF	\n
null character	NUL	\0
quotation mark	"	\"

All of these escape sequences may be used within character or string constants. The quotation mark can be used alone in a character constant (see Appendix E).

The *bit pattern sequence* enables the representation of any other character not shown. The backslash is followed by a sequence of up to three octal digits, where the value of the digits equals the character to be represented. Use the ASCII chart in Appendix A to determine the octal sequence for the character desired.

If the backslash is followed by a character not defined above, then the backslash is ignored and the character is used by itself.

PRECEDENCE
OF
OPERATORS

Operators are listed in order of decreasing precedence. All operators on the same line have an equal precedence level. Except where noted, all operators associate left to right.

```
() [] -> .
!  ~  + +  − -  (type)  *  &  sizeof                    (right to left)
* / %
+ -
<< >>
<  <=  >  >=
==  !=
&
^
¦
¦
&&                                                      (right to left)
¦¦                                                      (right to left)
?:
=  and other assignment operators

,
```

The commutative operators (* + & ¦ ^) may be rearranged by the compiler for convenience or efficiency. The expression

```
x * y * z
```

may be evaluated as (x * y) * z or as x * (y * z), depending upon the implementation. This may cause problems if x, y, or z is a function dependent upon the value of either of the other two identifiers.

CONVERSION

RULES AND

CONSTANT

FORMATS

All variables in C have a specified data type. Because variables of differing data types may be used within the same expression (where it is sensible to do so), there is a set of rules for converting all operands to one data type before any operations are performed and for determining the data type of the result. Variables will also have constant values assigned to them, and these constants should be in a format that will match the data type of the variable. This appendix lists the conversion rules and formats for constant values.

CONVERSION RULES

Conversion of operands within arithmetic expressions causes all data objects to be represented by the same data type. The primary effect of conversion is to change the data type with the smaller range of values to the data type with the larger range of values.

In an arithmetic expression, the rules of conversion are

1. All **char** and **short** are converted to **int**.

2. All **float** are converted to **double**. This conversion implies all floating point arithmetic is done in double precision.

3. After the initial conversion, both operands will be converted to the same data type in this order of decreasing precedence: **double, long, unsigned,** and **int**. In other words, if either operand is **double**, the other is converted to **double**; otherwise, if either operand is **long**, the other is converted to **long**, and so on. Whichever data type is chosen as common, that is the type of the result. This result will be converted to the type of the left-hand operator during an assignment expression.

CONSTANT FORMATS

Each of C's basic data types has an associated constant format. The proper format should be used to match the data type of the variable being assigned the constant value or to match the data type of the expression in which the constant is being used. If an improper data type is used and can be converted to the proper data type through the conversion rules explained above, then this will be done; otherwise the compiler will inform you that you have made an error (such as trying to assign a string to an integer).

INTEGER CONSTANTS

An integer constant consists of any sequence of digits. The sequence of digits can represent a numeric value in either decimal, octal, or hexadecimal notation. A digit sequence beginning with the digit zero (0) is taken to be octal. A digit sequence beginning with the digit zero and the letter "X" (0X or 0x) is taken to be hexadecimal and may contain the letters "a" through "f" or "A" through "F". Any other digit sequence is taken to be decimal notation.

If the digit sequence is followed by the letter "L," then the value is taken to be of type **long**. Whether the "L" is present or not, if the value of the constant exceeds the range of an **int**, the constant is taken to be of type **long**.

    Examples: 0542
              3211232L
              0x33ac

FLOATING POINT

A floating point constant follows the standard computerized form of exponential notation:

    +/− integer . fraction E/e +/− exponent

Each +/− indicates an optional algebraic sign, and the "E/e" means either upper- or lowercase may be used. A floating point constant must have an integer part followed by a decimal point and fraction or exponent portion (including the "E") or both. All floating point values are taken to be **double**.

    Examples: 3.2211
             − 0.222
              4.333E20
              43e − 3

CHARACTER CONSTANTS

A character constant has a character enclosed by apostrophes or single quotes (').

Examples: 'a'
'Z'
'\n'
'\012'

STRINGS

A string constant is a sequence of characters enclosed by quotation marks ("). The compiler automatically places the termination character (\0) at the end of each string constant. All strings, even those written identically, are treated as distinct constants.

Examples: "Hello"
"This \" is a quotation mark."

APPENDIX F

TRUTH
TABLES

The following truth tables indicate the values of the expressions on the right, given the values of "P" and "Q" shown on the left.

P	NOT P
T	F
F	T

P	Q	P AND Q
T	T	T
T	F	F
F	T	F
F	F	F

P	Q	P OR Q
T	T	T
T	F	T
F	T	T
F	F	F

P	Q	P XOR Q
T	T	F
T	F	T
F	T	T
F	F	F

APPENDIX G

GLOSSARY

The following glossary not only defines terms and phrases used in this book, but also contains terms relevant to the computing industry in general. Many definitions contain terms and phrases defined elsewhere in the glossary. In addition, note that while a definition presented here may not be the only possible definition for that word, it will be the one used throughout this text.

Abort
To stop processing.

Access
To get at. Data, both in memory and on disk files, may be accessed through various software.

Actual parameter
The expressions used within parentheses in a function call to provide that function with processing values.

Address
The numerical digits that identify a location in memory.

Algorithm
A set of calculating procedures. An algorithm can be thought of as a methodology or procedural exemplification of a situation.

Allocate
To set apart and designate for a purpose. In C we allocate memory for arrays and strings.

Alphanumeric
Any alphabetic or numeric character that can be produced using the standard keyboard. Alphanumerics do not include control characters.

ANSI
Acronym for American National Standards Institute. Used to indicate standardized items of computer-related material.

APL
Acronym for A Programming Language. This high-level programming language is used in specialized scientific applications where extensive matrix calculations are required.

Append
To add onto. The "append mode" in C will begin file access at the end of the file in order to allow immediate expansion.

Argument
A variable upon whose value a function depends. In functions, the parameter is a synonym for the argument.

Arithmetic expression

A combination of numbers, variables, and mathematical operators that forms an algebraic statement.

Array

A collection of data organized in matrix fashion, all of the same data type. Arrays use subscripts to indicate how many dimensions the array spans.

ASCII

The standard character set used on most microcomputers. ASCII is the acronym for American Standard Code for Information Interchange.

Assembler

A piece of software designed to translate assembly-language source code into directly executable machine code.

Assembly language

A very low-level language that uses macros and simple commands to perform single operations at the microprocessor level. Assembly language is one step higher than machine language, since in assembly language you are permitted to use commands, symbols, variables, and labels rather than the numeric representation of those commands.

Assignment operator

The (=) operator that sets the variable to the left of the operator equal to the expression to the right of the operator.

Assignment statement

A statement that equates what is to the left of an assignment operator to what is to the right of the assignment operator.

Auxiliary

An additional or supplemental item providing help or support through interaction. To compose your C programs, an auxiliary compiler is needed to translate your C source code into machine language.

Back-up

A copy of a file or entire disk physically separated from the original. Used only to restore or replace the original should it be damaged or destroyed.

BASIC

A programming language (Beginner's All-Purpose Symbolic Instruction Code).

Batch file
A file containing commands performed automatically and sequentially upon execution.

Binary
The base-2 numbering system, in which numbers are formed exclusively from the digits 0 and 1.

Bit
A common contraction for binary digit. A bit is the smallest unit of storage. Eight bits form a standard byte.

Bitwise
Performed bit-by-bit; using bits as they are encountered.

Bitwise operator
An operator that acts on an expression one bit at a time.

Black box
A process that produces output from given input by a process that is "invisible" from outside the box.

Boolean
A system of logic that evaluates expressions as true or false. A Boolean variable will contain either 1 for true or 0 for false. A Boolean expression will evaluate to true or false, and all conditional statements will evaluate to a Boolean result.

Boot
Usually a user-initiated process that causes the computer to load, from a disk, an operating system. Some computers have the ability to boot themselves when necessary.

Buffer
Something that serves to separate two items. Specifically, a temporary storage unit that holds information shared between two sources. A buffer is usually used between a secondary storage unit and the primary storage unit because of the difference in operating speed.

Byte
The basic unit of storage. A standard byte contains eight bits. A single character requires one byte of storage both in memory and on disk.

Call
To begin processing at a designated label or to begin execution through a specific function. The call is most often associated with

functions where parameters are used to pass data to the function. A return statement will be used to resume processing from where the call was initiated.

Call-by-reference

To pass the address of data to a function. In contrast to call-by-value, call-by-reference is designed to be able to return more than one value. The input data can be modified to reflect output data.

Call-by-value

To pass an actual value (numeric or string) to a function. In contrast to call-by-reference, call-by-value functions can return only one value.

Cast

A C operator that changes the size and representation from one data type to another.

Character

Any alphanumeric, control character, punctuation, or special symbol that requires one byte of storage space (both in memory and on disk).

Code

A group of meaningful symbols. In programming C, we use a compiler to translate source code into object (intermediate) code, and a linker to combine object codes to form executable code.

Comment

A message intended to explain or illustrate the meaning of the preceding or following instructions. A nonexecutable programming statement.

Compiler

A piece of software designed to translate source programs into object or intermediate code, which is then taken by a linker to produce executable code.

Compiler directive

A C source statement that begins with the number symbol (#), indicating a special command to the compiler.

Compiler error

A diagnostic message given by the compiler to the programmer indicating problematic source code. C compiler errors point out the nature of the error (syntax error, mixed-mode expression, and so on) and the approximate source code line number where the error was detected.

Computer

A machine that can accept, process, and output data.

Concatenate

To chain or add together. Several strings or files can be concatenated into one large entity.

Console

The default output device. When you boot your computer, the operating system assigns the console to the video display. Your C programs can direct output to this device, the printer, or to any other device connected to your computer system.

Constant

A numeric or string quantity that does not change throughout program execution.

Control character

Any character that causes special processing. The ASCII decimal value of a control character will occur between 0 and 31.

Control statement

A statement that directs execution to another portion of the program. A function call is an example of a control statement in C.

CP/M

An acronym for Control Program for Microcomputers. C/PM is the widely-accepted personal/small-business computer's operating system developed by Digital Research. It is available in both 8-bit (CP/M-80) and 16-bit (CP/M-86) versions.

CPU

The acronym for "central processing unit." This is the "brain" of your computer that is responsible for all data manipulation.

Cursor

A symbol (usually single-character) on the video display terminal indicating where the next keyboard character will appear if sent to the terminal.

Data

A collection of characters, symbols, or control codes that represent a logical item. The computer differentiates data in memory from program code by its memory location.

Data base

A large collection of (usually related) data. A data base represents a large matrix of data whose fields comprise records; several records comprise the data base.

Data file

Any named storage location on a disk or similar storage device containing either program code or other data.

Data structure

An organizational methodology for representing collections of data. The data may be of differing data types.

Data type

One of the classifications for designating data storage and representation.

Debug

To rid a program of errors. The process one undertakes to ensure program accuracy and completeness.

Declaration statement

A statement assigning a data type to a variable name.

Decrement

To decrease a numeric variable. By convention, a decrement is usually the subtraction of 1, but any value can be used. Opposite of "increment."

Default

A value used when no specific value is given. The value, whether string or numeric, automatically used if none is specified.

Delete

To remove. Files, memory, and other storage-oriented operations can involve deletion.

Delimiter

A boundary between two elements. Used to separate fields within a record.

Dimension

A property of arrays. A dimension is analogous to a direction in space: one dimension is linear; two dimensions are planar; three dimensions are cubic. When specifying an array, you must provide a subscript for each dimension.

Directory

A listing or index providing characteristics of files on your disk drive.

Disk

A floppy or hard storage medium with the ability to record programs or other data magnetically for repeated use. The storage capacity of a disk is usually measured in kilobytes.

Disk drive

A device that rotates a floppy or hard disk to provide your computer with access to the information on the disk.

Disk operating system

A piece of software that controls all input and output from the computer to its user. See "operating system" for more information.

DOS

An acronym for "disk operating system."

Dynamic memory allocation

A technique used by compilers and interpreters to reserve space for variables as they are encountered.

EBCDIC

An acronym for Extended Binary-Coded Decimal Interchange Code. EBCDIC is an alternative to ASCII. Both are methods of expressing characters or other data to a computer or any of its peripherals.

Edit

To refine and cause to conform to standards to suit a purpose. In this book you are asked to edit programming examples in order to change their actions and to observe those changes.

Editor

A word processor, line editor, or other software that can create and alter the contents of a disk file. You will require some sort of editor to produce your C programs.

Element

One of the members of an array, designated by a unique combination of subscripts.

Error

A statement or expression that does not follow the syntax regulations for that command. Your compiler will indicate where such source code errors exist, but logical errors that produce undesired results must be found through execution and debugging.

Execute

To run or begin a program.

Executable code
Program code ready to be used by your computer. It must be produced by compiling your source code into object code, and then linking the object code with referenced library functions.

Exponent
The power of a number. Specifically, the power of ten multiplied by the mantissa to yield a notation of the form: *n.nnn E exp.*

Expression
A group of characters (numbers and letters) that form a syntactically correct statement.

External function
A function defined outside of the current source file.

Factor
A divisor of a number that produces no remainder.

Field
A logically distinct unit containing zero or more characters that may be grouped together to form a record. A name, account number, address, or dollar amount can be a field.

File
A logically organized collection of data in which each record, field, or element is related to the other by some criteria.

Floating point
The classification of numbers that may contain fractional components.

Formal parameter
A placeholder in a function declaration used to receive data from a function call.

Formatted printing
Also known as "pretty printing." Used to produce tables, reports, and other printed documents within a predefined format.

FORTRAN
An acronym for *Formula Translation,* FORTRAN is a procedure-oriented programming language designed for mathematical operations. Used extensively in the scientific community.

Fragment
An incomplete programming statement.

Function

A program entity containing statements logically grouped to process one specific task. A function may be activated from any section of the program.

Global variable

A variable accessible to all statements within an entire program.

Hardware

Your computer, disks, printers, cables, and their subcomponents. All aspects of computers that are not software.

Hexadecimal

The base 16 numbering system using the digits 0 through 9 and the letters A through F to represent the numbers 0 through 15.

High-level language

A language that allows programmers to use symbols, labels, variables, and other complex concepts to express algorithms in ways a computer cannot directly understand; usually requires compilation. APL, FORTRAN, and BASIC are considered high-level languages. C is classified as a mid-level language.

Identifier

Any sequence of letters, digits, and the underscore. The first character must be a letter.

Include

To bring along. As a compiler directive, the #include statement reads source code into the compilation at the desired point.

Increment

To increase a numeric variable. By convention, an increment is usually the addition of 1, but any value can be used. Opposite of "decrement."

Indirection

Referencing by address; that is, using a variable's address instead of the variable itself.

Initialize

To set the value of. Initialization can be to any value. One can also initialize or "format" a disk.

Input

The information that comes to the computer from the outside. You will usually provide input to the computer through the keyboard.

Input/output

The process of communication between computer, operator, and peripherals. Often abbreviated as "I/O."

Integer

A numeric value with no fractional components.

Interface

A shared boundary. Often refers to the piece of hardware used between two pieces of equipment to facilitate communication between them.

Intermediate file

The file produced by the compiler from your source code. Also called "object files," these files must be linked with library files to produce executable code.

I/O

The standard abbreviation for "input/output."

Iteration

The process of repeating. Within the C language, iteration is implemented with **for** and **while** loops.

Kilobyte

One thousand bytes. Derived from the Greek prefix "kilo" meaning "thousand." Abbreviated as "K."

Label

A location within a source program. Program flow can be transferred to this location with a **goto** statement.

Librarian

A piece of software designed to take object files containing functions and concatenate them into "library files." The librarian adds, deletes, and modifies modules within library files.

Library file

A disk file containing object code created from many functions or procedures that can be linked to resolve references to external functions within a program.

Line

Any set of printable alphanumeric characters terminated with the carriage-return and linefeed characters.

Linefeed

Expressed numerically as ASCII code 10, it is used in conjunction with the carriage-return (ASCII 13) to form an end-of-line.

Link
To bring together. Specifically, to produce a large file (executable) from a series of smaller ones (object).

Linker
A piece of software designed to combine object and library files and produce executable code.

List device
The standard output device for receiving printed material; usually a printer.

Literal data
Any data item that appears "as is" repeatedly, regardless of the situation that uses it. A "constant" is an example of literal data.

Local variable
A variable accessible only within a defined block of programming statements.

Logical expression
An expression yielding a value of true or false.

Logical operator
An operator used to compare the truth values of two expressions.

Low-level language
A programming environment providing only the most basic microprocessor operations (addition, data movement, and so on).

Machine code
Commands directly executable by the CPU.

Machine language
A programming language with a very limited instruction set designed to directly control every function of the CPU.

Macro
An identifier used as a synonym for a set of instructions or a constant value.

Mantissa
The numeric portion of a floating point number or a number expressed in scientific notation. All numbers expressed this way have both a mantissa and an exponent.

Matrix
A collection of numbers or characters arranged in rows and columns and having "dimensions." Also known as an "array."

Megabyte

One million bytes. Derived from the Greek prefix "mega," meaning "million."

Memory

Storage space for data resident within the computer; measured in kilobytes.

Microprocessor

As the "brain" of your computer, the microprocessor is responsible for all calculations and hardware-controlling functions.

Mixed-mode expression

An expression involving at least two operands of differing data types.

Modular

Capable of being easily joined to. In this book we stress structured programming—that is, programming in complete functional units—as a means of giving programs modularity.

Module

Like a function, a module represents a single-step process that can be used by many other parts of a program.

Modulo

A mathematical function returning the remainder of an integer division. In C, the modulo operator is the percent sign (%).

Multidimensional

Having more than one dimension (planar, cubic, and so on). Arrays are often multidimensional.

Nesting

Putting loops inside loops, #include files inside #include files, and other repetitive functions inside themselves. In contrast with "recursion," a segment of code contained within a larger portion of code, whereas recursion causes the same portion of code to be reexecuted.

Nondigit

Any character that is not between 48 and 57 decimal ASCII; any character that is not a number.

Numeric

Any number; any character between 48 and 57 decimal ASCII.

Object file

The file produced by the compiler. Contains relocatable machine code to be linked with library files to produce executable code.

Octal
The base-8 numbering system, in which numbers are expressed with the digits 0 through 7.

Operand
A component of an expression that has a value.

Operating system
A piece of software that controls all functions of computer processing and peripheral communication.

Operator
A symbol or word performing some function upon one or more operands. Also used to identify the person using a computer.

Output
The information that goes from the computer to a peripheral. Output is presented to you on your video display terminal.

Parameter
The value or values required by a function, enclosed within parentheses.

Parse
To take apart. Programs must sometimes dissect strings or commands into separate data elements.

Peripheral
Any device connected to a computer that provides input, accepts output, or performs auxiliary functions (such as a storage device).

Pointer
A data type that holds the address of another variable.

Pointer operator
The * operator, indicating the use of the data at an address specified by a pointer variable.

Precedence
The order in which an expression will be evaluated.

Prompt
A character or group of characters used to notify the user that input is required. In programming, questions to the user are considered prompts.

RAM
An acronym for random-access memory.

Random-access file
A file whose organization permits access in a random fashion. Contrasted with "sequential file."

Random-access memory
Memory that can have its parts accessed in a random manner. More commonly, it is the reusable and volatile storage space within the computer.

Rational number
A number that is expressed as the quotient of two integers.

Read
To take as input. A program can read from the keyboard, a file, or from memory.

Read-only memory
Memory that cannot be erased, written on, or changed. Inherent capabilities of the computer and its start-up procedure are stored in read-only memory to provide permanent storage.

Real number
A number that may contain a fractional part. In the computer, real numbers can have values much larger than those of integers.

Record
A logical grouping of fields in a file. Records are composed of fields; files are composed of records.

Recursion
The process in which a portion of code begins to reexecute itself. The original executing version of code remains intact (but not operative), and the reexecuting code is initiated as a new entity.

Recursive function
A function that may call itself.

Register
A storage location within the CPU.

Relational operator
An operator performing some type of comparison between two operands.

Relocatable
Used to identify a file that can be inputted by a linker to be translated into executable code. Also known as "object code."

Returned value
The result of a function's processing.

ROM
An acronym for read-only memory.

Run-time
Occurring during execution as opposed to during compilation.

Sequential file
A file whose organization permits access only in a sequential manner, either from top to bottom, from bottom to top, or from any midpoint to an endpoint. Contrasted with "random-access file."

Software
Your compiler, word processor, line editor, operating system, any C programs, or other applications programs. That which controls hardware.

Source code
The statements you use to express algorithms in C. Source code must be compiled and linked to produce executable code.

Source file
A disk file containing programming statements in source code.

Statement
A line containing one or more expressions.

Stream organization
Arrangement in a sequential, one-directional manner.

String
Any continuous sequence of characters.

Subroutine
A procedure to which control can be transferred within a program. A subroutine performs one function and returns program flow to the instruction immediately following the call.

Subscript
One of the dimensions of an array. To specify an element of an array, one uses subscripts to uniquely identify the placement of the element within the array.

Syntax
The structure of a statement. The arrangement of commands in their proper usage.

Text

Any unit of alphanumeric characters.

Token

The identifier used as the pseudonym in a macro definition.

Two's-complement

A method of representing a negative number in the computer's memory.

Union

A data structure capable of holding different data types, but only one piece of data may reside in the union at any one time.

UNIX

An operating system written in C and developed for program development. Created by Bell Laboratories.

Utility

A piece of software designed for one specific purpose. A tool used to supplement a more important process.

Variable

Any valid identifier that can change value.

Whitespace

Any characters ignored by the compiler when translating a source file.

Word

The basic unit of addressable storage within the computer's RAM; usually 8, 16, 32, or 64-bits in length.

Write

Opposite of read; to write is to send information to a storage device.

APPENDIX H

BIBLIOGRAPHY

Bourne, S. R., *The UNIX System*. Menlo Park, California: Addison-Wesley, 1983.

Ghezzi, C. and Jazayeri, M., *Programming Language Concepts*. New York: John Wiley & Sons, 1982.

Kernighan, B. and Ritchie, D., *The C Programming Language*. Englewood Cliffs, New Jersey: Prentice-Hall, 1978.

Ralston, A., et al, *Encyclopedia of Computer Science*. First Edition, San Francisco: Van Nostrand Reinhold, 1976.

Wirth, N., *Algorithms + Data Structures = Programs*. Englewood Cliffs, New Jersey: Prentice-Hall, 1976.

INDEX

Selections from The SYBEX Library

Computer Specific

Apple II—Macintosh

THE PRO-DOS HANDBOOK
by Timothy Rice/Karen Rice
225 pp., illustr., Ref. 0-230
All Pro-DOS users, from beginning to advanced, will find this book packed with vital information. The book covers the basics, and then addresses itself to the Apple II user who needs to interface with Pro-DOS when programming in BASIC. Learn how Pro-DOS uses memory, and how it handles text files, binary files, graphics, and sound. Includes a chapter on machine language programming.

THE MACINTOSH™ TOOLBOX
by Huxham, Burnard, and Takatsuka
300 pp., illustr., Ref. 0-249
This tutorial on the advanced features of the Macintosh toolbox is an ideal companion to The Macintosh BASIC Handbook.

THE MACINTOSH™ BASIC HANDBOOK
by Thomas Blackadar/Jonathan Kamin
800 pp., illustr., Ref. 0-257
This desk-side reference book for the Macintosh programmer covers the BASIC statements and toolbox commands, organized like a dictionary.

PROGRAMMING THE MACINTOSH™ IN ASSEMBLY LANGUAGE
by Steve Williams
400 pp., illustr., Ref. 0-263
Information, examples, and guidelines for programming the 68000 microprocessor are given, including details of its entire instruction set.

Technical

Assembly Language

PROGRAMMING THE 6502
by Rodnay Zaks
386 pp., 160 illustr., Ref. 0-135
Assembly language programming for the 6502, from basic concepts to advanced data structures.

6502 APPLICATIONS
by Rodnay Zaks
278 pp., 200 illustr., Ref. 0-015
Real-life application techniques: the input/output book for the 6502.

ADVANCED 6502 PROGRAMMING
by Rodnay Zaks
292 pp., 140 illustr., Ref. 0-089
Third in the 6502 series. Teaches more advanced programming techniques, using games as a framework for learning.

PROGRAMMING THE Z8000®
by Richard Mateosian
298 pp., 124 illustr., Ref. 0-032
How to program the Z8000 16-bit microprocessor. Includes a description of the architecture and function of the Z8000 and its family of support chips.

PROGRAMMING THE 8086™/8088™
by James W. Coffron
300 pp., illustr., Ref. 0-120
This book explains how to program the 8086 and 8088 microprocessors in assembly language. No prior programming knowledge required.

PROGRAMMING THE 68000™
by Steve Williams
250 pp., illustr., Ref. 0-133
This book introduces you to microprocessor operation, writing application
programs, and the basics of I/O programming. Especially helpful for owners of the
Apple Macintosh or Lisa.

Hardware

FROM CHIPS TO SYSTEMS: AN INTRODUCTION TO MICROPROCESSORS
by Rodnay Zaks
552 pp., 400 illustr., Ref. 0-063
A simple and comprehensive introduction
to microprocessors from both a hardware
and software standpoint: what they are,
how they operate, how to assemble them
into a complete system.

MICROPROCESSOR INTERFACING TECHNIQUES
by Rodnay Zaks and Austin Lesea
456 pp., 400 illustr., Ref. 0-029
Complete hardware and software interfacing techniques, including D to A conversion, peripherals, bus standards and
troubleshooting.

THE RS-232 SOLUTION
by Joe Campbell
194 pp., illustr., Ref. 0-140
Finally, a book that will show you how to
correctly interface your computer to any
RS-232-C peripheral.

MASTERING SERIAL COMMUNICATIONS
by Joe Campbell
250 pp., illustr., Ref. 0-180
This sequel to *The RS-232 Solution*
guides the reader to mastery of more
complex interfacing techniques.

Operating Systems

SYSTEMS PROGRAMMING IN C
by David Smith
275 pp., illustr., Ref. 0-266

This intermediate text is written for the person who wants to get beyond the basics
of C and capture its great efficiencies in
space and time.

THE PROGRAMMER'S GUIDE TO UNIX SYSTEM V
by Chuck Hickev/Tim Levin
300 pp., illustr., Re.f 0-268
This book is a guide to all steps involved
in setting up a typical programming task
in a UNIX systems environment.

REAL WORLD UNIX™
by John D. Halamka
209 pp., Ref. 0-093
This book is written for the beginning and
intermediate UNIX user in a practical,
straightforward manner, with specific
instructions given for many business
applications.

INTRODUCTION TO THE UCSD p-SYSTEM™
by Charles W. Grant and Jon Butah
300 pp., 10 illustr., Ref. 0-061
A simple, clear introduction to the UCSD
Pascal Operating System for beginners
through experienced programmers.

Languages

Pascal

INTRODUCTION TO PASCAL (Including UCSD Pascal™)
by Rodnay Zaks
420 pp., 130 illustr., Ref. 0-066
A step-by-step introduction for anyone
who wants to learn the Pascal language.
Describes UCSD and Standard Pascals.
No technical background is assumed.

THE PASCAL HANDBOOK
by Jacques Tiberghien
486 pp., 270 illustr., Ref. 0-053
A dictionary of the Pascal language,
defining every reserved word, operator,
procedure, and function found in all major
versions of Pascal.

APPLE® PASCAL GAMES

**by Douglas Hergert and
Joseph T. Kalash**

372 pp., 40 illustr., Ref. 0-074

A collection of the most popular computer games in Pascal, challenging the reader not only to play but to investigate how games are implemented on the computer.

PASCAL PROGRAMS FOR SCIENTISTS AND ENGINEERS

by Alan R. Miller

374 pp., 120 illustr., Ref. 0-058

A comprehensive collection of frequently used algorithms for scientific and technical applications, programmed in Pascal. Includes programs for curve-fitting, integrals, statistical techniques, and more.

DOING BUSINESS WITH PASCAL

**by Richard Hergert and
Douglas Hergert**

371 pp., illustr., Ref. 0-091

Practical tips for using Pascal programming in business. Covers design considerations, language extensions, and applications examples.

Other Languages

FORTRAN PROGRAMS FOR SCIENTISTS AND ENGINEERS

by Alan R. Miller

280 pp., 120 illustr., Ref. 0-082

This book from the "Programs for Scientists and Engineers" series provides a library of problem-solving programs while developing the reader's proficiency in FORTRAN.

UNDERSTANDING C

by Bruce H. Hunter

320 pp., Ref 0-123

Explains how to program in powerful C language for a variety of applications. Some programming experience assumed.

FIFTY PASCAL PROGRAMS

by Bruce H. Hunter

338 pp., illustr., Ref. 0-110

More than just a collection of useful programs! Structured programming techniques are emphasized and concepts such as data type creation and array manipulation are clearly illustrated.

DISK OFFER

Now that you are familiar with C's many virtues as a development language for the Macintosh, you may want to make the process of mastering C easier by taking advantage of our Macintosh disk offer. A ready-to-go Macintosh disk containing all the full-length programs, programming examples, and program segments used throughout this book can be yours. By ordering our Macintosh C Programs disk, you can save yourself the trouble of typing all those programs and program samples into your Macintosh to see them run, and at the same time make it easier to begin immediately altering the programs for your own use. Our Macintosh C Programs disk is a great time saver!

To order your Macintosh C Programs disk, simply send your name, address, and $14.95 (price includes sales tax, if any, and all shipping charges) to

DATATECH Publications
Software Products Division
Post Office Box 8702
La Jolla, California 92038

Please indicate that you want the Macintosh C Programs disk. The disk will be shipped to you via First Class mail within five working days of receipt of your order. Thank you!